DESERT
HUMANITIES

Ron Broglio and Celina Osuna,
General Editors

SAND
WATER
SALT

MANAGING THE ELEMENTS IN LITERATURE OF THE AMERICAN WEST, 1880–1925

JADA ACH

TEXAS TECH UNIVERSITY PRESS

This book is typeset in EB Garamond. The paper used in this book meets the
minimum requirements of ANSI/NISO Z39.48–1992 (R1997). ∞

Designed by Hannah Gaskamp
Cover design by Hannah Gaskamp

Library of Congress Control Number: 2020950201
Printed in the United States of America
ISBN 978-1-68283-081-9 (cloth)
ISBN 978-1-68283-082-6 (ebook)

21 22 23 24 25 26 27 28 29 / 9 8 7 6 5 4 3 2 1

Texas Tech University Press
Box 41037
Lubbock, Texas 79409–1037 USA
800.832.4042
ttup@ttu.edu
www.ttupress.org

For Winona

CONTENTS

INTRODUCTION

RADICAL ELEMENTS

I n Claire Vaye Watkins's 2015 "cli-fi" novel *Gold Fame Citrus*, the American West has run out of water.[1] Depleted aquifers, dried-up rivers, prolonged drought, drained reservoirs, snowless mountaintops, and in general the breakdown of human-engineered landscapes trigger a mass exodus of individuals heading east in search of greener, more accommodating terrain. Watkins's story begins in Southern California, the heart of the "failed experiment," just a few years after the region ultimately "succumbs to salt" and "infinite sand."[2] In the apocalyptic passage that follows, the narrator breathlessly summarizes some of the many ecological disasters that contributed to the collapse of industries, municipalities, and infrastructures in the arid and semiarid West:

> [T]he Central Valley . . . went salt flat, as its farmcrops regularly drilled three thousand feet into the unyielding earth, praying for aquifer but delivered only hot brine, as Mojavs [Californians] sucked up the groundwater to Texas, as a major tendril of interstate collapsed into a mile-wide sinkhole, killing everybody on it, as all of the Southwest went moonscape with sinkage, as the winds came and as Phoenix burned and as a white-hot superdune entombed Las Vegas. (21)

This bleak vision of the Southwest set in the not-too-distant future is scarily alive with sandy, briny, and altogether animated environmental elements—elements that "kill" humans, squash their desires, and "entomb" entire metropolitan areas with what seems a blind indifference. The "gone water," as the narrator calls the now absent element, haunts the novel's dusty, contaminated

1

landscape. Humans could never manage in this "deadest place on the planet," readers might assume (192).

From a human perspective, Watkins's pavement-eating, city-smothering desert appears to orient itself toward death and destruction. In its aggressive rejection of human life, the novel's waterless West often comes off as the paradigmatic wasteland: if one lingers too long in its hostile sand and sweltering heat, she risks losing her life. However, *Gold Fame Citrus* also complicates readers' understanding of arid environments by imbuing desert materialities with a "throbbing" and, at times, enchanting kind of vibrancy (84). The Amargosa Dune Sea, a colossal ridge of ever-accumulating sand between Las Vegas and Los Angeles, exists as a case in point (117). Even though the "monstrous" dune is capable of blanketing entire towns in a matter of hours, the narrator also informs us that the Amargosa holds a queer and "curious energy," one that simultaneously attracts and vexes scientists, cartographers, and land management agencies (124).

> Still came the scientists: climatologists, geologists, volcanologists, soil experts, agriculturalists, horticulturalists, conservationists. . . . Still came the BLM and EPA and NWS and USGS, all assigned to determine why a process that ought to have taken five thousand years had happened in fifty. All tasked with determining how to stop the mountain's unrelenting march. All of them failed. (117)

The managers believe that scientific observation would lead to greater understanding of the dune's nature, which might allow them to develop more effective methods of control. However, despite their close surveillance—or perhaps because of it—they could not halt the Amargosa's "unrelenting march," the narrator concedes (85, 117). In other words, proximity to "environmental problems" does not always render mastery, especially when mastery entails subduing dynamic ecologies. The managers experiment with a variety of tactics to combat the dune, including spraying it with oil and even storming it with bombs, but these efforts fail to quell its power. The sand does not relent.

In addition to triggering diverse managerial responses from "khaki-capped" administrators, the ever-growing sea of sand "beckons the chosen" and foments feelings of "belonging" among desert outcasts and refugees (124). According to the narrator, the Amargosa, described in a Bureau of Land Management (BLM) report as "inhospitable, barren, bleak, and empty" (122), elicits a "pull . . . said to be far beyond topographic charm. It was chemical, pheromonal, elemental, a tingle in the ions of the brain, a tug in the iron of the blood" (124). Individuals in the novel who feel this near alchemical "pull" often experience sand as a dynamic entity that "moves through you" and changes a person from the inside out (172). Far from barren, Watkins's arid futurescape contains energetic elements that do not fit easily into the categories of waste, natural resource, or remediable problem. While management tends to read environmental matter as distant stuff whose value humans ascribe, the novel offers a more relational perspective on human-elemental engagement. In Watkins's twenty-first-century desert, elements intimately *live into* humans and, in doing so, refuse to let the human be. Sand, salt, and even water—when it finally does appear in the final pages—enter the skin, invade airways, choke the throat, stimulate desire, and, rather annoyingly, nestle in the "armpits and asscrack," resulting in recurrent managerial responses at multiple scales (7). While characters can easily "snap the infinite sand from" the bedsheets, they cannot prevent the giant dune from heading westward, in their direction (14).

Gold Fame Citrus reflects many of our own anxieties in the era of global climate change. In these opening pages, I refer to just a few of the novel's restless, sand-stirred moments because they call on us to consider the complicated legacies of scientific land management in the American West and beyond. *Sand, Water, Salt: Managing the Elements in Literature of the American West,*

1880–1925 tracks the impacts of these legacies via close readings of Progressive Era fiction, technical literature, national park documents, aerial photographs, Indigenous autobiography, and other literary and nonliterary texts. This diverse archive reveals how environmental elements *do* something outside of remaining *under control*. Often, the radical doings of sand, water, and salt test the authority of what Martha Banta refers to as turn-of-the-century "management culture," leaving us with a vision of administrative networks that are as unstable as they are pervasive.[3] For instance, even though water is scarce in Owen Wister's *The Virginian*, which would seem to put both humans and their water-dependent agricultural industries at risk, that same scarcity also amplifies the power of those who own the land or have the means to finance and supervise water diversion projects: namely, the ranchers and developers.

Administrative power, then, as I define it in this project, is contingent upon the same elemental uncertainty that threatens that power, making land management a queerly recursive enterprise. This vision of loopy management—or of controlling by slightly failing to control—provides environmental humanists with a counternarrative to more top-down, despotic depictions of Progressive Era land management, such as we see in popular environmental histories like Donald Worster's *Rivers of Empire* or Marc Reisner's *Cadillac Desert*, as well as more conventional histories like Robert Wiebe's *The Search for Order, 1877–1920*.[4] Instead of reading management as an all-consuming, highly abstract network of imperial power, which has the effect of severing humans from environments, the queer, messy, altogether interactionist vision of human-ecological relations I call attention to in the chapters that follow casts management in more porous, albeit still powerful, terms. For even though failure tends to stimulate the messy reproduction of the management apparatus, allowing its operation networks to sprawl and, not infrequently, fortify, those same failures offer a kind of hope. By highlighting those generative moments of supervisory breakdown, *Sand, Water, Salt* reveals spaces and moments wherein environmental justice activism and resilience might be possible.

The ecological and managerial failures Watkins vividly portrays in her novel—the salty ditches, empty reservoirs, crumbling aqueducts, and deteriorating dams—find their root in what historian Thomas C. Leonard refers to as Progressives' "extravagant faith in administration."[5] Through an examination of the eco-materials humans set out to manage in the arid, semiarid, and oceanic West, *Sand, Water, Salt* traces the contours of that faith while also shining a light on climatic and elemental incidents that breach that faith. Even though *Gold Fame Citrus* takes place in the twenty-first century and, therefore, seems far removed from popular *fin-de-siècle* depictions of the West as a "clean, blank page," prominent Progressive Era figures haunt both the structure and setting of the novel, demonstrating that history, unlike water, does not easily evaporate in the desert.[6] For example, William Mulholland, the engineer who, as his obituary reads, "almost single-handed [*sic*] and against . . . bitter opposition" designed and supervised the Los Angeles Aqueduct, visits Watkins's main character, Luz Dunn, in a dream.[7]

The ambitious engineer also emerges in epigraph form at the beginning of Book One with his famous words, "Go ahead. Take it," and thus reminds readers of the initial cascade of diverted Owens River water that stimulated development in Los Angeles and the surrounding Southern California region. At the beginning of Book Two, Watkins quotes a different kind of turn-of-the-century figure in the epigraph: nature writer and preservationist Mary Austin. When the words of these Western Progressives appear at the beginning of distinct sections of *Gold Fame Citrus*, they interrupt the novel's chronology, forcing readers to consider how the environmental reforms of the past continue to impact Western lands to this day. Other Progressive figures populate the novel's apocalyptic setting, such as John Muir,

Francis Newlands, and John Wesley Powell. We are even told that the eyes of Luz's "nerve-shaken" partner, Ray, resemble "the blazing prophet eyes of John Muir" (20). Watkins's resurrection of turn-of-the-century engineers, preservationists, federal managers, irrigation enthusiasts, and naturalists collapses time, making it difficult to distinguish the idealism of the past from what some ecocritics consider the melancholia of the present.[8] Though long dead, these reformers live on in the West via the vast networks of dams, highways, national parks, and other humanized landscapes they helped build and promote.

In the chapters that follow, I heed the implicit call in *Gold Fame Citrus* to reevaluate the Progressive Era's environmental and managerial legacy. By arguing that dynamic nonhuman materialities often challenge, frustrate, or resist managerial control, *Sand, Water, Salt* makes a crucial intervention in literary, cultural, and environmental histories that read Progressive Era management as an impervious force. In the diverse progress narratives I analyze in this project, management often imagines that it can achieve mastery over the environment. However, when we read such narratives through the lens of material ecocriticism, we discover that managers fail more often than they like to admit. While these recurrent failures often strengthen administrative and bureaucratic processes—after all, recurrent problems require innovative, often intensive responses, thus justifying the manager's continued presence—I contend that they might also invite possibilities for new, more compassionate ways of managing land and oceans in the Anthropocene.

Sand, Water, Salt investigates managerial engagements with animated elements in three particular Western environments: the arid deserts, the semiarid high plains, and the Pacific Ocean. At different times, and to varying degrees, Americans have deemed these environments economically unproductive, incompatible with Anglo-American settlement, or highly unmanageable. Despite these varied complaints, the United States has also intensely desired these "wasteland" spaces, perceiving them as sources of both national wealth and elite pleasure. Through close readings of a diverse management archive, *Sand, Water, Salt* will demonstrate how wasteland rhetoric has long been deployed in order to justify resource extraction, development, and the removal of Indigenous communities, problems that continue to plague western American regions to this day. When trying to justify the construction of his border wall along the US-Mexico border, for example, Donald J. Trump often described the biologically and culturally complex desert environment as mere "empty space," which has the effect of draining the arid lands of their human and nonhuman presences.[9] In the chapters that follow, I will argue that Progressive Era managers frequently deployed this same kind of rhetoric to appropriate valuable territory. As we will see, however, the elements that comprise those "empty spaces" often have a way of "engendering unanticipated forms" and interrupting the manager's plans.[10] *Sand, Water, Salt* is interested in pursuing those elemental eruptions and frustrations in the Western United States where exists the vast majority of the nation's publicly managed lands.

The three elements I've chosen to examine—sand, water, and salt—emblematize the three (wasteland) environments this ecocritical project treats. Turn-of-the-century writers depict these elements quite provocatively in their writings, imbuing these materials with a kind of liveliness that equals and, at times, even exceeds that of animals and humans. In their excess, scarcity, mobility, and/or obstinacy, sand, water, and salt exist as management problems in many Progressive Era works set in the American West. Characters in these works regularly struggle when exposed to the elements; after all, the elements this project pursues are capable of chiseling the skin, invading the nasal passages, flooding the lungs, and drying the blood. Though often relegated as "waste" elements in these works due to their failure to achieve valuable commodity status, these lively ecomaterials exhibit diverse methods of entering human lives, bodies, and policies. In other words, sand, water, and salt *matter*, but they do so queerly— and often entrancingly, as the writings of Yone Noguchi, Mary Austin, Frank Norris, and others demonstrate most clearly.

Furthermore, I argue that critical meditations on human-elemental engagements—particularly in the American West, a region that popular culture frequently regards as an intensely white-masculine space—force us to reconsider romantic representations of the rugged individualist who, because of his hard and impermeable body, supremely masters the climatically disobedient region. The ethical code of the Western, says Jane Tomkins, puts "adult white males on top with everyone else in descending order beneath."[11] It seems even the environment itself falls "beneath," and therefore exists apart from, the heroic white male body. However, when we track sand, water, and salt in turn-of-the-century works set in western wastelands, we begin to see that ecomaterials unendingly penetrate bodies—even tough and manly ones, such as Wister's Virginian—revealing an interconnected, bio-collective vision of the West. Other "waste" materials—wildfire smoke, cyanobacteria, uranium tailings, cow dung, biocrust, insecticide, etc.—would make compelling material for future elemental studies. Perhaps environmental humanists will investigate further these and other ecomaterials that *Sand, Water, Salt* overlooks.

The date range included in the title, 1880–1925, spans the cultural and political period in the United States known as the Progressive Era, a time defined by widespread social reform, urbanization, imperial expansion, mass immigration, Indigenous assimilation, technological innovation, and scientific management. Even though most of the literary works I explore in *Sand, Water, Salt* were published during this transformational forty-five-year period, not every author is on board with the cultural and developmental aims of the era. Therefore, when I refer to "Progressive Era American literature" in this volume, I do not mean to imply that such literature always endorses the movement's administrative objectives. While some of the authors I discuss certainly do promote explicitly Progressive agendas, others find queer and creative ways to critique or subvert the racist, classist, and xenophobic beliefs that often undergirded such agendas—even environmental ones.

Management is the guiding theme of this book. Each chapter focuses on management as a series of intimate human-environmental engagements in the contexts of American territorial expansion, trans-Pacific trade and travel, water development, the formation of national parks, ranching, scientific surveying, and forced removals of Indigenous peoples from ancestral lands. Management, as I define it in *Sand, Water, Salt*, not only refers to top-down efforts to regulate difficult or unproductive environments but also denotes human attempts to manage *in* harsh ecologies as workers, rangers, supervisors, natural scientists, travelers, or exiles. As ecocritic Tom Lynch says of human-environmental relations, "there is only and always engagement, only and always intimacy."[12] Try as we might, we can never manage our way out of ecological enmeshment. While each chapter examines the specific histories and philosophies of federal land management agencies and projects in the United States, such as the Forest Service and the United States Reclamation Service, I read these emerging administrative bodies alongside more granular attempts to manage (in) lively terrain. For example, in chapter 4 I track the corporeal transformations of pelagic seal hunters in Jack London's *The Sea-Wolf* as their bodies absorb the Pacific's salty waves. In contrast to the US Revenue Cutter Service, which we only witness from a distance at the end of London's novel, individual bodies are seen close up—and are altogether difficult to manage—in London's work.

In other words, *Sand, Water, Salt* asserts that managing environments and managing bodies are two sides of the same Progressive coin. To manage space was to make material an argument about which bodies both belonged and were permitted to have access to that space. In many Progressive Era works, especially those by naturalist writers such as London and Frank Norris, certain (non-white) bodies were often depicted as weak and permeable—and, hence, at greater risk of elemental contamination. Likewise, land and oceanic management, as projects administered by the state, were also very much invested in questions of racial and ethnic claim to western "American" environments. At the turn of the twentieth century, literary, artistic, and journalistic representations of the American West contributed to the country's white and manly vision of itself, and *Sand, Water, Salt* seeks to investigate how turn-of-the-century managers and the many artifacts they produced help generate, distort, and even dismantle that vision.

To say it more frankly, Progressive Era land management, as a cultural project, is also entangled with the environmental values of the white upper class—values that, according to queer ecocritic Catriona Sandilands, tended to promote "'clean' spaces for white folks" and opportunities for "elite recreation."[13] In the chapters that follow, I attend to the messy exchanges between bodies and wasteland elements in turn-of-the-century American literature in order to see how certain ecomaterials both reinforced and destabilized racial, gendered, and national "rights" to western lands. Often, human engagements with environmental elements were surveilled and policed in an attempt to safeguard white claims to public lands in the West. *Sand, Water, Salt* analyzes works by a diverse group of turn-of-the-century writers who, through a range of styles and genres, develop methods of upholding, critiquing, or rewriting these dominant modes of human-environmental belonging. Despite the obvious imprint that Anglo-American values of all stripes have made on the West, capital-M-Management is not a monolith; instead, *Sand, Water, Salt* pursues a spectrum of *situated managements* whose interests contradict nearly as often as they overlap.[14]

A literary studies approach to land and oceanic management in the West allows us to see, at ground level, how humans negotiate with—and, in a sense, *become*—the elements that surround them. Literature offers scholars across disciplines and fields opportunities to imagine what more adaptive and participatory modes of land and oceanic management might look like in an age when so much seems to be at risk. In particular, humanities-based approaches to environmental questions can help center our attention on the messy-and-profound transferences that occur between bodies and the lively elemental substances we always thought— and maybe wished—we were managing. Reading together in the same ecocritical project an Indigenous memoir, a children's fantasy novel, a collection of nature essays, two naturalist novels, a bestselling western novel, and a fictional diary written by a Japanese national, *Sand, Water, Salt* reveals that environmental management operated as a common theme for writers representing a range of turn-of-the-century styles and genres. While each genre and movement I examine in *Sand, Water, Salt* tends to hold particular attitudes toward elemental animacy, ranging from fear and anxiety to a queer kind of longing, every work, regardless of classification, depicts Western wasteland spaces as sites of meaningful, provocative, and, at times, radical human-elemental encounter.

According to environmental humanist Helen Feder, taking up environmental questions in literature can alert us to our "sense of kinship with the other inhabitants of the world"; I would add that those "other inhabitants" certainly include the material, the elemental.[15] This emergent kind of kinship is not always comfortable and harmonious. In fact, it is often downright exasperating and occasionally lethal, as many of the works in *Sand, Water, Salt* reveal. While some of the writers I treat in this project choose to live into and with the elements, such as Mary Austin, others, such as Frank Norris, read the elements as a kind of test to see what bodies should survive in the new century. Still others, such as

Paiute author and activist Sarah Winnemucca, read vibrant eco-materials as both extensions of the self and, when contaminated, as evidence of white encroachment on Indigenous lands. Stated simply, the elements are just *one* thing—resource, waste, source of pleasure, or annoyance. Instead, the Progressive writers I explore in this book expand, challenge, rewrite, and, taken as a whole, multiply what I term elemental values.

In addition to exploring the contours of human-elemental kinship, *Sand, Water, Salt* is deeply invested in questions of environmental justice. Julie Sze contends that "Literature offers a new way of looking at environmental justice, through visual images and metaphors, not solely through the prism of statistics."[16] The chapters that follow productively attend to Sze's important call to focus on ecojustice but do so by interrogating the settler-colonial roots of scientific management. By pursuing land management and elemental ecocriticism as joint fields of critical study, I argue that environmental and public humanities can gain "a new way of looking" at racist and exclusionary environmental practices and policies. Many of the turn-of-the-century literary and nonliterary works I pursue in this project reveal moments when a character's race, gender, class standing, sexuality, or ethnicity seem to determine the kinds of relationships they may have with elemental matter. For example, in Winnemucca's *Life among the Piutes*, which I take up in chapter 3, white, colonial violence is even compared to a furious and blinding haboob, a comparison that aligns settler-colonialism with destructive sand-energy. Reading Indigenous and minority literatures through an elemental lens unravels the complex ways that colonial violence is always already environmental violence.

In other words, the environment—particularly its reduction to resource, commodity, and wasteland, to name just a few ways settler-colonialism attempts to objectify dynamic ecologies—is often central to questions of social justice, as recent movements against uranium mining and energy pipelines in the West have revealed in sharp relief. Furthermore, when we ask ecojustice questions of Progressive Era American literature, it becomes evident that many of the land management issues that concern us today have a startlingly long legacy. Such issues include, but are certainly not limited to, the many challenges to tribal sovereignty, intensive extraction of "mineral wealth," overhunting, and water resource contamination. These problems are particularly alive in the American West, where the federal government currently owns nearly 47 percent of the land, the majority of which is managed by the BLM (formerly the General Land Office), which takes a multi-use, energy- and development-focused approach to land management. According to Traci Brynne Voyles, the concept of "wasteland" often operates as an effective weapon in these environmental justice debates, and the term's nineteenth-century roots inevitably link these ongoing power struggles between managers and communities to the Expansionist Era. Voyles says,

> Remaking Native land as settler home involves the exploitation of environmental resources, to be sure, but it also involves a deeply complex construction of that land as either always already belonging to the settler—his manifest destiny—or as undesirable, unproductive, or unappealing: in short, as wasteland.[17]

What this means is that, far from "wild" and "untrammeled spaces," Western environments operated as critical sites where social difference was both managed and, at times, challenged. In sum, the critical land management focus I take in this literary studies project offers environmental humanists another way of reading and reframing the captivating vibrancy of so-called tamed, regulated environments in the US West.

The literary and environmental stakes of this project's regional focus are many and frequently overlap. Over the past three decades, several critics have compellingly articulated the ways that Progressives' views on race, gender, and class permeate turn-of-the-century literary and cultural productions. Some of those critics include Lee Clark Mitchell, Jonathan Auerbach, Amy

Kaplan, Cynthia Davis, Gail Bederman, Andrew Hebard, and John Dudley. However, scientific land management's influence on turn-of-the-century American literature, especially literature set in the "unproductive" regions of the arid, semiarid, and oceanic West, remains largely unexamined in literary studies. Given land management's power to dramatically *reform* the Western American landscape at the turn of the twentieth century, it exists as a powerful heuristic with which to expand (and reorganize) the cultural and geographical contours of Progressive Era American literature. For example, critics like Nicolas Witschi suggest that the turn-of-the-century West existed as the "raw materiality" of the American imaginary and, as such, dramatically influenced art and writing in every region of the country—including the Northeast, which is often viewed as the nexus of literary regionalism and realism.[18] More recently, Neil Campbell has described the West as "rhizomatic," noting that its cultural influence extends well beyond the boundaries of the nation.[19]

Adding to these innovative critical and theoretical takes on Western literature's ever-expanding national and transnational influence, I argue that the West and its elements are, quite literally, on the move in nineteenth-century American literature. An elemental approach to literature highlights the ways that environmental matter moves through history, across borders and geographies, and through (human) bodies. As commodities, literary and cultural actors, atmospheric agents, and absorbed substances, Western ecomaterials are queer in that they never quite settle within the geographical boundaries of "the West."

Never has this emphasis on queer, mobile matter and "rhizomatic" regionalism been more relevant than it is now in the era of anthropogenic climate change. In a 2018 report, for example, climatologist Richard Seager suggests that climate change is causing Western American aridity to creep eastward, eerily reflecting the "steady march" of Watkins's Amargosa Dune Sea.[20] Until recently, geographers, developers, agriculturalists, and others had long agreed that the hundredth meridian—the longitudinal line that cuts through Nebraska, Oklahoma, and other central states—existed as the humid-arid divide, or the climatic line distinguishing eastern croplands from western rangelands. In his 1878 *Report on the Lands of the Arid Region of the United States*, John Wesley Powell first advanced this idea of a humid-arid boundary line, noting that it rains substantially less west of the hundredth meridian.[21] Over the last thirty years, Seager argues, this once relatively stable line has shifted from one hundred to ninety-eight degrees longitude, meaning the Western climate, as we know it, is, in a very literal way, migrating. "The west-to-east movement of this boundary," Joe Wertz reports, "could predict profound changes in farming, ranching, and the agricultural economy, including more wheat and less corn, and expensive irrigation in Eastern states."[22] As this roving West introduces new material agencies and environmental conditions to lands once considered "eastern," climatologically speaking, environmental humanists must develop methods for getting close to aridity—or of "desertifying" their work, as Tom Lynch suggests in the foreword of *Reading Aridity in Western American Literature*.[23]

Part of my aim in *Sand, Water, Salt* is to do just that: to trace the historical interactions between managers and "difficult" environments in hopes of seeking out management practices that are committed to environmental justice, nonhuman compassion, and what Stacy Alaimo refers to as "elemental love in the Anthropocene."[24] How can we manage with love, and what would the tools and outcomes of such a management style be? Can management effectively work when it radically embraces risk, encourages shared governance, and engages with the elements not as threats but as mutual stakeholders in environmental decision making? Literature provides a rich archive for observing and evaluating the diverse ways that humans and environmental matter have emotionally and physically touched, moved, and transformed one another. By building new literary archives that orbit around the theme of land management, we might also begin to develop new interdisciplinary and transdisciplinary communities that are invested in developing more ecologically attuned approaches to land management and activism. As *Sand, Water, Salt* moves through a variety of novels, memoirs, and cultural artifacts from the 1880s to the 1920s, it continues to ask what we can stand to gain, environmentally speaking, by looking back at *fin-de-siècle* American literature with a queer, ecological justice-oriented eye. What might it mean to manage without mastery?

Sand, Water, Salt extends arguments made by a range of literary critics and historians from the 1980s and 1990s who explore Progressive Era scientific management in American literature and culture. In particular, Martha Banta and Cecilia Tichi wrote innovatively about early twentieth-century management philosophies and the individuals who promoted them. While these critics do not specifically focus on land management, their interdisciplinary approaches to "management culture" and "machine-age texts"[25] provided me with a jumping-off point for examining human-elemental relations during the Progressive Era. Though incredibly compelling, Banta and Tichi's investigations rarely look West to see how managers directed their energies towards spaces deemed uninhabitable wastes, such as rural deserts and the deep ocean. *Sand, Water, Salt* picks up where these scholars leave off by insisting on a queerer, more elemental vision of turn-of-the-century management culture in the so-called waste spaces of the American West. Focusing primarily on the applications of Taylorism on urban, industrial environments, Banta explains that scientific management and Progressive reform projects permeated modern American culture, resulting in what she calls "the managed life," or a way of navigating the world on the basis of efficiency and human mastery. Each of my chapters considers how the managed life, as a modern American way of perceiving and relating to one's environment, both shaped and was shaped by *fin-de-siècle* land management policy in frontier spaces.

Management-focused literary and historical projects often focus on the impacts of Progressive ideals in urban, eastern settings, and in *Sand, Water, Salt* I ask how turn-of-the-century reformers engaged with and sought to "improve" Western wasteland spaces—spaces that proved integral in shaping the nation's modern vision of itself. In chapter 1, for example, I examine how the plot of L. Frank Baum's *The Wizard of Oz* follows a popular management philosophy known as the continuous improvement model. In other words, the novel's allegiance to a politics of perfectibility causes characters to view the strange settings of Oz as a series of problems that must be overcome. In this and other Progressive Era works, "the administrative state," as Thomas C. Leonard calls it, interacts with dynamic ecological materialities, resulting in radical modes of material and ideological becoming.[26] These lively ecologies I examine contribute to the making of what Linda Nash calls "the modern body," or a body whose borders are radically porous and, as such, perpetually at risk.[27] As an ecomaterialist project, *Sand, Water, Salt* builds from these and other compelling theories on societal and corporeal management to investigate the complex roles that Western wasteland environments played in both structuring and, at times, undermining "the managed life." At once a cultural construct and material reality, "the modern body" emerges as a potent question in turn-of-the-century Western American literature. Writers of the era contemplate both the dangers and the political possibilities of remaining open to the elements in contested geographies.

Due to this project's preoccupation with elemental animacy and human-environmental relationality, my readings integrate and extend various critical theories emerging from "the material turn," including new materialism, elemental ecocriticism, and transcorporeal materialism. New materialism offers invigorating methods for thinking about objects, environmental matter, human-environmental relations, and ethical attunements in the Anthropocene. Over the last fifteen years, the interdisciplinary nature of materially inflected literary approaches has encouraged critics to seek out new methods with which to consider the "presence" (Bill Brown), "thing-power" (Jane Bennett), or "explosive capacities" (Aaron Jaffe) of the non/human world.[28] In the chapters that follow, I track the "thing-power" of sand, water, and salt in turn-of-the-century literary and cultural artifacts while also considering how these elements animatedly enter, transform, disturb, awaken, create, and undo the humans who make contact with them. As Jeffrey Jerome Cohen and Lowell Duckert note in the introduction to *Elemental Ecocriticism*, a critical collection that stimulated my own interest in ecomaterial animacy, "You are never out of your element," meaning the elements are immanently with us, acting as "the perceivable foundations of which worlds are composed, the animated materialities with and through which life thrives."[29] In *Vibrant Matter: A Political Ecology of Things*, Bennett contends that

> the image of dead or thoroughly instrumentalized matter feeds human hubris and our earth-destroying fantasies of conquest and consumption. It does so by preventing us from detecting (seeing, hearing, smelling, tasting, feeling) a fuller range of the nonhuman powers circulating around and within human bodies.[30]

For Bennett, a kind of politics converges around objects, one that envisions "thing-power" as a potent response to imperialism and global capitalism. After all, since the instrumentalization of matter in a management context often coincides with the erasure of humans who live and work in close proximity to desirable *things*, my interactionist reading of sand, water, and salt allows for a greater focus on environmental injustice than does Bennett's study.

In *Elemental Ecocriticism*, Cohen and Duckert describe the risks of abstracting environmental elements via "mechanistic models": "Through active and recurring forgetting, the apprehension of material vibrancy evident in elemental theory has been obscured by mechanistic models that serve commodity capitalism well but license environmental devastation."[31] Cohen and Duckert's theoretical development of "elemental ecocriticism" aims to redirect our attention to environmental agency and thereby decenter the human, a move intended to cultivate an awareness of "unnoticed agencies" in the world around us.[32] In *Sand, Water, Salt*, I apply the authors' keen alertness to the gritty, granular, often unobserved materialities that surround us to turn-of-the-century scientific management, arguing that Progressives engage deeply and radically with the elements they claim to have mastered. *Sand, Water, Salt* adds a new voice to Cohen and Duckert's ecoelemental conversations by offering a sustained focus on the vibrancy of wasteland materials in an expansionist context. By situating human-elemental engagements in a specific geographical (Western US) and temporal (late nineteenth-/early twentieth-century) context, this project makes a unique intervention in elemental ecocriticism by insisting that environmental animacy is integral to the simultaneous breakdown (and development) of Progressive Era management culture.

Works by ecologically oriented new materialists such as Bennett, Alaimo, Heather I. Sullivan, and others also figure prominently in my examination of wasteland matter, as these theorists and critics resist reducing matter to its mere value as economic resource or metaphor. If one translates matter into resource, commodity, or abstraction, Bennett argues, one perpetuates the idea that objects exist for the taking. Bennett's insistence on matter's ability to captivate and act upon / in bodies is illuminating. *Sand, Water, Salt* extends Bennett's concept of "vibrant matter" to include managed environmental materials in order to observe the queer moments of elemental animacy in the regulatory discourses that tend to flatten matter. Even though Bennett's focus on "thing-power" gives breath to my own elemental study, I remain equally committed to highlighting the productive relationships ecomatter forms with humans, which is a dynamic Bennett sometimes overlooks.

Finally, given this project's interest in the intersections of new materialism with environmental justice activism, Stacy Alaimo's *Bodily Natures* stands as foundational text. Alaimo's "transcorporeal materialism" is a theoretical approach that traces "the interconnections, interchanges, and transits between human bodies and nonhuman natures."[33] Instead of reading environmental materialities apart from *the human*, which, as Alaimo explains, risks flattening matter into a "blank slate" and erasing certain human histories and communities, transcorporeal materialism charts "how race and class (and sometimes gender and sexuality) profoundly influence material, often place-based inequities."[34] In nearly every chapter of *Sand, Water, Salt*, I follow environmental elements as they absorb into and transform characters' habits, biology, management practices, and (racial, sexual, gendered) identities. "Social injustice," Alaimo explains, "is inseparable from physical environments," and in this project I explore the diverse ways that Progressive Era environmental reform efforts attempted to write white male supremacy into "wasteland" environments.

In sum, the thing-focused discourse these and other new materialists advance in their work has invigorated my own meditations on sand, water, and salt in the joint contexts of Progressive Era American literature and management policy. These scholars compellingly theorize "things," "objects," "matter," and "elements," often in relation to the human, in various cultural and historical contexts. *Sand, Water, Salt* productively adds to these lively conversations by interrogating management's relationship with animated elements during the Expansionist Era.

Central to my argument are the stories these elemental intimacies have to tell about "the environmental benefits versus environmental harms gained or suffered by different groups" as a result of scientific land and oceanic management practices.[35] Given Progressive Era preoccupations with public health, fitness, disease, and other bodily concerns, this book's intense focus on radical exchanges between bodies and ecologies at the turn of the century will shed new light on how modern humans came to define themselves in relation to the environment. New materialists have much to gain by looking back to the late nineteenth and early twentieth centuries when theorizing the nonhuman in an ecological context. From the rise and intensification of ecologically and corporeally destructive technologies to the proliferation of disposable consumer goods to the preservation of "aesthetic natures" for white upper-class Americans, the material impacts of Progressive Era land management policy remain inscribed on Western lands to this day.[36] New materialism provides me with a series of interdisciplinary tools from the humanities, social sciences, and natural sciences with which to read an entwined human-environmental history via the grains of sand, dried-out water tanks, and saltwatery currents.

The integration of queer theory, ecocriticism, and land management history operates as the quivering foundation of *Sand, Water, Salt*. These theoretical and historical fields help ignite the conclusions I draw about situated managements and managerial drift. Queer ecology gives us a way to push against—or, better yet, to play within—the language of environmental policymaking in an effort to disturb the masculinist attitude of environmental mastery that insists that capital-N-Nature is separate from, and therefore immune to, people. Even in spaces that are heavily marked by ideological and physical imprints of the nation, such as our national parks and monuments, innumerable experiential possibilities exist. Calling attention to sensual human interactions with the environment in literature can help us to better understand and develop nonnormative modes of citizenship and environmental belonging. If we view environmental materialities not as distant entities to be controlled but as participants in a near infinite variety of human and nonhuman assemblages, our current hierarchical management methods might begin to feel incompatible with the always-interactive ontology. Queer theory and queer ecology give us a language for rethinking the way we manage (in) public lands. Throughout this project I fuse my own insights with those from critics and theorists like Benjamin Bateman, Catriona Sandilands, Timothy Morton, and others as a means of imagining what compassionate and collective approaches to land management might look like.

Although not a queer theorist, Louise Westling articulated very early on the ways that gender and sexuality *matter*, in very literal ways, when it comes to environmental thinking. Westling's groundbreaking *The Green Breast of the New World* ended with a call to resist "destructive gender oppositions" that, for too long, have shaped the way "European/Mediterranean/Mesopotamian" traditions have described landscapes, including Western American ones.[37] Instead, she advises writers to depart from "the heroic masculine codes" in order "to shape new metaphors for the land that are neuter and nonanthropomorphic."[38] *Sand, Water, Salt* builds from Westling's central premise: that gender oppositions often result in both human and environmental harm. However, in this ecoelemental project, my aim is to reach beyond metaphor and into materiality. Metaphors, even so-called "neuter" ones, as Westling proposes, still distance the human from the nonhuman and thereby risk environmental objectification. A word like "resource," for example, operates as a stand-in for lively matter; such a term quickly reduces thing to use-value, vibrant matter to flattened metaphor. What is more, a "neuter" metaphor implies an absence rather than a profusion of ecological possibilities. *Sand, Water, Salt* instead reads the elements as lively forces that make queer contact with other beings. These queer encounters can make it difficult to manage; often, they throw us off course and make us lose our physical and emotional footing, thus leading us to manage in new and unanticipated ways.

This project builds off of these foundational critical, historical, and theoretical works and pushes for more elementally grounded readings of human-environmental interactions in literature set in the American West. Over the past ten years, nineteenth-century literary scholars have excitedly begun taking up environmental questions related to waste, toxicity, and extinction in their work. Energized by the expanding fields of the environmental humanities, energy humanities, and Indigenous studies, the Society of Nineteenth-Century Americanists, known as C19, chose "Climate" as its 2018 conference theme. In its call for papers, C19 articulated the environmental urgency of its theme:

> The conference theme of "Climate" invites us to explore the term's various layers of signification from its meteorological relation to weather, atmosphere, and storms to its metaphoric association with mood, variability, and time. In our own highly contested political climate when environmental, social, economic, and racial justice represents an ongoing struggle, what does it mean to explore the climates of the nineteenth century?[39]

C19 hosted its first environmental humanities cluster in 2016, and many who attended, including myself, expressed a need for an enhanced focus on the environment in nineteenth-century literary studies. Despite this growing interest in asking environmental questions of nineteenth-century American literature, more ecocritical attention is needed that focuses on realism, naturalism, and other late nineteenth- and early twentieth-century literary movements. Progressive Era literature set in the arid, semiarid, and oceanic West remains ripe territory for ecologically oriented literary criticism, especially given that period's intense interest in questions of conservation, waste, civil engineering, federal infrastructure, and resource management. In the chapters that follow, I pursue the movements and provocations of sand, water, and salt in order to more clearly envision the relationship and (highly untidy) nature of turn-of-the-century management.

Due to the project's interest in scientific land management's attempts to suppress environmental animacy and human-elemental intimacy, I have arranged the chapters by ecomateriality rather than by region, chronology, genre, or literary movement. Organizing the project by element highlights the diverse stories that human engagements with sand, water, and salt have to tell about the dreams, shortcomings, and enduring environmental legacies of Progressive Era land management. Furthermore, I examine a range of late nineteenth- and early twentieth-century literary modes and genres, including Indigenous autobiography, a children's fantasy novel, a bestselling western novel, naturalist novels, nature essays, and a fictional diary written by Yone Noguchi. Looking at this diverse range of genres enables me to compare how writers from various movements respond to unmanageable environments both thematically and structurally. Human-elemental intimacy was not an idea relegated to a specific author or movement, which is why *Sand, Water, Salt* reads across broad genres and geographies.

How to manage difficult cultural and ecological terrain is a central concern in both the literary and nonliterary works I explore in this project, and each chapter follows characters as they touch and, in a sense, become dynamic ecomatter. To that end, *Sand, Water, Salt* is organized into four chapters that move across various regions and environments in the West—and beyond. Chapter 1 offers an introduction to late nineteenth-century land management practices and tracks how "the forester's eye," a term I adopt from Gifford Pinchot, attempts to supervise and arrest dynamic ecomaterials in "management literature." Each chapter thereafter focuses on how a single element frustrates, beckons, overpowers, or transforms in a management context the humans who interact with it. I organize each chapter in three distinct parts, beginning with a historically situated overview of the element or technology in question and continuing with close readings of works by two turn-of-the-century authors. In each chapter, I attempt to bring together works by two writers of the West who, at least at first, might seem to have little in common.

My hope is that these unlikely pairings will illustrate how gender, race, sexuality, ethnicity, and nationality shaped human-environmental relations during what was often a hostile time for women, immigrants, non-Anglos, and others who felt that they were positioned on the cultural fringe. Within each chapter, I put literary works in conversation with nonliterary artifacts such as maps, dry-farming manifestos, travel guides, and park foundation documents in an effort to build an interdisciplinary archive around the concept of land management. Furthermore, by analyzing Progressive Era literary works alongside these diverse cultural and political artifacts, I am able to chart a lineage of scientific management through various turn-of-the-century discourses and movements. The management archive represented in this book is one of many, and I hope other scholars will feel encouraged to curate, question, and reimagine other management archives that speak to the range of ways individuals connect with their environments.

Unlike chapters 2 to 4, each of which focuses on human engagements with a dynamic eco-element, chapter 1 will examine the diverse ways that the managerial state structures knowledge. As an overview chapter, "Under 'the Forester's Eye': Overseeing the Elements in Progressive Era Management Utopias" argues that turn-of-the-century scientific land management's increasing power coincided with its deployment of a variety of aerial camera technologies. Aerial vision is, therefore, central to the modern management project, and in this opening chapter I argue that this surveilling "eye of the forester" shapes both the theme and the structure of a variety of turn-of-the-century utopian works, including L. Frank Baum's *The Wonderful Wizard of Oz* (1900). Baum's fantasy novel, which takes place both in Kansas and in the mythical Land of Oz, consistently offers readers panoramic views, map-like depictions of difficult landscapes, and scenes depicting flying animals and various aviation technologies. When combined, these aerial moments in the novel privilege the view from above as a way of understanding—and, therefore, managing—challenging landscapes that are reminiscent of the vast "wasteland" spaces of the turn-of-the-century West. Not only does Baum favor aeriality in terms of plot and point of view, but the manager's all-seeing, future-oriented eye also permeates the novel's structure. In other words, for the plot to progress, characters must recursively engage with and overcome a series of environmental problems. By reading the novel alongside aerial photographs, parakite technical manuals, and nineteenth-century cloud studies, I argue that Progressives' reform-oriented way of seeing the world both produces the concept of the wasteland and requires such a concept for its survival.

Chapter 2, "'Left All Alone in This World's Wilderness': Queer Ecology and Managing Desert Sand," further complicates scientific land management's recursive logic by exploring the queer, interactive relationships between humans and desert sand in two very different turn-of-the-century works: Frank Norris's naturalist novel *McTeague* and Mary Austin's collection of nature essays *The Land of Little Rain*. Both works offer glimpses of individuals who *desertify*, or literally become the desert, when they make contact with Southern California's lively grains. Despite their generic and tonal differences when writing about "desertness," as Austin calls it, Norris and Austin figure desert sand as a queer, almost agential material that provokes desire in the manager and refuses to behave. By and large, Progressive managers viewed arid environments as obstacles to Western development and, hence, maintained that desert spaces "bordered on anarchy."⁴⁰ Additionally, in the American imaginary, deserts have long been perceived as the quintessential wasteland in that they contrast starkly with the lush, green, Thoreauvian landscapes often associated with more Romantic conceptions of nature.

The cultural artifacts I cite in the first section of this chapter demonstrate Progressives' urgent efforts to eradicate the pesky grains of sand from their communities, homes, and bodies. The Death Valley scene in Norris's *McTeague* illustrates how desire (for distance, for understanding, for control) both undergirds and threatens administrative power. By reading McTeague's clumsy march through the desert through the lens of queer ecology, I argue that management's enduring presence in American wastelands requires that the manager intimately engage with so-called managed elements. McTeague's grapplings with the pesky elements—elements that choke, exfoliate, and dry him out—urge him on, albeit a bit recklessly, revealing that management is as vulnerable as it is persistent. Austin's reflections on the arid lands surrounding her home in the San Joaquin Valley mark her as a different kind of manager, one who attempts to decelerate the anxious rush of managerial time via close examinations of sand and other desert actants. In chapter 2, I argue that management's endurance hinges on its ability to make itself appear essential in the future tense via short- and long-term planning. In *The Land of Little Rain*, however, Austin examines the possibilities of what I refer to as "sand-time" to question what land and environmental management might look like without the future tense.

The third chapter, "'Under the Ditch': Managing Bodies (of Water) in Western American Literature," heads to the semiarid high plains and asserts that the desire to channel and divert water across vast distances and at great costs underscores the agentive power of both aridity and water in the West. The book's water chapter reads Owen Wister's bestselling western novel, *The Virginian*, alongside Sarah Winnemucca's memoir, *Life among the Piutes: Their Wrongs and Claims*, in an attempt to view western expansion and water development from two different cultural perspectives in the arid and semiarid West. Both authors depict water and water infrastructure as more than a mere backdrop in their writing; however, while Wister reads dams and ditches as artifacts of national progress, Winnemucca's situatedness as a displaced Paiute causes her to view these same structures as symbols of environmental injustice. For settlers, farmers, ranchers, developers, and politicians, Western water development emerged as a potent creed at the turn of the century. By using a diverse set of critical theories, including envirotech history, maintenance studies, and transcorporeal materialism, I demonstrate how Progressives' often troubling views of race, gender, and sexuality at once saturate and come undone around the sites of federal water infrastructure.

Finally, chapter 4, "The Salt Cure: Brining Soft Bodies in the 'Wild Waste' of the Pacific Ocean," heads into the turbulent waves of the turn-of-the-century Pacific and asks how characters in Jack London's *The Sea-Wolf* and Yone Noguchi's *The American Diary of a Japanese Girl* experience salt as a penetrative, transformative, and altogether queer agent. In these works, salt(water) and sea-sickness threaten the bodies of those who venture into the "wild waste" of the Pacific Ocean, and these salty penetrations offer insight into gendered and ethnic anxieties during the Progressive Era.[41] In the first sections of chapter 4, I provide a historical over-view of "the salt cure," a turn-of-the-century medical procedure whereby "nervous" patients—who were often white and upper class—received hypodermic injections of saltwater in an effort to revitalize the body and mind. From this view, salt is both a per-meative and corrective element, and I argue that London uses saltwatery immersions in a similar way in his novel: to manage and restore masculine whiteness. While London's main character, Humphrey Van Weyden, attains strength and masculine hardness as a result of his body's radical absorption of Pacific saltwater, Noguchi's fictional diarist, a young Japanese woman named Miss Morning Glory, loosens up when her body makes contact with Pacific elements. This loosening—or what I refer to in the chapter as a "productive drift"—allows her to manage by not-really-man-aging when she arrives in the strange new land of California. These two very different Pacific tales offer a unique take on the ways that unmanageable environmental elements, such as salt, (re)articulate Progressive conceptions of masculinity and ethnic belonging in the United States at the turn of the century. Pursuant to the masculinist logic of London's naturalist novel, race and gen-der determine one's ability to successfully manage (in) the elements, highlighting the close relationship between early twentieth-century oceanic mobility and white male supremacy in the United States.

Informed by my own commitment to the environmental humanities, in the coda I assert that Progressive Era environmental thinking, as it is diversely expressed in turn-of-the-twentieth-century American literature, continues to inform human-environmental relations in the twenty-first century. Building from Benjamin Bateman's notion of "lateral agency," I argue that climate change calls on us to seek out queer ways of managing by *not* managing—or of drifting, oceanically, into moments of intimacy, activism, and pleasure.[42] These more adaptive approaches to management should act not as replacements for but as supplements to already established practices and policies. In other words, what we need are situated managements that invite mutual care and shared governance.

It is easy to overlook sand, water, and salt both in literature and in our daily lives. We might think of these elements—when we think of them at all—in largely economic terms: as "passive matter" that achieves value via the marketplace. At other, more immersive moments, these elements might strike us as nuisance materials, such as when sand blows into our eyes or rainwater leaks into our homes. Unless we contemplate these elements for more than a few seconds, we might perceive them as dead and discrete particles—*a drop of water is just a drop of water*—instead of as highly mobile members of hyperobjective assemblages in their own right. *Sand, Water, Salt* encourages environmental humanists to give into "the pull," as Watkins calls it, of sand, water, and salt in Progressive Era American literature. When we imaginatively surrender to the pull, we gain the powerful ability to see wasteland for what it is: a capitalistic concept that rhetorically deadens environments and, in turn, rationalizes extractive industrial practices. Even in the desiccated West that Watkins imagines in *Gold Fame Citrus*, readers discover moments of strange liveliness—and possibility. "But there is life here," one character says as the sand continues its steady march in the distance. "That's what I'm trying to tell you. There is so much life" (192).

CHAPTER 1

UNDER "THE FORESTER'S EYE"

OVERSEEING THE ELEMENTS IN PROGRESSIVE ERA MANAGEMENT UTOPIAS

But we were careless and happy and full of fun, and enjoyed every minute of the day. This was years ago, long before Oz came out of the clouds to rule over this land.

—L. FRANK BAUM (1900)[1]

There are no trees, there are no deepwater lakes. There are no mountains like those in the video. . . . This image of a flat, white nothingness is what you would see the majority of the year. . . . I intend to uncover the facts for you as clearly and as graphically as time and the Committee's audio-visual technology will permit.

—INTERIOR SECRETARY GALE NORTON, TESTIFYING ON BEHALF OF OIL AND GAS EXPLORATION IN THE ARCTIC NATIONAL WILDLIFE REFUGE BEFORE THE US HOUSE COMMITTEE ON NATURAL RESOURCES (2003)[2]

Google Maps tries to fill in holes only to end up revealing that much more is missing than geographical coordinates. We are still missing a philosophy.

—ELENA GLASBERG (2012)[3]

S cientific land management greatly depends upon the ability to observe, apprehend, map, and closely analyze the natural world, and *fin-de-siècle* innovations in aerial photography and applied microscopy certainly aided in these perceptual efforts. Whether a geological surveyor is gazing at the striations of a distant glacier through a telephoto lens, or an entomologist is spying the egg sac of an "injurious" bark beetle through the eyepiece of a compound microscope, there is no doubt that vision plays a key role in modern "knowledge projects."[4] In this introductory chapter, which begins by sketching a historical and theoretical framework for the rest of the book, I argue that Progressive Era American literature experiments with the possibilities of the scientific administrator's totalizing eye, an eye equipped to oversee environmental matter from an elevated vantage point. Then, in the second half of this chapter, I will investigate visuality's fundamental role in regulating wasteland ecologies in what I consider to be an archetypal management novel, L. Frank Baum's *The Wonderful Wizard of Oz* (1900).

According to theorists Mark Dorrian and Frédéric Pousin, the aerial view "is central to the modern imagination and, indeed, might even be claimed to be its emblematic visual form."[5] Baum's novel in particular highlights this Progressive fascination with what I term an eco-managerial optics, or an intense desire to control difficult, dynamic terrain by way of seeing. Through both theme and structure, this work promulgates what seems the infinite vision of the surveyor, manager, developer, or expeditionist and mirrors innovations in modern visualization apparatuses. In particular, aerial camera technologies, which existed as tools of choice for modern land managers, operate as the narrative eyes in Baum's novel, granting characters the ability to manage environments at both macro and micro levels. However, I contend that an administrative approach to seeing the world risks perpetuating what Jane Bennett refers to as "fantasies of conquest and consumption," thus resulting in exploitative, divide-and-conquer relations with humans, animals, and ecologies.[6] What's more, this chapter's engagement with both cultural and literary artifacts reveals that the lively presence of elemental activity at once clouds and distorts the manager's "synoptic gaze," even, and maybe especially, when he purports that his vision is exact.[7] An understanding of these complex human-environmental relations in the context of Progressive Era management helps give shape to the three element-focused chapters that follow.

What exactly is the manager's vision, and what does it see? Early promoters of scientific land management, such as Gifford Pinchot and John Burroughs, were firm believers in "the seeing eye" of the ranger.[8] In his treatise on scientific forestry titled *The Training of a Forester* (1914), Pinchot, often referred to as the father of American forestry and conservation, asserts, "No man can be a good Forester without that quality of observation and understanding which the French call 'the forester's eye.' It is not the only quality required for success in forestry, but it is unquestionably the first."[9] Throughout this work, which reads like an occupational manifesto for future foresters, the first chief of the US Forest Service elevates the power of sight over all other senses as the ranger's most important tool for managing America's burgeoning forest preserves. Pinchot calls on rangers to develop "the forester's eye," or an ability to keenly understand, scan, separate, and assign value to the features of the managed environment, thus reinforcing the primacy of sight in the management project. If a ranger wishes to be successful, Pinchot argues, he must develop "the seeing eye," "an immediate eye," and the "unassisted eye," all of which contribute to "his silvical knowledge by observation."[10] Moreover, he stresses that trees, mineral resources, and waterways exist "under the eye . . . of the technical forester, whose duty is to see that the future of the forest is protected by enforcing the conditions of the sale."[11] Unlike the country's national parks, whose vast tracts were to be managed according to a preservationist ethos, the national forests, guided by the philosophy of conservation, were intended to be used wisely and sustainably for the long-term benefit of the American people. In other words, the job of a modern forester was to ensure the inexhaustibility of the nation's valuable resources, which meant that the modern forester needed to acquire "a far-sighted attitude," or the unique ability to both foresee and efficiently manage the nation's future.[12] The eye of the forester, as Pinchot understood it, was as literal as it was visionary.

In addition to simultaneously surveilling his surroundings *and* keeping an eye on the future (no easy feat!), the Progressive manager must also learn to distinguish between waste material and valuable resource, or to individualize and particularize matter via the lens of commodity capitalism, according to Pinchot. In "what time he can spare," the forester must occupy himself "with studies of injurious insects or fungi, of the reasons for the increase or decrease of valuable or worthless species of trees in the forest," and other issues related to the forest's apparent worth as resource.[13] Tasked with so many duties already, the eye of the ranger had to double as the eye of the developer-capitalist, since a significant part of the job of a forester involved "classifying the economic woods of the United States," Pinchot adds.[14]

This description of the woods as "economic" aligns with those who espoused conservationist views at the turn of the century, such as John Burroughs. Burroughs, a well-known naturalist and contemporary of Pinchot, seems as invested as Pinchot in an eco-managerial optics and avers that one's eye should be well trained before the naturalist conducts serious work in the field. In his 1908 essay "The Art of Seeing Things," Burroughs asserts that a trained eye is one whose "purpose goes to the mark."[15] "The things that pass before [the eyes of close observers]," he says, "are caught and individualized instantly."[16] To "instantly" catch and particularize environmental objects in the messy ecological assemblage—to identify "the mark" of importance amid matter-in-motion—speaks to the techno-visual imperative that guides Burroughs's work as a naturalist. Nature writing, for him, is an art of focus that involves tracking and extracting *significant matter* from the unfolding expanse, much like a photographer homes in on her animated subject or a biologist adjusts the lens of a microscope to achieve focus. These same optical impulses, motivated by complex desires to see (clearly), permeate Baum's writing as well, aligning his narratives with the goals of scientific land management while also revealing the inherent weaknesses of the management project.

OVERSEEING UTOPIA

Using Pinchot, Burroughs, and other modern conservationists as illustrative proponents of what Donna Haraway calls the "doctrine of objectivity,"[17] the remaining sections of this chapter pursue the machinations of the totalizing eye of the Progressive Era land manager—an eye charged with policing and overseeing substance, temporality, and cultural value—in a quest narrative that grants a utopian vision of land management in the turn-of-the-century American West. I use the word "oversee" deliberately here, as we often think of the physical eye of the land manager as hovering above the environment, such as from a mountain peak, a topographical map, a microscope, a drone, or even a satellite.[18] (It comes as no surprise, for example, that the very first photograph that appears in Pinchot's *The Training of a Forester* depicts an imperial-looking forester peering across a denuded landscape through a set of binoculars.)[19] However, both mechanical and ocular failure inherently undermine the authority of the overseer, and in the remaining sections of this chapter I pursue moments when weather, light, and mechanical and bodily complications inhibit vision. As aerial photographer William Eddy noted in an 1897 *Anaconda Standard* article regarding his experiments with kite photography, "I don't wish to appear too sanguine . . . as the chances of failure in any attempt at aerial picture-taking are at least one in three in spite of every precaution."[20] Failure,

I contend, does not necessarily result in the dissolution of the management project; on the contrary, failure serves to motivate the management apparatus by justifying continued surveillance, instigating technological innovation, and eliciting more extractive environmental practices in the name of "progress." To that end, I suggest that the compulsive problem-solution structure of *The Wizard of Oz* reflects this managerial fixation with a politics of endless improvement.

Finally, since I am framing *The Wizard of Oz* as a *management utopia* while simultaneously considering the book's more specific literary classification as a fairy tale, it is worth explaining what I mean by "utopia." Scholars of utopian studies refer to the years between 1865 and 1917 as the "Golden Age of Literary Utopias" in the United States.[21] According to the *Historical Dictionary of Utopianism*, 120 utopian novels appeared within this Golden Age, nearly a third of which were published in the 1890s.[22] Much criticism exists that ties the revival of the utopian genre in the nineteenth century to longings for racial justice or Black liberation, female emancipation, economic equality, and, in some cases, white supremacy.[23] However, few critics have contemplated the imbrication of Progressive Era literary utopias to the ideals of land management, especially as these ideals manifested themselves west of the Mississippi River. Since literary critics in utopian studies often frame the utopian impulse as a yearning for "a good place," as Mary Ellen Snodgrass suggests, then a land-oriented approach to the genre may help to align utopianism with an eco-managerial ethos.[24] In *The Wizard of Oz*, Baum provides glimpses of characters who, at first, seem to achieve a kind of mastery over their environments via diverse tools, methods, and virtues, including aerial surveillance technologies, maps, bodily training, and a strong work ethic. While the author offers unconventional—and, at times, fantastical—approaches to *knowing the land*, his distinct takes on human-environmental relations frequently coincide with the utopian aspirations of scientific land management, particularly as such efforts were realized in the "unproductive" wasteland spaces of the American West. While the aerial view, as it emerges in this work, would seem to render a "totalizing utopic view" for the modern overseer, Baum instead reveals that optical distortions, elemental interferences, cartographical limitations, and biological and technical failures compound and disrupt total control.[25] After all, the eye cannot manage its way out of a cyclone, the natural disaster that initiates Dorothy's expedition through the Land of Oz in the first place.

"THE HITHERTO IMPOSSIBLE IN PHOTOGRAPHY IS OUR SPECIALTY"

Baum was certainly not the only Progressive fascinated with what William L. Fox terms "aereality," or an "aerial view of reality," that began to dominate modern perception at the turn of the century.[26] For example, in his 1897 article in *Scribner's* titled "Unusual Uses of Photography," Gilbert Totten Woglom explains that the "pervasive vision" of the aerial camera proves more dependable than the unreliable eye of man:

> Instead of sending up a man or men . . . and relying only on their eyes and powers of memory, it is evident that a camera may be sent aloft with much less trouble. A camera has a pervasive vision, its impression is of everything within its view, its memory is infallible and it needs no quizzing except with a magnifying glass.[27]

Woglom, who wrote extensively about the advantages of kites for surveying purposes, sees in aerial photography the dream of a perfect, inescapable vision.[28] Unlike the unassisted human eye, which is prone to error and forgetfulness, photographic memory is "infallible," he stresses, and he devotes the remainder of his article to examining the various scientific purposes to which kites and kite photography could be applied. From attaining "valuable meteorological information" and reconnaissance in times of war to providing an "accurate perspective with exact details" of *terra incognita*, aerial technologies facilitate the bird's-eye view that management has thus far lacked, Woglom believes.[29] Therefore, before analyzing the implications of the eco-managerial eye in Baum's novel, it is worth investigating in greater detail modern Americans' faith in aerial-visual technologies.

Throughout the nineteenth century and into the twentieth, scientists, surveyors, and developers experimented with capturing a view of the land from above via a variety of devices and locations, including camera-equipped pigeons, towers, ropes and trapezes, ladders, hot-air balloons, helium balloons, mountain peaks, roofs, ship masts, kites, flag poles, telephone cables, "captive airships," and even rockets.[30] Ranging from aiding in commercial and military operations to assisting with urban planning and even infrastructural development, aerial photography gave modern individuals opportunities to engage with "hitherto impossible" visual pursuits.[31] Land managers and surveyors found much to admire in these new ways of seeing, and they quickly adopted aerial camera equipment due to the "accurate perspective" and "exact details" it was believed to render.[32] In fact, from its inception in the mid-nineteenth century, photography was thought to hold particular advantages in the field over other modes of visual representation, such as painting and drawing, because of its "rigorous precision."[33] In *Photography and Exploration*, for example, James R. Ryan asserts that whereas the nineteenth-century expeditionary sketcher "might be tempted to omit or ornament some detail to enhance the picture, the photographer had no option but to capture nature completely."[34] The term "capture" here at once resonates with the technical procedure of snapping a photo and the expansionist ambition of claiming new country, which seems to imbricate exploratory photography with an imperialist spirit, or what Haraway refers to in more disparaging terms as the "unregulated gluttony" of the "technological feast."[35]

In the 1890s, innovations in aerial camera technologies certainly gave the manager-explorer a larger buffet from which to feast. In writing about the advantages of aerial photography for the modern explorer, Woglom explains that the "folding parakite," an aerial camera device "which may be rolled as compactly as an umbrella and carried in a tin case," would allow one to capture more "untracked" terrain than ever.[36] With such a device, a surveyor would "be able to choose beforehand the best routes over unknown mountain ranges and through yet untracked jungles, and by this means make accurate detailed maps of wide districts that now must remain *terra incognita*."[37] Not only would portable parakites save surveyors both time and space, thus resulting in a more efficient expedition, but this exceptionally portable device would also allow hikers to cross the threshold into the unknown without the risks or difficulties associated with actually *being* there. Erwin Hinckley Barbour, surveyor for the Morrill Geological Expedition of 1897, shares Woglom's excitement about the portability and scope of modern visualization technologies when describing the agential nature of the crew's telephoto lens in the Badlands of South Dakota: "Our telephoto lens looked directly over the heads of these same hills and brought the distant object to us, instead of us going to it."[38] Instead of wandering into unknown spaces, the enhanced lens of Barbour's camera does the job for him, thus saving him both time and energy. Similar to today's camera-equipped drones or Google satellites, whereby a machine acts as a stand-in for or extension of the flesh-and-bone human body, turn-of-the-century aerial cameras gave American explorers an opportunity to see, control, and manage one's way into future-space. In other words, land could be seen, mapped, and claimed well in advance of contact.

Even though experimentations with aerial photography occurred well before Woglom carried out his tests with parakites—in fact, as early as 1855 French balloonist Gaspard-Félix Tournachon processed what many consider to be the first aerial photograph from the basket of his tethered hot-air balloon—rapid innovations in both aeronautics and photography in the 1890s improved the art, thus promising photographers and managers

more clarity, portability, and technical flexibility. One such inno-
vator in the arena of aerial-visual technologies in the United States
was George R. Lawrence, from whom the title of this section
derives. As the first commercial aerial photographer in the United
States, Lawrence's business motto was "The Hitherto Impossible
in Photography Is Our Specialty," a phrase that encapsulates the
modern photographer's desires to push his or her cameras to new
limits—and, in Lawrence's case, to new altitudes.[39] Among other
innovations, he devised the world's largest camera, improved
flash powder technology, and developed a relatively stable train
of camera-lifting kites, the latter of which piqued the interest of
President Theodore Roosevelt, who met with Lawrence to discuss the benefits of aerial photography for wartime purposes.
Lawrence referred to his own seeing kite as "the Captive Airship"
and used it to take one of his most famous photographs, "San
Francisco in Ruins" (1906). This realist rendering of environmental disaster proved just how valuable aerial photography could be
to Progressive Era land management and urban planning.

Following the 7.8-magnitude earthquake that struck San
Francisco on April 18, 1906, a series of fires broke out across the
Bay Area, resulting in the deaths of over three thousand individuals. Determined to document "the true magnitude of the disaster," Lawrence and crew arrived in San Francisco a few weeks later
with the Captive Airship, a series of seventeen kites connected by
a main kite line that was capable of elevating a heavy panoramic
camera two thousand feet into the air.[40] The launch proved successful, resulting in the production of four large contact prints,
three of which averaged a whopping forty-seven by nineteen
inches.[41] Both the size of the prints and their surprising clarity
led many to question whether the images were indeed real.[42] In
describing the impact these panoramic photographs would have
had on viewers at the time, historian Simon Baker notes, "Each
one invites close inspection of its details: people in the streets,
horses, wagons, tents, piles of rubble, and remains of buildings.

Everything but the horizon is in sharp focus." Lawrence's photographs, he continues, "showed perspectives of landscapes few humans had ever seen," which might be why individual copies sold for $125 each.

Baker's inventory of the distinct elements that populate "San Francisco in Ruins"—gridded roadways, various modes of transportation, and makeshift buildings—highlights one of the key appeals of aerial vision, especially as we consider the implications of these surveillance technologies in a management context. What Thébaud-Sorger describes as the "atmospheric approach to seeing," or the act of looking down upon the world from above, cultivates a narrative of order in the presence of overwhelming disorder, and Lawrence's photograph certainly delivers on this effect.[43] On the ground, the "piles of rubble and remains of buildings" might seem insurmountable—the dust yet too thick to see through, the toppled bricks still impeding the flow of traffic. From above, however, as previously noted, "everything but the horizon is in sharp focus." The tents sheltering the homeless present themselves in "neat rows," and the city below "slowly return[s] to normal life."[44] Not only does "San Francisco in Ruins" allow us, as viewers, to peek in on disaster from a safe spatiotemporal distance to sate our curiosity—we hover above the "ruins" well after the earthquake, the fires, have ended—but the camera's removal from ground-level interferences, such as people, ashes, broken water pipes, and the dead, generates a message of organization and resilience. If one were living in one of those "neat rows" of tents or, perhaps, still searching for a loved one in all that rubble, would such a message seem true?

Lawrence's camera, an eye "floating disconnected above the earth and above the melee," revises the city's "ruins" by containing and compressing disaster into a manageable frame.[45] Or, as Susan Sontag notes in *On Photography*, "To photograph is to appropriate the thing photographed. It means putting oneself into a certain relation to the world that feels like knowledge—and, therefore, like power."[46] Revision, the somewhat privileged act of adjusting the angle and seeing anew, promises a way out of failure, disaster, waste, or inefficiency, allowing the manager—the literal overseer—to continue plotting a path toward improvement, even and maybe especially when the obstacles seem insurmountable. Aided by digital and satellite technologies, today's aerial imagery continues to elicit these same revisionary narratives of control even when the photographers' intentions are to raise awareness about environmental disaster. For example, many of the aerial photographs taken of the 2015 Gold King Mine wastewater spill, which sent 3 million gallons of heavy metals into the Animas River watershed and impacted habitats and communities across regions in Colorado, Utah, New Mexico, and Arizona, render the contamination as simultaneously devastating *and* containable.[47] Even though the yellow-tinted water, when seen from above, alerts us that a toxic event has taken place, the bird's-eye view obscures the rhizomic seepage; the vast, messy dispersal; and the current and future ingestions of arsenic, zinc, and other metallic agents. When we are located above the disaster, the lines between poisoned and unpoisoned appear clear, distinct; eventual containment seems possible. As "hyperobjects," entities so large they become "impossible to hold in mind," the earthquake in 1906 and the contaminated river in 2015 are nearer to us and, perhaps, more agentive than the camera makes them out to be.[48] "Hyperobjects are not just the stuff of charts and simulations," Timothy Morton says, "but rather are huge objects consisting of other objects," and their sprawling interconnectedness makes them inherently illegible, inaccessible, and therefore highly unmanageable.[49] Playing with an aerial metaphor, Morton adds, hyperobjects are "responsible for pushing us out of the plane," eradicating the distance between the overseeing human and the messy ground below.[50]

Lawrence's own failures to sever the seeing eye from unruly terrain are perhaps most evident in a series of government reports produced in response to his Captive Airship. Following the popularity of "San Francisco in Ruins," Lawrence put his Captive Airship to a variety of other uses, including irrigation photographs for prospective development companies and wildlife photography in East Africa. However, it was the attention he received from the US Navy in 1905 and 1906 that perhaps best demonstrates the optical limitations and consequential failures of modern visualization technologies, especially when these technologies confront agentive ecologies. Having caught wind of Lawrence's successes in kite photography, the Navy invited him to conduct a series of experiments off the coast of Virginia to see if the Captive Airship could deliver reliable reconnaissance during times of war. In addition to providing detailed technical descriptions of the Captive Airship, as well as providing some of the only existing diagrams and photographs of Lawrence's craft, the two Navy reports exude excitement about the prospects of aerial surveillance while, strangely, also reading like an inventory of instrumental failure. Rough winds, hazy skies, rain, humidity, poor lighting, and other atmospheric annoyances hindered Lawrence's experiments on both occasions, leading the reports' authors to doubt the efficacy of his design.

"Accidents of different kinds occurred and would be likely to occur under any ordinary conditions," reads the 1906 report, "though the whole system could be improved in many particulars. Kites were lost or blown to pieces, some falling in the water. On one occasion the steadying line carried away, tilting the camera but fortunately not losing it."[51] The 1905 report also comments on the problem of weather, noting that "Rain squalls and light winds *full of flaws* greatly hampered this test."[52] The flying camera—angling, waterlogged, and at times "blown to pieces"—ultimately misses the mark at achieving "pervasive vision." The pesky elements, ever "full of flaws," cloud the managerial eye, underscoring Morton's claim that "'distance' is only a psychic and ideological construct designed to protect me from the nearness of things."[53] But can eco-material agencies really undermine Progressive Era management, or do these generative interferences merely activate or justify the enhancement, entrenchment, and prolongation of the management project? According to Woglom, the "special difficulties and new problems" born from aerial-visual pursuits—problems like light, air, and weather interacting with scientific instruments—require new and improved solutions, a message that reads more like an enthusiastic call to action for managers and engineers than a sign of an ultimate administrative defeat.[54] As a novel devoted to capturing the land via observation and "aereality," *The Wizard of Oz*, similar to other management novels this book explores, demonstrates that problems with (seeing) nature perpetuate managerial desires.

MANAGING IN THE CLOUDS: THE AERIAL OPTICS OF L. FRANK BAUM'S *THE WONDERFUL WIZARD OF OZ*

In the visual and literary arts, the modern desire to go airborne at the turn of the century engaged writers and artists in new aesthetic orientations and points of view and, according to some, liberated the terrestrial eye from what Victor Hugo described as the "universal tyranny of gravity."[55] Be it an aerial photograph of San Francisco following the 1906 earthquake, an impressionistic oil painting depicting a collage of puffy cumulus clouds, or an exhilarating description of a young trick pilot "diving earthward" above a "silent, motionless, gazing" crowd, Progressive Era artists and writers, similar to their land management counterparts, grew increasingly captivated by the possibilities of liftoff.[56] In his own fiction, Baum began to ask how a bird's-eye view, especially when *captured* and then interpreted by the trained eye of a manager, might enhance one's understanding of and mastery over unruly terrain. This section argues that the rising popularity of aeronautics, and aerial photography in particular, as a land management tool stimulates the seeming illimitable gaze in Baum's *The Wizard of Oz*. Even when Dorothy and her friends are traveling by foot, they often achieve vistas of vast, open spaces, almost as if they were viewing the land from a balloon. While camera technologies themselves fail to appear in the novel, the book's deep interest in (and anxieties about) narrative mapping, visual manipulation and interference, and what Haraway terms the "infinite vision" of masculinist science resonates with the developing practice of aerial camerawork.[57] Given Baum's own interest in amateur photography, especially his collection of Dakota cloudscapes, the novel's recurrent desire to capture the land from the sky finds a biographical root as well.[58]

Baum shared his deep interests in technological innovation, aeronautics, and photography with other Progressive-minded individuals, including Charlotte Perkins Gilman, who excitedly anticipates the "coming conquest of the air" in her essay "When We Fly" (1907).[59] "Behold man," Gilman says, "winged and engined, buzzing off, like a huge cockchafer, to soar and circle, dip and rise as he will!"[60] Likewise, Gilman's utopian novel *Herland* begins with a biplane exploration; the passengers, who made sure to pack their cameras and glasses, believe that flight will afford them "the lay of the land."[61] In his fiction, Baum explores these "winged and engined" possibilities of the new century, linking mechanical flight, as Gilman does, to individual will and determination. For example, nearly eleven years after writing the first of his *Oz* novels, Baum produced two works for young adults titled *The Flying Girl* (1911) and *The Flying Girl and Her Chum* (1912), both of which centered on a young girl named Orissa Kane who rose to fame as a trick pilot in Southern California.[62]

Writing under the pseudonym Edith Van Dyne, Baum notes in the preface of the initial book that he looks forward to a future where airplanes will be the dominant mode of transport in the United States: "The world is agog with wonder at what has been accomplished; even now it is anticipating the time when vehicles of the air will be more numerous than are automobiles to-day" (11). Similar to other flight-oriented novels written for young adults at the turn of the century, such as Harry Lincoln Sayler's *The Airship Boys* and *The Aeroplane Boys* series,[63] *The Flying Girl* both marvels at "the awful audacity of man in building these mechanical birds"[64] and encourages future innovations in aviation design. Several pages in *The Airship Boys* series, for example, are devoted to technical diagrams and detailed instructions on how to assemble modern aircraft. Even though *The Wonderful Wizard of Oz* was published in 1900, just three years prior to the first official flight of an airplane by Orville and Wilbur Wright, Baum's interest in modern air travel figures prominently in the fairy tale, beginning with Dorothy's ride in the cyclone that "felt as if she were going up in a balloon" (8) and ending with her journey in the Silver Shoes that "can carry [her] anyplace in the world," including over the notoriously treacherous desert of Oz to her home in Kansas (104). When combined with the diverse forms of flight experienced in the novel, these panoramic views allow characters to render extreme, nearly impassable terrain in cartographical terms, thus making it more manageable—or so it would seem.

Baum, who wrote *The Wonderful Wizard of Oz* a little over ten years after living in drought-stricken South Dakota, introduces flight and the wide-lens imperial gaze as keys to managing the unruly environments Dorothy encounters in Oz.[65] From the Winged Monkeys and the helpful stork to the leaping lion and hot-air balloons, Dorothy and her crew are able to evade severe landscapes and dangerous situations with the help of flying bodies and machines. Even though various types of flight appear in this and other Progressive Era novels, here I wish to focus my attention on the environmental implications of Baum's aerial vision.

Critics like Laura Barrett have examined the managerial imperative of *The Wizard of Oz*, making a case that its emphasis on the development of roads and infrastructure underscores the Progressive Era's administrative ethos. This section builds on this extant criticism by asserting that Baum's atmospheric approach to seeing helps to define turn-of-the-century land management as a visual-aerial enterprise, one that continues to inform how land managers relate to, and are perhaps even overcome by, dynamic ecologies. It is especially worth considering how the seemingly innocuous and pleasurable views characters gain from elevated vantage points—the sky, hilltop, cliff, treetop, and wall—reflect the reductionist ways scientific managers often engaged with so-called difficult environments in the American West.

In one scene we are even told that the Wicked Witch of the West "had but one eye . . . that was as powerful as a telescope, and could see everywhere," aligning a somewhat sinister force "of the West" with all-seeing surveillance technologies. With this eye, she oversees her territory and plans violent attacks on trespassers. *The Wizard of Oz* privileges this ability to visually capture and, therefore, manage land, people, animals, and biota from hovering locations, and characters frequently gain higher ground in an attempt to broaden their scope of vision over indeterminate landscapes. In one scene, for example, Dorothy can be observed "riding easily" (71) in the arms of Winged Monkeys over a land that, just moments before, had frightened and disoriented her at ground level. Having lost their way to the Emerald City in a strange land with "no road," the group "did not know which was east and which was west, and that was the reason they were lost in the great fields" (70). Their vision struggles in this perceived no-man's-land, as "they still saw nothing before them" after days of travel (70). "'If we walk far enough,'" Dorothy announces to the group, "'we shall sometime come to *some place* I am sure'" (70, emphasis added). In a land without pathways or built infrastructure—a *no place* that contrasts with the "some place" of the city—their progress slows and grows unfocused. What is more, with the sun "behind a cloud" (70) and "big fields of buttercups" (69) blocking their sight, they cannot see a way forward. Visual obstructions, such as unmanaged foliage and poor lighting, interfere with clear vision, turning their once energized march into a distracted wandering. What they need is a new perspective, a chance to rise above the inhibiting over-growth and map a way out of nothingness.

When the Winged Monkeys happily come to Dorothy's aid, optimism returns to the group. From above, the once impervious landscape takes on a more disciplined appearance, revealing how an aerial perspective grants the overseeing eye an element of control. While in flight, "they had a fine time looking at the pretty gardens and woods far below them. Dorothy found herself riding easily between two of the biggest Monkeys. . . . They had made a chair of their hands and were careful not to hurt her" (71). Sitting comfortably at such a great height, Dorothy marvels at how the unruly "no place" suddenly takes on the appearance of a humanized and nonthreatening landscape, such as "pretty gardens and woods." As spaces that are managed for both practical (cultivation of food) and aesthetic (art) purposes, gardens tend to communicate order, intention, and the nearby presence of humans. Likewise, the reference to "woods" might remind readers of the green and inviting Thoreauvian landscapes associated with New England, where Baum happened to be raised.[66] In other words, gliding above the sticky, thorny elements in "rapid flight," Dorothy achieves a kind of visual mastery over the environment. Her newfound ability to see out and over all that space allows her to interact with the land in both cartographical and economic terms. After all, both garden and woodland spaces yield consumable goods for humans, such as food and timber. Here we might also be reminded of Pinchot's "economic woods," a description that reflects capitalism's embeddedness in the discourse of environmental management. To use a popular Progressive term, wilderness *reforms* into wealth when viewed from the arms of winged animals.[67]

In *Aereality*, a collection of essays on the evolution of aerial vision, William Fox argues that seeing or capturing the land from above, as Dorothy does in this moment of flight, initiates the process of transforming unknown space into knowable "territory" or property: "Picturing a space is not just part of creating place, but of claiming it, of converting the terrain into territory."[68] In technical management literature, authors often refer to these emergent "territories"—a label denoting political and economic claim—as "tracts" or "swaths of land." This terminology acts to rhetorically apprehend, bracket off, and, in general, contain indeterminate ecologies. Since Dorothy, too, observes the wild land beneath her as already-garden, even when no gardens currently exist there, we sense the Progressive operations of her eco-managerial vision: figuratively, she presses her eye to the camera's viewfinder, perceives the land through the square, focuses, and captures space. When she develops the mental image, place-as-property emerges.

In this way, flight and the panoramic gaze it enables facilitates Dorothy's ability to navigate the strange land that exists "beyond" Kansas—land that, in many ways, resembles the diverse regions of the American West. For example, Baum's treatment of "the great desert," which is described as so hostile that "none could live to cross it," frames the arid ecology as a flyover region, which is why Dorothy seems so perplexed as to how to traverse its insufferable topography by foot (13). Unlike the green, "rich and pleasant" (17) environments located in more familiar and pastoral parts of Oz, such as the Land of the Munchkins, Baum presents the desert as a management problem without an immediate solution, which, as the next chapter explains, is largely how developers, surveyors, and settlers viewed Western desert spaces at the turn of the twentieth century. In a 1903 *Topeka State Journal* article titled "Plowing the Desert," for example, the author describes the construction of a segment of the Los Angeles and Salt Lake Railroad (SLR) in San Bernardino using the heroic language of warfare:

> Out in the appalling desert country . . . is a sight of strenuous endeavor to stir the heart of a strong man. There, unheralded to the swarming world, far beyond the boundaries of that death-still region, an army is laboring toward a conquest so arduous that only one who has seen the slow, stubborn battle waging can understand the magnitude of the task. There the wilderness is being probed with steel, driven by brawny arms, directed by masterful minds.[69]

This passage paints the arid desert lands of California's Inland Empire as an antagonistic and highly unnatural force, for not only is this particular environment "appalling," but it is also "death-still," or devoid of movement and life. A successful conquest of this waste space requires "masterful men"—the managers, architects, engineers—to "direct," or oversee, the energies of both labor and steel. Similar to military captains, these great minds of management are to hover above the fray, the author intimates, surveilling and controlling the persistent battle from a removed location.

A similar kind of desert surrounds the Land of Oz on all sides, creating no easy escape. One Munchkin even tells Dorothy that, as noted above, "none could live to cross it," a statement that causes her to sob since her only wish is to return to her family in Kansas (13). Dorothy is told that the only individual known to have survived a desert passage is Oz, who, only by sheer accident, passed over the unnatural terrain in his hot-air balloon (89). Since characters merely contemplate the desert's terrors at its borders and refuse to access it directly, it remains a hostile, blank, and therefore unbeautiful waste space, one we can only imagine from a distance and imperfectly map.

The power of flight, however, could lift Dorothy above the desert's disorder, thus rescuing her from the chaos of the unmanaged geography, or so it would seem. For example, when Dorothy learns that she has to cross the arid lands in order to return to her home in Kansas, she asks Oz how such a journey could possibly be made. He responds, "[W]hen I came to this country it was in a balloon. You also came through the air, being carried by a cyclone. So I believe the best way to get across the desert will be through the air" (84). As an unpeopled ("no one could live to cross it"), uncharted, and seemingly unnatural environment, Oz introduces balloon travel as Dorothy's only option. However, even flight is not without risks, as Oz makes sure to warn her that "if the air should get cold the balloon would come down in the desert, and we should be lost" (84–85). This fear of being lost in unmanaged spaces, which is also a fear of seeing unclearly—or of failing to process that which we are seeing—pervades the novel; in other words, when one is lost, one loses the ability to see a way out of the unfamiliar. In several scenes, for example, the group encounters large plants, "thick wood" (91), intoxicating poppies, and even "fighting trees" (90) that block the sun and make travel difficult. Not only do these biotic obstacles hinder movement, but they also impair vision and, thus, momentarily throw the group off track.

As a "great" unknown in the novel, the desert is especially liable to cause visual impairment and disorientation. In *Terra Antarctica*, William Fox asserts that arid environments can play tricks on our eyes; not only are we at risk of falling for thermal illusions, but the lack of humidity actually interferes with our ability to perceive distance.[70] In hyperarid environments, he says, "the air is so clear things appear closer than they really are."[71] Fox also suggests that in regions devoid of noticeable landmarks or chartable referents, the mind becomes easily confused. "A severe challenge . . . is trying to develop a sense of place where our ability to sense the space itself is so compromised," Fox says.[72]

To be lost in the vast desert spaces surrounding Oz, in other words, would mean a failure to manage on a grand scale. Lost without a map in "an environment that looks the same in all directions" could mean death for the overseer.[73] Attempting to come to terms with the immensity of the "death-still" desert, a perceived negative space not unlike the arid regions of the American West, perhaps poses the most overwhelming management obstacle in Baum's novel. Given Baum's own inability to make a living in Aberdeen, South Dakota, during a time of extreme drought (1888–1891), as well as his "almost mystical" belief in Western irrigation, the novel's hostile depictions of the desert emerge from human-environmental struggles that were close to home for the author.[74] Nancy Tystad Koupal writes that "Baum believed strongly, almost mystically, in irrigation as the salvation of Dakota farmers," noting that his

"optimism about opportunities in the West could not survive" following the worsening of the drought, the failure of crops, and many
settlers' eventual abandonment of Dakota in the late 1880s.[75]

Despite the risks involved with crossing the desert via air,
flight presents itself as Dorothy's only option. However, just
as soon as she decides to brave the crossing, she discovers additional limitations with modern air travel. Her only two modes of
escape—the Winged Monkeys and a hot-air balloon—fail to assist
her in the goal of being shuttled over the arid waste. Despite the
help the Monkeys offer Dorothy in other parts of the novel, she
discovers that they also are ill-equipped to handle the desert's difficult atmosphere. "We shall be glad to serve you in any way in our
power," they tell Dorothy after she beckons them with the Golden
Cap, "but we cannot cross the desert. Good-bye" (89). Likewise,
as a nondirigible and, therefore, somewhat unmanageable device,
the Wizard's hot-air balloon takes off without Dorothy, and the
helpless pilot-engineer can do nothing but wave good-bye to the
girl. In this moment of managerial failure, both wind and heat
deliver a kind of animacy to the balloon, revealing it to be stron-
ger and more powerful than the "masterful mind" of Oz. The
narrator tells us that the balloon "was tugging hard at the rope
that held it to the ground" until, finally, it "rose into the air without her," leaving Dorothy and Toto to find their own way back to
Kansas (87). As the agentive subject of this passage, the uncon-
trollable machine—motivated by the hot "air within it," like a
breath—becomes a force not even Oz, the professional balloonist,
can tame. Both animal and mechanical flying devices fail (to be
managed) in these moments; the next section examines how these
technical errors, when combined with visual distortion, at once
constrain and further entrench the modern management project.

OZ UNCLEARLY: FAILING TO CAPTURE UTOPIA

While flight seems to aid what Thomas C. Leonard and other
historians refer to as "the administrative state" by enhancing

the legibility of the ground below, it also distorts and even erases environmental particulars, as various scenes in the novel demonstrate; such distortions, I contend in this section, challenge the authority of the atmospheric eye.[76] As animated matter, environmental elements threaten the authoritative gaze of "the forester's eye" throughout *The Wizard of Oz*, and the characters must then adjust and respond to Oz's always-stirring ecology. Not only do rain, humidity, aridity, cloud cover, tree cover, wind, and other elemental and biotic nuisances challenge the aerial view in Baum's fantastical work, but the characters' own perceptual limitations— the rapid changes in scale, the obfuscation of difference, and a general warping of the senses—contribute to a host of vision problems that impact their abilities to manage the supposed utopia. In other words, when humans take to the sky, "the eye is . . . constantly challenged," Marie Thébaud-Sorger argues, leaving readers to question the veracity of managerial surveillance in the field.[77] By focusing on the moments in the novel when the eye of the forester-manager-engineer blurs and falters, we might discover that management often transforms failure into possibility and bureaucratic longevity.

One of the strangest scenes in the novel involving the strengthening of management via warped vision occurs in "The Dainty China Country," a short chapter where the characters encounter an enclosed village made almost entirely of fragile porcelain. The vibrant land of China Country, composed of ecomaterials unfamiliar to the travelers, begins to play upon the eye of Dorothy and friends.[78] Since China Country is surrounded by a "high wall" whose surface is described as "smooth, like the surface of a dish," the Tin Woodman decides to construct a ladder so that he and his friends may climb over the structure that stands "higher than their heads" and annoyingly limits both vision and mobility (92). Once the ladder is built and the characters reach the wall's summit, each traveler individually voices disbelief by exclaiming, "Oh my!" at the enchanting landscape that outstretches before them

(93). Only after all of the characters achieve the ledge is the reader granted a vision of the Dainty China Country, a place that perplexes the eyes of all newcomers. At "the top of the wall *they looked down*," we are told, "and saw a strange sight."

> Before them was a great stretch of country having a floor as smooth and shining and white as the bottom of a big platter. Scattered around were many houses made entirely of china and painted in the brightest colors. These houses were quite small, the biggest of them reaching only as high as Dorothy's waist. There were also pretty little barns, with china fences around them, and many cows and sheep and horses and pigs and chickens, all made of china, standing about in groups. (93, emphasis added)

Here the narrator separates the land below into a series of knowable objects and relations, a taxonomical move that, consequently, aligns one's skills as a keen observer with the aims of federal land management practices in frontier spaces. Land management, particularly as it is practiced by agencies such as the Bureau of Land Management, requires that distinctions be made between *the parts* (objects, people, animals, natural resources, commodities, landmarks) that together constitute an environment.[79] When divided into individual elements, the value of each element can then be assessed and hierarchized, preserved, or exploited, according to the economic determinations of the observer. The repetitive use of the word "and" in place of a comma ("many cows and sheep and horses and pigs and chickens"), otherwise known as a copulative conjunction, mirrors the hurried eye of the manager making quick inventory of the country's valuable resources. He scans quickly, hoping to document all in one glance.

In sum, this visual inventory of both living and nonliving things reflects and facilitates the continuation of the divide-and-conquer ideology of turn-of-the-century expansionist thought, especially since each object in the list appeals to Western hunger and pleasure. When the narrator looks to this "dainty" country, he sees distant, desirable matter—matter that satisfies the eye, invigorates the soul, and tempts him to breach the wall to make contact.

As a consequence of this expansive view from above, the land appears to both invite and deem inevitable resource commodification and consumption. Even "the pretty little people" who occupy this country look to be "made of china, even to their clothes" (95). Additionally, their miniaturization in the eyes of the narrator marks them as fragile, and hence highly valuable, commodities. At one point, Dorothy meets a "china girl" with a "frightened little voice" who twice is described as "beautiful" (95–96). Viewing the young girl as a precious and pretty ornament, perhaps similar to a porcelain figurine, Dorothy asks, "Won't you let me carry you back to Kansas and stand you on Aunt Em's mantel-shelf? I could carry you in my basket" (96). When the girl refuses, telling Dorothy that in other countries "our joints at once stiffen, and we can only stand straight and look pretty," the group decides to move on with their journey, leaving a broken cow and church in their wake—not to mention the ladder capable of facilitating the entry (or invasion?) of future surveyors (96).

The recurrent use of the term "china" to describe the country's dominant environmental (and possibly biological) substance reduces what would be a complex, dynamic ecology to a mono-elemental resource. However, since we only see the world via the eyes of the narrator and central characters, we must question their porcelain vision of this new terrain. As Fox notes, "[W]e use cultural means to augment our neurobiology in order to overcome the perceptual difficulties we experience when exploring large spaces."[80] In other words, when we encounter radically unfamiliar environments, our vision is often tested, triggering us to compare the profound unknown to familiar cultural referents. In difficult-to-see environments, such as Dainty China Country, the manager's eye struggles to make sense of what seems a profound difference and thus likens the "great stretch of country" to a desirous cultural material: china, also known as porcelain enamel (93). The word "china" appears sixteen times in this brief chapter, underscoring its material importance in the mind of the narrator.[81] Porcelain enamel emerged as a common industrial building material at the turn of the twentieth century, and its predominance in the narrator's visual-cultural catalog reflects the conversion of lively ecological materialities—including sentient beings—to objects of imperial desire.[82]

From the top of the wall, the distant objects in Dainty China Country appear small, vague, and without life. Hovering above the terrain, assuming the position of the surveyor, the narrator perceives the country below unclearly. Oddly, this warped, smeary vision at once impairs his ability to manage and reinforces the capitalist underpinnings of the management apparatus. In other words, a failure to see can ultimately lead to highly extractive or consumptive relations with dynamic ecologies. Take, for example, the synonyms the narrator uses at the beginning of the chapter to describe Dainty China Country. At one point, he refers to the land beyond the wall as "smooth and shining and white as the bottom of a big platter" (93). To envision the new environment as a "platter" resonates with a photographic distortion known as "dishing," a technical issue Baum, the amateur photographer, might have been familiar with in his own camerawork.[83] Dishing, which is caused by a poor camera lens, makes landscape photographs appear warped and rounded, similar to the concavity of a bowl. Thébaud-Sorger considers dishing a problem of perception particular to those who take to the air, reinforcing the narrator's supervisory position in Baum's novel. "The balloonist," Thébaud-Sorger says, "perceives himself within a concave space, as if he were inside a bowl and as if the lie of the land were like a miniature painted inside the bowl's rim, while the edges smooth out all around into a linear flatland."[84] "Platter" and "china" resonate with this common photographic distortion. Contrary to what we might expect, however, this distorted view does not always weaken management. After all, by perceiving Dainty China Country as a platter, the narrator reads it as already-commodity. One need only languorously gaze from the top of the wall to see the future objects of commerce.

Moreover, visual distortion, or the inability to connect on the same level with what seems a profound Otherness, leads to detrimental, potentially unmitigable environmental impacts, as evidenced by the great "clattering" Dorothy and her friends make upon the "china ground" when they first leap down from the boundary wall. If Mr. Joker, a clown who is "completely covered in cracks," offers any indication of porcelain's ability to regenerate, then it seems the group's forceful rattling of the fragile ground could lead to irreparable ecological damage. Following their clumsy entrance into the new country, the travelers fail to synchronize the movements of their bodies with their eyes, which leads to significant cultural and psychological disruptions for the inhabitants of Dainty China Country; one wonders what the lasting impacts of such an encounter might be. After all, the narrator tells us that before exiting the country, the Lion "upset a china church with his tail and smashed it all to pieces." Though supposedly accidental, the decimation of a spiritual site could be devastating for the citizens of Dainty China Country. However, Dorothy and her friends never look back to assess the damage they caused, nor do they claim any kind of responsibility for what might be read as acts of aggression—or even terrorism. Instead, the travelers swiftly move onto the next territory, overlooking the wreckage that continues to accumulate. The group's rapid progression into always-new environments resonates with the nineteenth-century idea that the American West contained boundless resources to exploit and endless futures to inhabit.

REVISIONARY FORM AND "CONTINUAL IMPROVEMENT": READING ABOVE THE LINES IN OZ

In *The Wizard of Oz*, not only do the characters' desires to control the world from above reflect the remedial motives of the eco-managerial eye, but this same ethos of perpetual improvement also permeates the novel's structure. When Dorothy and her friends encounter dense, dark forests, heavy rainstorms, or other problems with nature, they rely on problem-solving as a way of overcoming the environment. Flight, for example, provides what the Lion calls "a quick way out of our troubles," and in this section I argue that the quick fix or swift escape, as a recurrent maneuver in this utopian novel, directs the course of the Progressive Era management plot (74). Just as soon as the characters navigate one environmental obstacle, a "new problem," to use Woglom's words, animates itself into being, calling upon the characters to think, act, and, hence, propel themselves further toward their goal.

Cecilia Tichi notes that *fin-de-siècle* environmental and economic policy viewed the "destabilizing energy" of the natural world ("the fire and ice, the snow, the waves, infestation of insects, cyclones, etc.") as a force to be contained or subverted, and such obstacles to human progress came to be identified as unnatural in their supposed opposition to development: "The well-regulated environment began to be felt as the natural environment, and vice versa. Severe wind and wave, tremors and geomorphic upheavals were perceived increasingly as anomalies, aberrations in nature."[85] This might be why the authors of the report on Lawrence's Captive Airship referred to unpredictable wind as a "flaw" that further technological improvements could hopefully overcome. Likewise, when Dorothy and crew enter a "disagreeable country, full of bogs and marshes," they remark that the sticky environment is "rank," "difficult," "tiresome," and "so thick that *it hid them from sight*" (97, emphasis added). According to the novel's managerial ethos, soft, gummy environments such as swamps pull people into the muck, preventing them from managing from a stable, elevated vantage point. In Progressive Era management novels, untamed wilderness, extreme weather patterns, and dirt lack discipline and require correction—nothing a little structure can't cure!

The somewhat compulsive problem-solution structure of Baum's fairy tale highlights this Progressive distrust of environmental "anomalies" that social reformers of the time equated with "disease, immorality, and disorder," according to Daniel Eli

Burnstein. In *Next to Godliness: Confronting Dirt and Despair in Progressive Era New York City*, Burnstein argues that Progressives' devotion to health and social well-being "reinforced acceptance of the concomitant need to foster environmental conditions that brought physical and moral improvement."[86] Baum's novel shares this same wariness of unregulated nature and, as a response, engenders what I call a revisionary logic that proves necessary the perpetuation of management systems. To put it quite literally, Dorothy and her traveling companions repeatedly revise (or see again, and again, and again) a way out of nature; however, each character's growth and eventual success depend on their constant encounters with new problems to surmount. When a crisis emerges, such as a gap in the road or a stranded friend, the team considers all of their options and methodically implements an action plan, one that ultimately allows them to master nature-danger.

Not only does Baum's ratiocinative structure function as an example of what Tichi has termed "the machine-age text," a work that "does not just contain *representations* of the machine—it too *is* the machine," but I contend it also engenders what today's management leaders call the continuous improvement model (CIM), a management philosophy that promotes "the ongoing improvement of products, services, or processes through incremental and breakthrough improvements."[87] As a linear quest tale whose narrative eye remains ever fixed on the goal of returning (home), *The Wizard of Oz* follows the "plan-do-check-act" process of CIM, firmly aligning it with the reformist doctrines of modern scientific management.[88] Similar to many of the management-oriented novels I explore in *Sand, Water, Salt*, Baum's novel ironically insists upon elemental animacy for the management project to survive. Over the course of the novel, we expect that problems (with nature) will work themselves out. Correspondingly, we expect problems with nature: cyclones, storms, swamps, deserts, cloud cover, weather-worn roads, fissures, rock-clogged ditches, unnavigable rapids, and on and on. To avoid the obsolescence of the manager-engineer, a little wildness needs to linger and occasionally erupt into generative geomorphic disturbances. In other words, environmental "aberrations" are fundamental to management's existence—and persistence. After all, doesn't the cyclone initiate Dorothy on her path to becoming a manager in the first place? Similar to how dirt, dust, trash, and bacteria motivated Progressive sanitary reformers to develop systems for achieving what Burnstein calls "the good society," Baum introduces environmental obstacles to both stimulate and train the future land manager.[89]

What I'm terming the "management novel" follows a resolution-oriented structure that lays bare the "internal workings" of the text as a kind of model for incremental improvement. This means that the structure of the narrative operates as a lesson in managerial vision. For example, when a dilemma presents itself in *The Wizard of Oz*, such as how to cross a turbulent river, the group pauses, identifies the problem via inquiry ("How shall we cross the river?"), brainstorms possible solutions, chooses the most efficient plan, and then acts. Baum reiterates the importance of this pragmatic process through signposting and repetition (36); for instance, the very same process repeats itself on the following page when Dorothy and friends lose their path to the Emerald City. "'What shall we do now?'" the Tin Woodman asks, and his query promptly elicits a list of suggestions from others in the group (38). These questions express a dual purpose: they announce that a problem exists *and* create an opportunity for collaborative decision-making, both of which allow for the reader to observe and even admire the working out of each new problem. Tichi discusses a similar mode of structural exposure in modern building design. In describing "the world of girders and gears," she notes that modern architecture "invites the onlooker to see its internal workings, its component parts. It insists upon the recognition that it is, in fact, an assembly."[90] In other words, "the world of girders and gears" makes visible its formal traits, emphasizing its *madeness* as a tribute, of sorts, to the technologies and human ingenuity that contributed to its construction.

Similarly, *The Wizard of Oz* renders hypervisible its trusty scaffolding, enabling readers—or "onlookers"—to be mesmerized by the characters' wide-ranging problem-solving abilities. For example, while on their way to the Emerald City, the group encounters "a great ditch that crossed the road and divided the forest as far as they could see on either side" (34). It is then that Dorothy, the engineer-in-training, begins to hatch a management plan, which she elicits with a simple research question: "What shall we do?" Through dialogue, readers get to listen in as the group registers what is and is not possible in such a scenario. Noting the impossibilities of flying over, seeing their way around, or climbing into and out of the ditch as methods of arriving at the other side, it seems the travelers may not reach the Emerald City after all. However, just when we think their journey will cease, the Lion introduces a solution. After "measuring the distance carefully in his mind," which tells us he has contemplated the mathematics of his proposal before making it public, he states, "I think I could jump over it" (34). The Scarecrow validates the Lion's management plan by responding, "Then we are all right," therefore quelling any doubts about the plan's efficacy (34). One by one, the Lion carries each character to the other side of the immense gap, and the quest is able to continue. Interestingly enough, flight comes to the rescue yet again, as we are told that Dorothy experiences the giant leap "as if she was flying through the air" (34). Aerial transport offers individuals the unique opportunity to pass over aberrations instead of engaging with them more materially, saving them time and allowing them the opportunity to observe the environment from new vantage points.

Just as soon as they arrive at the other side, however, a new—and even greater—obstacle presents itself: a gap in the road "so broad and deep that the Lion knew at once he could not leap across it" (35). While this current problem does, in fact, resonate with the previous dilemma, the new, even wider gap in the road demands collaborative innovation. Given the width of this particular fissure, familiar solutions will not suffice. The proximity of these two infrastructural problems, I suggest, is no accident, as it demonstrates the revisionary structure of Baum's continual improvement text. Were the problem the same in every situation—the gap in the road *always* as deep and as wide, the leap-of-the-Lion *always* the solution—management technologies would never advance and progress would flatline. The constant working out of details, of revising old methods to accommodate new and greater "aberrations," allows for the group to continue performing the rites of continual improvement. Management in the novel expresses an ongoingness, as one can always depend on a new problem whose presence further installs administrative networks into lives, bodies, environments, and economies. After all, one of the key tenets of CIM reads, "If the change was successful, implement it on a wider scale and continuously assess your results. If the change did not work, *begin the cycle again*."[91]

Science historian Roger Turner argues that the pervasiveness of management—its diffusion across vast networks, its deep-rooted institutionalization in modern society—is contingent upon the "repetitious production of constantly expiring knowledge," which quickly renders solutions obsolete.[92] Strangely, "expiring knowledge" is what gives management its power, he stresses. Citing modern weather forecasting as an example of a globally entrenched management apparatus, Turner notes,

> Since the value of forecasts and observations degrade as quickly as the weather changes, many workers in meteorology spend their careers producing tiny chunks of expiring knowledge about the atmosphere. Around the world, thousands of weather observing stations measure local conditions. They send this information to central offices . . . where the observations are plotted on maps, allowing forecasters to visualize the weather at different scales. Forecasters interpret these observations in light of meteorological theory, using ideas about how the atmosphere behaves to create predictions for specified locations at specified times.[93]

Since weather and atmospheric conditions change daily, weather managers are never at a loss for new data to process, he notes, revealing how expiring knowledge leads to the expansion and entrenchment of meteorology's management network. Turner goes on to say that synoptic meteorology "involves tens of thousands of people, spread around the world, keeping tabs on conditions that affect every person."[94] The existence of this vast global system demonstrates that when it comes to dealing with ever-changing environmental systems, management continues giving birth to more management, and the data never end. Or, to use the words of CIM, one must always "begin the cycle again." Even though Dorothy's management team exists on a much smaller scale than the global network Turner describes, its own growth and progress as a community require the "repetitious production" of knowledge that swiftly expires or becomes irrelevant when dealing with the always-new challenges that lie ahead. In a novel that orients its vision toward the perpetual future, the narrator refuses to linger long in one scene. Hesitations and prolonged layovers would signal a managerial breakdown, and so the narrator economizes the tale by focusing on progressive movements into the utopian vastness that is future-space.

After the characters' struggle to overcome the two gaps in the road, the narrator brings us quickly up to speed in the following chapter: "Behind them was the dark forest they had passed safely through, although they had suffered many discouragements; but before them was a lovely, sunny country that seemed to beckon them on to the Emerald City" (37). Panoramic vision is again achieved after having been lost in the "dark forest," and there is no use in looking back, or of assessing the impacts their journey has thus far effected on the Land of Oz.

Caught up in the rapidly unfolding, episodic plot, readers might also fail to look back in order to contemplate how Dorothy and her friends have altered environments deemed difficult or foreign. In their wake, "our little party of travelers" (37) leaves behind new bridges, ladders, rafts, wheeled carts, and other managerial artifacts, and it remains to be seen whether these objects will be maintained or hold any useful value to the inhabitants of Oz.[95] Some of these items, such as the wheeled cart and raft, risk falling into irrelevance, and, if left unused, will likely convert to waste for unseen others to contend with. We must also remember that the group's path has been marked by often severe impacts on beings and environments, not unlike the destructive consequences of colonialist encounters in the American West and elsewhere. For example, they leave in their wake "little heaps" of killed wildlife (61), injured livestock, destroyed buildings, imposed political and economic structures, and new gateways into once-isolated villages.

Just as the scope of an aerial photograph has a tendency to miss, or overlook, the homeless who occupy the tent cities following an earthquake, or the fish that ingest heavy metals following a spill, Baum's aerial vision orients the narrative away from what the narrator might consider the "unnecessary data" that accumulate at ground level. As a contemplative observer, the narrator is, as W. J. T. Mitchell might say, "safe in another place—outside the frame, behind the binoculars, the camera, or the eyeball, in the dark refuge of the skull."[96] His eyes at once scan, select, ignore, imagine, and assemble elements that culminate in a particular racial, economic, and cultural vision of nineteenth-century frontier spaces in the West. However, we must keep in mind that the land the narrator so desires also exists, vibrates, and beckons as a thing to be wanted. Something about it, some "impersonal affect," enchants or disturbs him in the first place.[97] In turn, he continues to look down, always hungry for more.

CONCLUSION: "FLAT, WHITE NOTHINGNESS": THE MAKING AND MANAGING OF VIRTUAL WASTELANDS

When interviewed during the Dakota Access Pipeline (DAPL) protest at the Standing Rock Sioux Reservation in 2016, water protector and Native American activist Winona LaDuke equated the aerial perspective to colonialist disregard both for Indigenous lives and remote regions of the United States. "Everybody in the country flies over North Dakota and looks down and says, 'Well, that's North Dakota.' Nobody comes out here. And so stuff continues out here for a hundred years."[98] The "stuff" LaDuke alludes to includes the expropriation and pollution of Indigenous land and water, "high rates of abuse and violence," and other social and environmental ills she connects to a nineteenth-century expansionist worldview. She believes the high plains exist as a flyover zone for many Americans, meaning "stuff" can carry on out of view and, therefore, out of mind.

The representation of the "great desert" as a largely unseen but very present space in *The Wizard of Oz* connotes a similar kind of colonial erasure, one that seems to invite intensive human impacts. As a region that "none could live to cross" (13), and, hence, where no humans could possibly dwell, Baum's wasteland operates as a vast site of future disposal. In fact, when Dorothy finally uses the magical powers of the Silver Shoes to fly home, the shoes slip off her feet "and were lost forever in the desert," adding more trash to the arid trash heap. Artifacts that bear evidence of Dorothy's presence in Oz, possibly viewed as inutile to Oz's inhabitants, line the path of her journey from beginning to end. And even though Dorothy never sets foot on the sandy ground, the Silver Shoes stand as proof of her presence in, and subsequent mastery over, the so-called impassable expanse of the great desert surrounding Oz. As desert trash, the Silver Shoes amount to what seems an insignificant environmental impact, especially when we consider the types of toxic, "hyperobjective" materials that communities are grappling with in today's Western regions, such as uranium, magnesium, crude oil, natural gas, copper, and methane. However, when we follow the shoes' descent to the ground—from a magical accessory to so much rubble—we begin to better understand the relationship between Dorothy and her waste object—or, better yet, between Dorothy and the waste space into which she passively, and without responsibility, "loses" her trash. As a space she never enters but fears intensely, Baum's desert—the ecological Other, so to speak—causes individuals to lose their real and proverbial shit.

While much of the present chapter, as well as the next, focuses on deserts as cultural and agricultural wastelands in the American imaginary, especially when individuals gaze upon these environments from aerial or cartographical perspectives, it is important to consider how those whose interests often side with intensive resource extraction mobilize wasteland rhetoric in pursuit of political and economic gain. In addition to the arid West, many other biotic communities, such as the Arctic and semiarid high plains, have been disparaged in order to justify "wastelanding," a term Traci Brynne Voyles uses to describe the detrimental effects of uranium mining on environments and Indigenous populations in the American Southwest.[99] In this project, I wish to hold onto Voyles's specific regional and historical vision of wastelanding while also expanding the term to include other physical and rhetorical acts of human and environmental disregard, such as Baum depicting the great desert as a blank space wherein Dorothy can toss her trash, or energy lobbyists proclaiming that public lands exhibit little value when not generating profits.

This latter example of wastelanding poses significant social and ecological problems in these Anthropocene times, and Alaska's Arctic National Wildlife Refuge (ANWR), a wilderness area roughly the size of South Carolina, is a prime example of a public land currently at risk of losing its protected status to energy development. Using the language of barrenness and desolation, energy enthusiasts often speak of ANWR as a desert even though it is not a desert in the categorical sense. Not surprisingly, those who support oil and gas exploration in ANWR's coastal plain, otherwise known as the "1002 area," regularly deploy aerial imagery of this region to depict Arctic spaces as lifeless, unproductive deserts. When Gale Norton, former secretary of the interior under George W. Bush, described the 1002 area to the House Committee on Natural Resources as a "flat, white nothingness"—and provided her own aerial images as proof of claim—a special kind of landscape was made, one that appears particularly hostile to human bodies.[100] Norton's equation of the Arctic to a profound "nothingness," or a space where there is nothing to see, resonates with Baum's vast, impassable desert. As a blank, *somewhere-out-there* space "in which the brain struggles to create place," ANWR easily transforms into an exploitable locale, as has much of the American West.[101] In an effort to bring oil and gas exploration to a portion of ANWR's coastal plain, Norton had much to gain by promoting an inhospitable image of the region. If we are unable to see ourselves in ANWR—a region that, as Norton emphasizes, contains "no trees," "no deepwater lakes," "no mountains," and no people—then why should it matter what happens there?[102] This was the message Norton presented to the committee in 2003, and she brought along her own photographs of ANWR to combat the "emotionalism," as she called it, of those who oppose drilling.[103] "Now, let's take a look at what the Coastal Plain of Alaska *actually looks like* most of the year, with a video produced by Arctic Power," she said to the committee. "*This is what I saw* when I was there the last day of March 2001" (emphasis added).[104] Norton cannot help but remind us of her authority as one who was there, who saw the wasteland, and who knows what Alaska's remote coastal plain "actually looks like." Despite her confession that she had only visited ANWR on the "last day of March," she assures the committee that the video—produced by a private energy company, no less!—represents what the refuge is like "most of the year."

Nearly fifteen years after Norton presented "nothing" to the committee, the Trump administration similarly painted the Alaskan refuge as an unproductive absence, a view on par with how many Progressives either dispraised or failed to see the multitudinous other values that American "wastelands" provided to Indigenous inhabitants, animal life, and other stakeholders. Echoing Norton's attempts at rhetorical erasure, President Donald Trump voiced his own irritation about withdrawing public lands from energy development when discussing his thoughts on ANWR—or what he referred to as "one of the great sites of energy"—at the National Republican Congressional Committee Dinner in March 2018.[105] In his speech, Trump recalls a friend praising Republicans' inclusion of an energy leasing provision in the 2017 Tax Reform Bill:

> [O]ne day a friend of mine who was in the energy business called. "Is it true that you have ANWR in the bill?" I said, "I don't know. Who cares? What is that? What does that mean?" They said, "No, is it true?" I said, "What does it mean? What's the big deal that they put it in?" He said, "Well, you know, Reagan tried, every single president tried, and not one president was successful in getting it. . . ." I said, "You got to be kidding. I love it now." And after that we fought like hell to get ANWR.[106]

The string of semiannoyed questions in this quotation (*Who cares? What is that? What does that mean? What's the big deal?*) underscores ANWR's inconsequentiality-as-refuge in Trump's mind. "Withdrawn from appropriation or disposal under the public land laws," which is how the 1980 Alaska Lands Act describes ANWR's purpose, the refuge, as a real place, did not register for the president until it had something to offer him: profit and prestige. As both wasteland and sanctuary, depending on who you ask, ANWR obviously remains a highly contested site, or a place that many stakeholders "fight to get," to use Trump's excited, colonialist language.[107] In December 2017, President Trump signed a tax bill that included a provision to make portions of ANWR available for lease sales, and as recently as April 2018, the Department of the Interior initiated a sixty-day environmental review process to study the potential impacts of drilling in the refuge's oil- and gas-rich northern coastal plain. While litigation from pro-environmental groups, Indigenous activists, and others will likely delay, if not prevent, the actual drilling, energy exploration in the 1.5-million-acre "North American Serengeti" would irreparably impact local and global ecosystems, many biologists say.[108]

In *Aereality*, Fox suggests that Americans have long justified treating rural or remote locations as waste disposal sites, and only when viewing these regions from the air do these harsh impacts become noticeable. In this way, the aerial view has the potential to be a force for good in its capacity to make us aware of severe environmental impacts. When describing a recent flight around Salt Lake City, for example, Fox noted, "To my right is desert interrupted by an occasional industrial facility. To Mike's left is desert interrupted by an occasional industrial facility. Most of what's out here has to do with waste disposal."[109] He continues,

> When you fly over this desert what you see is a network of roads the sole purpose of which is to transport waste to remote sites for storage and disposal. You see another and parallel network built by the military in order to reach bombing target areas. From a jetliner at thirty-five thousand feet, most of these lines are visible, but inscrutable, as are the bulls-eye targets inscribed by bulldozers on the ground, another kind of earthworks.[110]

From the air, Fox calls attention to the visibility of these vast networks of waste, regions where entire roadways and "earthworks" are designed for the sole purpose of transporting and burying Americans' unwanted, often highly noxious materials. Paradoxically, Fox reveals how aerial vision, once considered the tool of the (waste) manager, could be apprehended for more radical purposes: to document the sprawling unsustainability of our current land and waste management practices, and to potentially aid in the remediation process. If nothing else, Fox invites readers to project their own vision (*"you* fly over," *"you* see") onto these locations we both create and overlook. By practicing an "aesthetic alertness to the violence and evil written on the land, projected there by the gazing eye," a space of possibility—one that orients itself to ecology instead of death—might be attainable.[111]

The chapters that follow offer a variety of ways that Western environments, and the lively elements of which they are composed, make contact with human bodies and help shape modernist ideologies in a diverse set of management texts and artifacts. In order to manage and survive in harsh, unfamiliar, or otherwise demanding locales, characters in these works attempt to master, connect with, or—as the next chapter demonstrates—surrender to overwhelming "wasteland" ecologies. Additionally, these works reflect how turn-of-the-century conceptions of race and sex came to be intertwined with Progressive Era land and environmental management, ostensibly granting certain bodies—mostly white, mostly male—direct contact with and subsequent claim over new territories. Characters come to learn—some sooner than others— that management is a far riskier, more relational enterprise than they first imagined.

CHAPTER 2

"LEFT ALL ALONE IN THIS WORLD'S WILDERNESS"

QUEER ECOLOGY AND MANAGING DESERT SAND

Nearly everywhere on earth, sand is principally made up of one element—in some places silica, in others limestone. Ninety percent of a grain is almost always just one of those two elements. But the other 10 percent is the percentage with a difference—the percentage that, in its difference, matters—the percentage that can tell us something about the history of a place.

—VANESSA AGARD-JONES (2012)[1]

Can you describe that vast and holy desert, a desert that is so old that it once was the sea? No, you can't. But does that stop you? Never.

—MICHAEL COBB (2012)[2]

But you have not known what force resides in the mindless things until you have known a desert wind.

—MARY AUSTIN (1903)[3]

This chapter explores the irritatingly seductive, somewhat deviant nature of nineteenth-century American desert ecologies, with a particular emphasis on the animacy of sand in Frank Norris's *McTeague: A Story of San Francisco* (1899) and Mary Austin's *The Land of Little Rain* (1903).[4] At once oppressive and "radiant with the color of romance" (Austin, *Land*, 10), the sand, sun, and wind of Norris's desert, much like the material forces at play in Austin's writing, generate an embodied discourse that both supports and thwarts national projects of American identity-making at the turn of the twentieth century. As one of the desert's many queer actants, sand operates as a metonym for arid geographies and, as this chapter reveals, is the material that emerges most frequently to identify a region as a desert.[5]

Far from a manageable geography, the antipastoral desert lands of Southern California and Western Nevada, as they are presented in these Progressive works, are alive with eco-matter that elicits what Heather I. Sullivan calls "material environmental immersion."[6] Our survival on Earth, Sullivan says, "depends on our full immersion into our earthy, bacteria-laden surroundings."[7] Furthermore, Sullivan contends that "the challenge of shaping dirt and negotiating with its mobile grit functions as a metaphor for the project of modernity."[8]

As a character in Ednah Aiken's *The River* notes of the sand that perpetually invades her Southern California home, "There's no use in trying to be clean"—but that doesn't stop her from deliriously trying.[9] Desiring a "control over dirt" through the institutionalization of various sanitation and waste management projects, Progressives sought to overcome, or at least mitigate, human engagements with the sticky, gritty stuff of their modern environments.[10] In addition to the spread of local anti-dirt and "spotless town" campaigns, such as promptings by the Phoenix Vigilance Committee to "erect barriers against dirt and insanitation," federal engineers and land managers were often charged with the messy task of building a nation on a foundation of itinerant grounds composed of mud, erosive rock, and sand.[11] This chapter examines human attempts to work with the latter. If, as Nicolas Witschi argues, the West exists as the "raw material" of the American imaginary, what role does the region's raw materiality play in that national project?[12]

As a response to that question, I argue that in America's arid desert spaces, the "mobile grit" that is sand at once tested and engendered a Progressive vision of modernity. In other words, management likes to think its success depends on securing impervious boundaries between humans and the wily elements, that working *against* instead of *with* the land safeguards the longevity of administrative authority. However, this chapter asserts that management's enduring power in the arid West derives from its unending, radically intimate engagements with agentive eco-matter. This is not to say that sand's only role is to merely solidify the Progressive project in the American West. In addition to energizing the administrative apparatus, both Norris and Austin reveal that sand can occasionally undermine or hinder human attempts to manage altogether, imbuing the element with revolutionary potential, or a vitality that "can never be predicted or controlled."[13]

Ecofeminist Elizabeth Grosz refers to these moments of potentiality—when bodies and/as things encounter one another and experience ontological conversion—as "zones of cohesion," or a kind of queer commingling of subjects and objects wherein sensations are both exchanged and shared.[14] Management, then, does not merely assert its power from above, as some historians and ecocritics have argued, nor does it effect change upon the landscape from a safe and separate realm.[15] Instead, management exists as a series of desires (for control, for power, for distance) born from its sticky relationships with indeterminate, frustrating, and vibratory matter. To state it in more granular terms, people will manage sand so long as sand remains a problem; management is people's confession that they are inextricably mired in "vibrant" sand.[16] For example, in Norris's novel, McTeague exists in a perpetual state of becoming-sand despite his frustrating attempts to control it.

Nowhere is the strange relationship between the human-manager and animated eco-matter more apparent than in the story of the construction of roads and highways in the arid West. At the turn of the twentieth century, the nation's "desert wastes" were both a temptation and a frustration to developers and policymakers. Projects that aimed to reclaim land for agriculture and settlement were under way in hopes that the West could become what many were calling the "empire of the desert."[17] However, such projects required access in the form of dependable roads and highway systems. Weather, erosion, and drifting sand made many of the existing dirt roads and trails impassable. Local newspapers and other periodicals of the period are full of reports detailing the progress of highway labor and upkeep in remote, hitherto inaccessible parts of desert country. In describing the creation of a stretch of the Lincoln Highway in Nevada, for example, Claus Spreckles, secretary of the Savage Tire Company, describes the difficulties of sustaining visible roadways near the Fallon Sink, a region he refers to as "the nightmare spot of the whole state."[18] The road is "at least a foot deep with sand in the middle of the summer," he says, "and the rest of the year it is a quagmire where a car often sinks up to the hubs." He continues, "It is nothing unusual for an auto or truck to become so mired that it takes 30 mules to pull the car out."[19]

Frustrations with desert sand continued during the construction of the Bankhead Highway, the nation's first paved interstate highway connecting Washington, DC, to San Diego. In 1920, Senator John H. Bankhead of Alabama organized a convoy expedition that would traverse the Bankhead Highway from coast to coast. Among other tasks, the convoy's team, which included thirty-two Army officers and 132 enlisted men, would assess the state of the roadway, make repairs when needed, and promote the economic benefits that an improved national highway system could deliver to regions like the Southwest that had been neglected by previous federally funded works projects. Even though the "black gumbo" of Mississippi mud created a few delays for the convoy, a member of the Bankhead Highway Association noted that the crew encountered few problems until it reached New Mexico and Arizona, where it had "difficulty in extracting itself from the clinging sands."[20] The report elaborates even further on the environmental nuisance by stating that "from Sentinel [Oklahoma] to Wellton [Arizona] heavy sandy road was encountered in spots which caused the convoy's speed to be materially reduced."[21] In these excerpts, it seems as if sand has the upper hand—it renders invisible modern infrastructure, slows mobility, and often stalls progress. The author of the Bankhead report even imbues sand with what Mel Chen calls "linguistic animacy" by maintaining that it "clings" to modern technology, making it the primary agent of the sentence—and therefore a force with which to be reckoned.[22]

Countless historical examples reveal that Progressive Era management tends to react to these ecomaterial challenges on the highway with more management, better road surfacing, and sturdier, more agile vehicular technologies. A perfect illustration of these techno-managerial responses to pesky sand is the creation of the Death Valley Dodge, a car capable of "smashing its way through the cactus, mesquite brush and greasewood through which the car is forced."[23] Having journeyed "into and through almost every desert in western America," which included descending to the base of the Grand Canyon, the Death Valley Dodge, a stock car equipped with a special bumper, a video camera, and a "spot light for night driving in the mountains," operates as a precursor to today's powerful off-road vehicles.[24] In a 1916 *Evening Capital News* article titled "Car Performs Thrilling Feats," the author details a thousand-mile excursion meant to showcase the strength of the Dodge, explaining that the car's perilous tour across the sands of Death Valley "was probably the most strenuous trip ever recorded in the annals of western motoring." After traversing "eight miles of sand dunes and terrific heat on the floor of Death Valley," the author stresses that the car has proven its ability to overcome extreme temperatures and harsh terrain, as well as antagonistic elements. Sand and rock, often considered a nuisance to highway engineers and motorists in the arid West, at first seem no match for the Dodge. After all, the car succeeds in rolling into Los Angeles, its final destination, bearing "desert trophies of Gila monsters, rattlesnakes, and side-winder skins," all of which stand as evidence of its supposed conquest over desert nature.[25] A 1915 *Los Angeles Times* article even notes that as the Dodge made its way through the nascent coastal city, it was "covered in alkali dust." None who observed the dusty Dodge as it paraded down the green, tree-lined boulevards of Los Angeles could now doubt that it survived the inland desert lands, the author suggests.

However, the dust that clings to the Dodge perhaps reveals something more remarkable about the way humans interact with the earthy, inescapable stuff of their environments. "Alkali dust" coats the body of the Dodge, accumulating in tiny corners of the floorboard and engine; as the car's tires kick up clouds of sand, the driver—an engineer named O. K. Parker—is unable to resist the body's need for air, and so he breathes in, inhaling tiny particles of desert dust; camped on the side of the dirt road at night, Parker scratches at his scalp and feels small grains of sand collecting under his fingernails. The sand, it seems, is everywhere, and the engineer-driver fails to prevent its rapid accretion. In his modern machine named after a sandy space he thinks he has mastered, Parker makes his mark in the sand, only to have those marks disappear with the next monsoon or gust of wind. In Austin's *Earth Horizon*, published in 1932—nearly thirty years after the publication of *The Land of Little Rain* and seventeen years after Parker's dusty adventure—she comments on the now predominance of highways in her beloved desert environment: "All told, I have had little travel in my life which has yielded so much profit on the exertion as the old Mojave stage. I understand that the road is well furnished now with gas stations and hot-dog stands, and the trip can be made in a few hours without incident. Which seems on the whole a pity" (263).[26] As Austin notes, drivers in the 1930s could now travel upon Southern California's vast, streaming networks of paved highways and interstates "without incident." However, while one was more likely to run out of gas than be thwarted by an interloping sand dune on these well-maintained systems, wind, sandstorms, and increasingly frequent flash floods continued to agitate even the most agile of vehicles, leaving Progressive Era highway managers and car manufacturers at the design table.

It is no mystery why the makers of the Dodge decided to name the vehicle after what was considered, at the turn of the twentieth century, a veritable waste space. The difficulty of managing (and managing in) Death Valley cannot be overestimated. Located on the border of Nevada and California in the Great Basin, Death Valley, known as the driest ecology in North America, exists as one of the hottest places on Earth. Austin, a California transplant from the Midwest, considered Death Valley "the remotest place in California," and this out-of-the-way region was of particular interest to early twentieth-century readers who craved stories written by "husky men with adventurous temperaments."[27] Newspapers, literary magazines, and book publishers were quick to print travel narratives set in the arid bioregions of Southern California, and Death Valley often operated as the setting in such works.[28]

Both works I examine in this chapter take place, at least in part, in Death Valley, a contested space that both Norris and Austin describe as largely separate from the American nation-state. Despite their clear differences in genre and tone, Norris's naturalist novel and Austin's collection of regionalist essays highlight the significant role arid environments played in defining regional and national belonging, especially for Anglo-Americans. In *McTeague*

and *The Land of Little Rain*, published just four years apart, characters become "saturated with the elements," to use Austin's words
in *Land*, an act that registers not only as a kind of radical openness
to eco-matter, but also as an aggravation to the management apparatus (28). After all, saturation signifies porous boundaries and a
watering down of the body; in contrast, management prefers its
bodies watertight, nimble, and machinelike.[29]

While McTeague tries hard and then fails to prevent the inevitability of elemental saturation, Austin seems to invite permeation,
understanding it as a way for outsiders to connect intimately with
place. Contrasting herself with prospectors and "Indians" who
develop a "weather shell" that prevents the "dust-heavy winds"
from penetrating—and, hence, further altering—their forms,
Austin admits that as a relative newcomer to the San Joaquin
Valley, she "can never get past the glow and exhilaration" of a sandstorm (28). Her inability to keep sand at a physical and emotional
distance, similar to McTeague's radical openness to Death Valley's
agential dust, mesmerizes her, prompting her to write enthusiasti-
cally of "desertness" as a way of understanding the new region in
which she found herself.[30]

Through an examination of Southern California sand in these
two works, we might be able to better understand the longings
and frustrations of Progressive Era management as it deals with
animated environments. Sand is matter, but it is unstable matter;
it is made of rock, but it often behaves like air and water. In environments composed of such matter, national ideals of masculinity
and sexuality hover like hazy mirages on the horizon; McTeague
can't help but reach "his hand forward," an act of interminable
longing that serves to complicate and sustain the relationship
between self and nation at the turn of the twentieth century
(235). Responsive to this kind of longing, queer ecology merges
queer theory with ecocriticism and offers a new way of viewing
the late nineteenth-century desert as a complicated location of
liveliness and human/nonhuman longing, which runs counter to

how Norris's critics have thus far conceived of *McTeague*'s Death Valley.

When we do naturalist or regionalist criticism from American desert spaces—spaces that, as this chapter shows, have historically been depicted as unproductive tracts of land that exist on the fringes of the national imaginary—the solidity of the national project begins to erode like so much sandy soil. What we are then left with is a vision of the nation that appears not as an indestructible, inherent geography but as an idea that we collectively imagine into being and can potentially undo. At the same time, we should resist thinking of these arid geographies as remote, removed, and untrammeled wilderness areas wherein a new and improved national or ecological consciousness will emerge to save us all. Romantic thinking such as this falls into the frontier-fantasy trap and, as such, washes the desert clean of its people, its history, and its ecological complexities. Just because many non-desert-dwelling Americans hold deserts out of mind, regarding them as intangible and untouchable *out-theres*, does not mean that these spaces have not been thoroughly and, often, devastatingly regarded as a resource by extractive industries financed, or at the very least permitted, by the state. Even today, over five hundred abandoned uranium mines exist on the Navajo Nation's lands alone, and the uranium mining industry is "renewing a push" in Utah's soon-to-be-downsized Bears Ears National Monument.[31] As zones of both possibility and precariousness, deserts—and the sandy, potentially radioactive elements they contain—call on environmental humanists to read into the dark natures of both our past and present moments. The continuities between then and now suggest that Norris and Austin might not be as removed from contemporary concerns as we think.

SHIMMERING "SOMETHING" OF THE DESERT IN *MCTEAGUE*

"There was no change in the character of the desert," observes the narrator near the end of *McTeague*. "Always the same measureless leagues of white-hot alkali stretched away toward the horizon on every hand" (236). Just a few sentences later, the narrator describes the "horrible desolation" of Death Valley, where "[n]ot a rock, not a stone" interrupts "the monotony of the ground" (236). In almost every paragraph in *McTeague*'s final chapters, the narrator notes the desert's refusal to cultivate life and deliver topographical diversity, and at times Norris seems to go out of his way to emphasize the stasis of this region: "on the face of the desert not a grain of sand was in motion" (232). Not a one. However, Norris's desert may be more complicated—and more erotic—than what appears "on the face." Despite its harshness, its relentless invariability, Norris also depicts the desert as uneven, "dazzling," and shimmering with the "glitter of sand and sky" (236). How is it that the desert can simultaneously contain all these contradictory characteristics? In one passage, we are told that the landscape is both "flat" *and* marked by "low mounds"; in yet another passage, the "dazzling surface" of the desert instantaneously fades into oblivion (236). An indeterminate landscape that occupies both eastern California and southwestern Nevada, Norris's Death Valley is a generative "[s]omething—something or other," to use McTeague's recurrent utterance, that cannot be reduced to management's binary systems of classification (226). It is this mesmerizing "something" of the American West that simultaneously propels and frustrates McTeague, just as it did countless individuals who "looked westward for the fulfillment of American promises" in the second half of the nineteenth century.[32] But unlike cowboys, outlaws, miners, prospectors, artists, writers, and others who wandered these regions before him, McTeague turns eastward from the western edge of the nation and stumbles upon the sandy wilderness.

However, McTeague's unpredictable Death Valley is a different kind of wilderness than what John P. O'Grady playfully refers to as the "holiday side of the wild" depicted by other nineteenth-century writers such as Henry David Thoreau and

John Muir.[33] In *Pilgrims to the Wild*, O'Grady uses words including "recreational," "privileged," and even "dilettantish" to describe environmental writing born from the nineteenth century's burgeoning conservation movement, which aimed to preserve the nation's wilderness areas for future use.[34] In such writing, "wilderness" is synonymous not with desert lands but with the "forested, well-watered landscapes" of New England, coastal California, and the American Northwest.[35] Rooted in anxieties "leveled at cities... urbanization, industrialization, and environmental contamination (not to mention immigration)," Theodore Roosevelt's wilderness ethos defined the wild spaces of the American West as "elite and remote" corrective zones where Anglo-Saxon men could seek refuge from modern urban influences.[36] Urban anxieties, when combined with the perceived threat of an increasingly feminine national identity, culminated in what Denise Cruz has called "the hypermasculine discourse of westward-moving imperialism."[37] This growing interest in the (gendered) West contributed to the federal management of wilderness spaces under the designation of national parks, beginning with Yellowstone in 1872. According to Catriona Mortimer-Sandilands and Bruce Erickson, editors of *Queer Ecologies: Sex, Nature, Politics, Desire*,

> Parks were a curative response; with clear biopolitical overtones, they were created in part as places in which heterosexual masculinity could be performed and solidified away from the dramatic upheavals of American social and economic transformation, a restoration of the dominant social body through rigorous, health-giving recreation.[38]

Threatened by "women's increasing economic independence," as well as "rapidly changing racial and ethnic politics," the idea of national wilderness enclaves embodied much promise for white manhood at the turn of the century.[39] In other words, what white men were at risk of losing in the American city, they could find in the unspoiled "pleasuring-grounds" of the nation's vast woodlands.[40]

But what of the "empty, solitary" wilderness that is the desert in Norris's *McTeague* (235)? While critics of *McTeague* frequently underestimate the novel's desert space as an impotent no-man's-land—a vast, "monotonous," "static yawn"—here I read Norris's Death Valley as a frustrating though generative realm of becoming for McTeague and others.⁴¹ Despite the prevalence of desert spaces in turn-of-the-century writing of the American West, the desert ecology has received very little attention in naturalist and regionalist scholarship, and in this chapter I call for deeper critical engagements with arid wild spaces. The remoteness of these spaces, I argue, offers unique opportunities for considering the masculinist desires of land management and undoing the exclusionary, heteronormative logic of the nation-state.

QUEER ECOLOGY: AN ENVIRONMENT WITH/ WITHOUT

In our contemporary imagination, the desert is still often perceived as an environment *without* (water, vegetation, animal, human, resources) and not a place where people can survive, or at least not easily. When describing areas that lack access to food in the United States, we think "food desert." When a community lacks theaters, music venues, libraries, or institutions of higher learning, we think "cultural desert." In many ways, the desert has become synonymous with death, shortage, and absence. According to Tom Lynch, who writes of the "sensuous presences" of arid spaces in *Xerophilia*, the word "desert" "encodes an absence, not a presence, and implies that deserts are inherently and by definition deficient."⁴² The desert landscape, unlike the tangled, wooded landscapes celebrated by American Romantics and transcendentalists, is ripe subject matter for the antipastoral; in other words, it is *natural* space, but it is also perceived as *unnatural*, and aggressively so, in that it reputedly refuses to harbor life. This may be why Death Valley, along with Arizona's Saguaro and California's Joshua Tree, did not become national parks until 1994, more than one hundred years after Yellowstone and Sequoia. On the surface, it seems as though Norris's novel contributes to the notion that the desert equals death. After all, both Marcus and the mule are killed in this "measureless" expanse, and we might assume that McTeague and his "half-dead canary" will reach the same fate (243).

Despite the near absence of ecocritical engagements with Norris's work, many critics reference the strangeness of *McTeague*'s Death Valley episode. Investigating consumerism and class in the novel, David McGlynn remarks that "while Muir portrays the wilderness as 'a noble mark for the traveler' within accessible reach of San Francisco, Norris' landscape is remote, 'very hot,' and 'magnificently indifferent to man'—a terrain fit to rival the wiles of the city."[43] While it would be difficult to find fault in a critical description of Death Valley that is both harsh and remote, I argue that the novel's desert space is not *only* that; it is also, as *McTeague*'s narrator tells us, "magnificent," "beautiful," and "radian[t]" with "intense" color (230). Critics of American naturalism have long interpreted *nature* and *natural spaces* in these works as vulgar, overwhelming forces against which an individual has not a chance; however, a more nuanced reading of the desert in *McTeague* might reveal a different kind of ecology, one that deviates from how naturalist scholars generally characterize environments in these works.

McGlynn suggests a more complicated reading of the desert when he says that "the landscape awakens in McTeague a kind of sixth sense."[44] Norris refers to McTeague's "sixth sense" on two occasions in the novel and remarks that this "instinctive" sense grows keener in remote locations.[45] However, McGlynn then elides the creative potential of this unique *desert sense* by aligning it with words like "rational" and "deliberate."[46] Denise Cruz offers a similar view of the novel's arid spaces. Providing a nuanced reading of the same-sex desire between McTeague and Marcus, she explores the significance of their final meeting in the hot sands of Death Valley:

> [The novel] forecloses the viability of McTeague and Marcus's relationship by trapping them in the middle of nowhere, with no foreseeable

future and the present rapidly slipping away. . . . The novel thus closes
with McTeague and Marcus forever linked in a futureless partnership,
their desire successfully imprisoned within the isolation of Death
Valley.[47]

Similar to McGlynn, Cruz conceives of Norris's desert as a zone
of "isolation" and rural irrelevance. McTeague and Marcus are
"trapp[ed] in the middle of nowhere," which is to say that they are
nowhere. One is only "somewhere" when one is in the city, or at
least in close proximity to one. In such a parched landscape, the
men's relationship cannot take root, Cruz argues. Her exquisite
reading of this connection between male-male desire and place
calls attention to the shifting views of homosocial relations at the
turn of the twentieth century. From Cruz's perspective, desire is
born from humans and felt between humans, and Norris's desert
happens to be the unfortunate stage and prison where such desire
is tragically enacted. However, when we inquire into desire's con-
tingency upon place and relationship between the human and
nonhuman, a new way of considering desert spaces opens up, one
that requires queer critical methodologies.

So how can we conceptualize a *desert desire*? How might a
more nuanced understanding of the desert and desert sand in
McTeague broaden our understanding of land management at
the end of the nineteenth century? And how, exactly, does one
approach a queer reading of a landscape, especially one as seemingly "nowhere" as Death Valley? In this chapter, the term "queer"
functions as a destabilizing apparatus that is meant to "undo nor-
mative entanglements and fashion alternative imaginaries."[48]

In order to unpack and reimagine the difficult space that is
the nineteenth-century American desert, it is worth considering what queer theory and environmental criticism might be
able to offer one another. In *Queer Environmentality*, Robert
Azzarello proposes a more relational vision of the environment
than we might find in traditional ecocriticism.[49] His queer environmental approach merges environmental theory with queer
theory in order to see "the other-than-human world in all its

non-human-ness, its poetic complexity and queerness."[50] Similar to other self-described queer ecocritics like Timothy Morton, Erickson, and Mortimer-Sandilands, Azzarello considers earlier strands of ecocriticism ill-equipped to narrate a vision of the environment that is not steeped in heteronormative conceptions of nature and desire. Since nineteenth-century wilderness areas became understood as spaces where "whiteness, masculinity, and virility could be explored" and managed, Mortimer-Sandilands and Erickson contend that white heteronormativity has "left a clear imprint on the landscape," an imprint that political, cultural, scientific, economic, and literary discourses have reinforced.[51] As a result, queer ecocritics argue that bodies have been disciplined to interact with these national "nature-spaces," which are nearly always pristine green spaces, according to a paradigm that leaves little room for mystery or experiential plurality.[52] In other words, bodies may trespass into these environments, but the established management rubric, my term for the state's paternalistic attitude toward and treatment of public lands, may leave little room for those bodies to change or become. In an attempt to challenge the dominant national imprint of heteronormativity, queer ecocritics attempt to reenvision the multiplicity of ways that humans and environments interact and perhaps even *merge* with one another. Few critics have argued this point by way of nineteenth-century literary examples, nor have they paid much attention to works set in arid desert spaces. The relative absence of queer readings of the American desert perpetuates the notion that arid ecologies are no place for humans, meaning they are *no place* at all.

In *McTeague,* human bodies and eco-matter engage in these ongoing exchanges throughout the desert episode, and by the final scene the environment can hardly be relegated to a distant *over yonder.* As experienced in the novel, sand is nothing less than unmanageable queer matter that insists on blurring the border between McTeague and the landscape. Sand scratches, chisels, enters, and ultimately changes his body. In the novel, sand interacts with every one of McTeague's senses, thus providing an opportunity to read "against the commodification of nature as resource and as spectacle."[53] For example, when the narrator in *McTeague* describes Death Valley's "illimitable leagues of quivering sand and alkali," sand becomes a peculiar source of energy that calls for a new way of recognizing one's body in relation to the land (232). The word "quivering"—an odd word to describe sand—complicates a landscape that at first appears both unchanging ("illimitable leagues") and scientifically understood ("alkali"). To think of sand as "quivering," a word that is often linked to sensations of both fear and sexual pleasure, is to think of the desert as a complex, dynamic space that is alive and intimately engaged with McTeague. Vibrating with energy, the "quivering" sand refuses to be any *one* thing, including virginal, spoiled, or "under . . . exclusive control."[54] Such discourse has often been applied to national parks and wilderness spaces, suggesting a kind of environmental vulnerability and defenselessness that is foundational to what Morton calls "Masculine Nature" or "Organicism."[55] In Norris's novel, however, the desert challenges the need of human dependency and reveals itself, instead, as a zone of unbridled "infinite strangeness." When one tries to manage (and manage in) these lands, sand responds, often irritatingly. For McTeague, the amateur manager, sand is sensory-rich matter capable of communicating pleasure, pain, and an unexplainable "something" that propels him deeper and deeper into the country.

"*LORD!* WHAT A COUNTRY!"

In "What the Sands Remember," ethnographer Vanessa Agard-Jones takes a queer, interdisciplinary approach to sand on the shores of Martinique, a former French territory in the Caribbean. By studying the capacious nature of sand—how it "both holds geological memories in its elemental structure and calls forth referential memories through its color, feel between the fingers, and quality of grain"—Agard-Jones argues that sand is an appropriate metaphor for the "messy," generative interplay between body and environment:

> [S]and is the less embraced referent that returns us to the body's messy realities. Water washes, makes clean. Sand gets inside our bodies, our things, in ways at once inconvenient and intrusive. It smooths rough edges but also irritates, sticking to our bodies' folds and fissures.[56]

Even though Death Valley in the nineteenth century may seem to have little in common with the tropical ecosystems of today's Martinique, Agard-Jones's ruminations on sand resonate with how "the less embraced referent" functions in *McTeague*'s desert space. Throughout the Death Valley episode, sand reminds McTeague that he has a body, and that that body exists in an always unfinished, never fully managed national space. Engaging with and transforming every sense, sand blurs and "mess[es]" the line between body and land, resulting in a continuous epistemological quandary: McTeague is always becoming-sand. At first, McTeague views Death Valley as a space that exists outside himself, which is not surprising given the language of the national parks project at the turn of the twentieth century. For example, the Yellowstone Act of 1872, which drafted Yellowstone as the first national park, describes the wild space as a "tract of land" that is "set apart" from the rest of the country.[57] Political rhetoric renders this space divisible and therefore manageable. Additionally, the document warns those who visit Yellowstone to not "settle" or "occupy" the land contained within the borders of the park, lest they be considered "trespassers."[58] In other words, the Yellowstone Act safeguards the "natural condition" of the park's "natural curiosities," regulating the space so as to prevent people from inhabiting it or experiencing it intimately.[59]

This same rhetoric of distance works within *McTeague*; however, the desert-logic presents various challenges to the federal management of park and wilderness spaces. Not only is McTeague at first "set apart" from the desert, but the apparent vastness also works to separate him from his "pursuer": "He would strike straight out into that horrible wilderness where even the beasts were afraid. He would cross Death Valley at once and put its arid wastes between him and his pursuer" (233). Even though McTeague is the subject of these two sentences—"he" is the one with the power to *do*, or at least it would seem—the use of conditional verbs ("would strike," "would cross") implies that action depends on a grand delusion: McTeague's ability to dominate and divide the "horrible wilderness." He would strike, *if*—; he would cross, *if*—. Since the "merciless lash" of sand and sun prevent him from existing beyond the so-called tract of land, McTeague's ability to dominate Death Valley never comes to fruition. As a result, he is left to "grasp," "chase," and "reach," gestures that indicate desperate, erratic movements into the unknown, but that are movements nonetheless (235). As active and elusive matter, Norris's sand prevents men from orienting themselves or getting a "grasp" of the landscape. In a dynamic, agentive environment, and not merely a measurable "tract," McTeague reaches for understanding that never arrives. The sand and wind, among other animated elements, refuse to allow his *weathered* body to rest, let alone achieve mastery. In this environment, management remains an aspiration only. The land may be mapped, but the desert-logic smudges the map at every turn.

The difficulties of controlling an ever-changing environment continue to trouble McTeague throughout the Death Valley episode. Far from inert substances, sand and sun penetrate McTeague's body with ease. He and the desert trespass into one another, which calls attention to the weakness of both corporeal and political boundaries. Despite McTeague's perpetual desire to uphold distinct borders, or to position his body at a safe distance from sand, the desert ecology undermines his attempts and thus thwarts his managerial desires. As he wanders even deeper into the unmanageable "thing of terror," desert eco-matter acts on and in McTeague, resulting in what the narrator describes as a "tortured body" (234). The narrator attempts to wrangle the ever-changing landscape into the logical container of temporality, but this effort is immediately undermined by the indeterminacy of the place:

> *By eleven o'clock* the heat had increased to such an extent that McTeague could feel the burning of the ground come pringling and stinging through the soles of his boots. Every step he took threw up clouds of impalpable alkali dust, salty and choking, so that he strangled and coughed and sneezed with it. (234)

This passage reveals an interesting discursive tension between McTeague and Death Valley. In a place without signposts, recognizable landmarks, maintained trails, or reliable maps, the narrator reaches for the intangible marker of time—"[b]y eleven o'clock"—as a means of dividing the landscape into knowable moments. Chronological "mapping," along with references to estimated distance ("eight miles") and direction ("steadily eastward") occur frequently throughout the Death Valley episode, especially early in McTeague's journey. Imposing these directional markers onto the "immeasurable tide" that is Death Valley serves as a reminder that the wilderness, though large and supposedly remote, exists in the context of an even larger political territory that is framed by coasts and gridded by borders and "circuits" traveled by men (229). As he travels "steadily eastward," for example, the text locates McTeague's movements in the geography of the American nation-state. However, these efforts to measure and govern both time and geography prove ineffectual when the sand, the language of the desert, becomes particular, which is to say *a particle*, and intimate. Now "burning" with the heat of the sun, the sand "pringl[es]" and "sting[s]" McTeague's feet. Once a boundary between McTeague's body and the sand, the soles of his shoes now operate as conduits; McTeague's feet absorb the heat of the sand *and* sun, further troubling McTeague's ability to deter the trespassing matter.

But the sole is not the only interface between McTeague and the environment. In this same scene, "clouds of impalpable alkali dust," grains too fine to even feel between the fingers, penetrate every exposed opening on McTeague's body: his nose, eyes, ears, mouth, and pores. The dust is also "salty," charging it with the ability to pull fluids from McTeague's skin and mucous membranes. This gradual drying-out is nothing less than *desertification*, a term that expresses a process of transformation and not necessarily a process of depletion, which is often how the word is used in an environmental context. McTeague spasmodically responds to the cloud of dust by "strangl[ing] and cough[ing] and sneez[ing] *with* it." The use of the word "with," a preposition that cultivates new associations and intimacies, exhibits the desert's sensual agency in this passage. Instead of merely expelling these foreign particles as a means of protecting, and separating them from, the vulnerable body, the sneeze initiates a different kind of process: McTeague's biology begins to merge *with* the desert matter, further challenging his ability to manage in this space.

Although obviously irritating, given the coughing and choking the sand provokes, the experience does not lack desire for McTeague. Coughing and sneezing involve quick muscular contractions followed by release, much like the physical sensations elicited during orgasm. When McTeague sneezes, he gives back to the desert his changed cells, his changed bacteria, and his changed mucus. In other words, the dust operates in and against McTeague's body in an almost alchemical fashion, and then he returns this new matter to the desert. In this way, desertification can be read as sex without form, or what O'Grady refers to as a "presence charged with a powerful eroticism."[60]

McTeague's sneezing and choking exemplify how sexual intimacy interrogates the borders of the body, reminding individuals that they have a specific body. In other words, Norris's sand, like sex, simultaneously dissolves *and* rearticulates the body's form, a seemingly contradictory effect that defies heteronormative taxonomies of gender and sexuality. After the desert has burned through his "sole" and entered his body, McTeague responds to the arousal by exclaiming, "*Lord*! What a country!" pointing out that the political territory that contains Death Valley is embedded in every dust particle of his desire. Death Valley may feel far removed from the American nation-state, but as "the repository of memory," sand preserves traces of country in its ever-moving grains.[61]

Throughout the novel, Norris infuses the desert with enigmatic agency. The desert is always felt but never named. "[T]hick and heavy," the air elicits a palpable presence in the Death Valley episode, and the narrator frequently describes the work it does within McTeague's body: it "was hot to his lips and the roof of his mouth" (230–31). At every step, the narration informs us that sensorial consumption, and "consummation," are inevitable in this space. In Death Valley, even the silence—not an empty thing in the least—enters McTeague and begs to be recognized:

> As soon as he ceased his tramp and the noise of his crunching, grinding footsteps died away, the silence, vast, illimitable, enfolded him like an immeasurable tide. From all that gigantic landscape, that colossal reach of baking sand, there arose not a single sound. Not a twig rattled, not an insect hummed, not a bird or beast invaded that huge solitude with call or cry. (231)

Once again, the desert emerges as an erotic, generative presence for McTeague. Strangely, the narrator tells us that the silence "enfold[s] him" as an ocean would in its "immeasurable tide." The startling use of water metaphors to describe a land made of "baking sand," in addition to the list of sounds that are *not* heard in all that silence, reveals a world full of queer rhetorical possibilities. Silence is not dead in this passage, nor is it empty. Instead, it is "gesturing and rippling in an infinite number of directions, in an infinite number of ways."[62] To conceive of Death Valley as an oceanic space is to convert dry granular matter into new matter, or, in Austin's words, to embrace the "odd contradictions" of place. Norris's desert, the landscape that enters McTeague's body "from all sides" (231), defies nineteenth-century understandings of the wilderness as inert "tracts of land" waiting to be managed.

To envision the desert as "the other of consummation" is to recognize its ability to both consume and obliterate, as well as its power to make again. "To be shattered by (our being in) the world," writes Michael O'Rourke, "is facilitative of a creation of the world, a redesigning of it."[63] Such an intimate relationship with eco-matter challenges the solid outlines of things, specifically between one's body and the environment. Sullivan, who coined the term "dirt theory" to describe intimate relations between humans and the animated particles that "surround us at all scales," observes that "dirty nature is always with us as part of ongoing interactions among all kinds of material agents, and thus is, in other words, more process than place."[64]

To McTeague, the desert is always "something or other," an utterance that, in its very construction, contains traces of both the human "other" and the nonhuman "some*thing*." The tangled ecology that flourishes in *McTeague* presents a real challenge to federal control. Anglo land management regimes both create and take as a given clear demarcations between matter, whether human, animal, or natural resource, but the novel's ecological meshwork disturbs the possibility of a stable national taxonomy. Instead of a distinct and separate body or citizen, McTeague emerges as a plexus of beings. Neither his body nor the desert landscape can be abstracted into easy data as a result of this sandy intra-action. If anything, the McTeaguean "something" reveals just how vulnerable human bodies are to the elements they wish to subdue.

The line between McTeague and his environment, or between the human and the nonhuman, is a hazy one at best in the novel, and it becomes even hazier in the final scene. Cruz argues that the novel "unravels into comedy" and "restrains homosexual desire" as Marcus and McTeague commence to fighting over Trina's money in the middle of "the valley's suffocating heat."[65] McTeague and Marcus, she argues, are left with "no options" in such a place, and so it becomes inevitable that the two men must meet their death in Death Valley.[66] However, the "Western showdown" may in fact be queerer than even Cruz argues.[67] When the fight initiates, both men begin to take on physical characteristics of the desert. Sand erupts with much agency in this scene, and it continues its work of chiseling and entering the men's bodies. "Rolling and struggling upon the hot white ground," Marcus and McTeague immerse themselves in the sand and, thus, instigate a kind of elemental penetration that reflects the potential desire the two men have for one another (243). Given the lacerating effects of the desert floor against the skin, such scratches and scrapes would allow the sand to merge with the blood, thus accelerating the process of desertification. Just as sexual climax stimulates the release of ejaculate, which causes the body to essentially lose liquid, so, too, does this sandy infiltration result in a radical drying-out. As the struggle continues, the narrator remarks that "[c]louds of alkali dust, fine and pungent, enveloped the two fighting men, all but strangling them" (243).

Words like "hot," "blindly," and "strangling" demonstrate that there is another agent in the fight, one capable of "wrestling with every human sense." The word "pungent," which suggests a smell that is penetrative and overpowering, is an especially odd description of sand. We hardly think of sand as having any scent at all. The use of this word further exposes the transformation that is taking place, for the desert even overcomes the men's sense of smell. As active matter, these desert grains refuse to be consigned to static, measurable tracts of land. When humans find themselves in the midst of these agentive grains, the promise of both federal control and heteronormative directives seem unattainable.

The desert-actor rouses with even more presence in the last few paragraphs:

> McTeague's right wrist was caught, *something* clicked upon it, then the struggling body fell limp and motionless with a long breath.

> As McTeague rose to his feet, he felt a pull at his right wrist; *something* held it fast. (243, emphasis added)

The unnamed subject in this scene, "something" both "clicks" and "holds" the dead man to the man who is still alive. Even though readers know that the agent that "holds fast" in this passage is a set of handcuffs, the recurrence of the vague "something" hints at the presence of another force, one that mirrors the queer "something" of McTeague's desert.

Linked now by a chain, Marcus and McTeague have merged into a new, united form. This synthesis both challenges the notion that the body is an independent form *and* interrogates the existence of a wholly predictable future. McTeague is bound, now literally, to a dead past. "[A]lways . . . dictated to a function of the nation," always unreachable, the future-horizon appears even more unattainable now that McTeague is weighed down by Marcus's dead body.[68] Marcus has, quite literally, completed the cycle from *dust to dust*, reflecting the biblical associations between corpses and granular matter. McTeague—or whatever the "something" is that he has become— is left in the disturbing, ever-consummating present where history and the future converge to make and unmake the nation. In other words, McTeague remains caught in the anxious space between the end of one century and the beginning of another. "[T]he movement between tradition and innovation," writes Erickson, "is always fluid and uncharted."[69] At the end of the novel, Norris's desert is the indeterminate space articulated by Erickson as the "movement between." Queering the desert in this way, *McTeague*'s Death Valley becomes anything but "sterile," but neither is it wholly alive.[70] Instead, it is a "half-dead" (Norris, *McTeague*, 243) performative space that moves both within and against a fixed national identity. Despite the fact that this region had been explored, mapped, and *naturalized* as a national, though allegedly unproductive, land by the end of the nineteenth century, experience with this environment on the ground was a different thing entirely, as McTeague's constant grappling with the granular ecology demonstrates.

DESERT-SPEAK: A NATIONAL LANGUAGE

Unlike McTeague's former role as a dentist in the city, in Death Valley he is unable to either anesthetize or extract meaning. As he continues to wander in this strange space, his purpose grows less and less clear. As a result, his language, full of stutters, stammers, and confused exclamations, becomes an extension of Death Valley. "If it gets much hotter," says McTeague, "I—I don' know—" (231). Unable to escape the steadily increasing heat or to "strike" and "cross" the multivalent terrain, McTeague is propelled into an interminable threshold, which his speech reflects. "I don' know" serves as the only way McTeague can articulate "all that gigantic landscape," and this recurrent uncertainty takes on many stylistic forms throughout the Death Valley episode (231). Variations on "I don' know" appear throughout the novel's final chapters, emphasizing the generative potential of the body's relation to the unknown. In just two pages in the Death Valley section, McTeague utters the following statements:

> "Lord! . . . I never knew it *could* get as hot as this."
> "If it gets much hotter, I don' know what I'll do."
> "Ain't it *ever* going to let up?"
> "Good *Lord!* What a country!" (231–32)

While all these pronouncements speak to the strange incomprehensibility of the sandy desert, each one reveals a variation on the same idea: that Death Valley is beyond McTeague's understanding and out of his control, and amazingly so given the persistent use of exclamation marks. Indeterminate words like "could" and "ever" are even italicized, further emphasizing McTeague's inability to rein in meaning from a land as outlandish as Death Valley. It is worth noting that until Marcus arrives, there is nobody around to hear McTeague's declarations, but neither is there no *one*; instead, the "evasive Something" of the desert, to use Austin's description, responds by expanding even further in every direction.

Elaborating on how desert landscapes evoke this kind of "relentlessly unspecific" rhetoric, Michael Cobb argues that in its attempt to render coherent the inchoate, it approximates the religious.[71] Cobb writes,

> Something about gorgeous vistas occasions a "peculiar form of plea-
> sure" and aesthetic arrest, which begs for the kind of description
> that cannot, will not, describe: something like the sublime meets the
> romantic clichés about nature meets New Age spiritualism, which will
> utterly fail to capture the view. So we're left straining to express the
> grandeur we're seeing and feeling.[72]

While McTeague rarely resorts to "romantic clichés" in the Death
Valley episode, the "relentlessly unspecific," generalized language
that Cobb calls attention to characterizes accurately McTeague's
desert-speak. Just as McTeague "reaches his hand forward" toward
the horizon, his words also reach out, even though no one is listening. It is within the communicative space that is the abstract zone
between his fingers and words and the vague "something" in the
distance he desires that McTeague ceaselessly becomes sand. Since
his words never arrive at certainty, and since his fingers never touch
the "receding horizon," McTeague remains a being propelled into
"flight" by enduring escape and desire (235). The fact that readers
do not witness McTeague's inevitable death underscores Norris's
refusal to arrive at closure. We can predict that McTeague will die
in the desert, but the novel ends before his expected death.

Furthermore, McTeague's desert-speak elicits frequent openings of the mouth, allowing environmental particulates to enter
the body and nudge him further into the sandy valley. Even when
McTeague announces to the desert that he is ready to give up
his march, the generative act of speaking provides him with the
energy to "rouse himself again," as we see in the following passage:

> "I *can't* go on," groaned McTeague, his eyes sweeping the horizon
> behind him, "I'm beat out. I'm dog tired. I ain't slept any for two
> nights." But for all that he roused himself again, saddled the mule,
> scarcely less exhausted than himself, and pushed once more over the
> scorching alkali and under the blazing sun. (235)

When followed by narrative descriptions of action—"he roused
himself" and "[he] pushed"—the statement "I *can't* go on" illustrates the generative tension that exists between McTeague's failure and his steady propulsion. Just as "I don' know" continues to

fuel his unfocused desire to dive further into the mystery that is Death Valley, the frustration embedded in the phrase "I *can't* go on" spurs him even further into the desert.

While a primal urge, or "sixth sense," continues to propel our brutish sojourner ever deeper into the Southern California desert lands, the strangeness of the place—and McTeague's inability to navigate that strangeness—produces endless speech. McTeague's speech never rises above vague utterings, but that vagueness keeps him plodding ever deeper into unmanageable terrain. Clumsy and unfocused, McTeague never "arrives" at *someplace*. Instead, he merely continues to generate more movement, always desiring to be where he is not—or, as Lee Clark Mitchell says of naturalist characters, they "are no more than events in the world."[73] Even if possibility exists in that reckless desiring for rest that never arrives, McTeague never attains absolute fulfillment. Such is the logic of naturalism, whereby novelists often reduce characters to what Mitchell describes as "mere scenes where external events coincide with internal reflexes."[74] McTeague's desert—a generative, though highly disappointing, space—is a sandy amalgamation of rhetorical and physical desiring, which a decidedly masculine national promise borders: *You will arrive if you are strong enough and brave enough.* Despite the fact that McTeague "swing[s] forward in great strides" toward this masculine ideal, the (national) landscape continues to dissolve and then regenerate, indefinitely, into a profound sigh: "I don' know" (235).

POLICY PLAY

The harsh, intractable desert that Norris introduces at the end of *McTeague* cannot harbor life. Instead, characters are lured there by a vague *something*, wither away, and die. Unlike the American mythos of Manifest Destiny, whereby heroic individuals tirelessly do battle with the untamed wilderness in order to attain the promised land that is civilization, Norris's novel works in reverse. Once a city-dweller—and a dentist, no less—McTeague wanders from west to east from a thriving coastal metropolis to the heart of the body-numbing desert. As a brute, a common figure in literary naturalism, McTeague cannot manage his way into productive futures. Instead, the backward desert seems a fitting habitat for a character ill-equipped to handle the intellectual and professional pressures of modernity. It is therefore important to consider Norris's choice of making Death Valley McTeague's final *place of unrest*, especially since, even today, many continue to write lifelessness and alterity onto American desert spaces. In its promotional materials, for example, Death Valley National Park capitalizes on conceptions of extreme uninhabitability by advertising itself as "a land of extremes," and the official park website boasts that it is 120 miles from the nearest city. Branded as the "Hottest, Driest, [and] Lowest," Death Valley sells an identity marked by "steady drought" and "record summer heat."[75] An aerial shot of the vast, multicolored ashfalls of the park's "Artist's Drive," the website's banner photograph further stresses the overwhelming desolation of this desert landscape. In the image, a road can barely be seen cutting through the middle of the valley's clay formations, demonstrating a way of *knowing* the landscape from the safety and speed of an automobile. The artist-traveler who seeks inspiration from this terrain is invited to pass through but not linger. In fact, the majority of the photographs on Death Valley's official website favor images of panoramic vastness over the intimacy of close-up shots at ground level. This is a land we can only experience, know, and marvel at from a drone-hovering distance, and that distance renders very few traces of life.

However, beyond the headlines and the wide-lens photography on the park's official website, Death Valley sustains more life than we might have first imagined. Take, for instance, the one-paragraph summary from the website's home page:

> In this below-sea-level basin, steady drought and record summer heat make Death Valley a land of extremes. Yet, each extreme has a striking contrast. Towering peaks are frosted with winter snow. Rare rainstorms bring vast fields of wildflowers. Lush oases harbor tiny fish and

refuge for wildlife and humans. Despite its morbid name, a great diversity of life survives in Death Valley.

Remarkably, this passage insists on environmental extremes ("steady drought," "record summer heat") and subsequently refuses to claim that it is *only* lifeless. Even though the language here is consistent in its devotion to extremity—the contrast is "striking," the peaks are "towering," and the fields of wildflowers are "vast"—the desert here becomes stranger and more complex than mere "measureless leagues of white-hot alkali" (Norris, *McTeague*, 236). Snow, rainstorms, and "towering peaks" are hiding in the shadows of the park's motto: "Hottest"/"snow," "Driest"/"rainstorms," "Lowest"/"towering peaks." Even more confusing is the idea that in a place named Death Valley, "life survives."

When the California Desert Protection Act (CDPA) redesignated Death Valley as a US National Park in 1994, Congress used familiar language to describe the region: *Death Valley is a problem that we know how to solve.* The CDPA states, "The California desert is a cohesive unit, posing difficult resource protection and management challenges."[76] Along with Joshua Tree and the Mojave National Preserve, Death Valley has both "public and natural values," which must be protected. What are those values? we might ask. And how do we distinguish a "public" value from a "natural" value given the "messy reality" presented to readers in *McTeague*? Congress attempts to answer these questions in the CDPA with language seemingly untouched by doubt:

> Congress found that: federally owned desert lands of southern California constitute a public wildland resource of *extraordinary and inestimable value* for current and future generations; these desert wildlands have unique *scenic, historical, archeological, environmental, ecological, wildlife, cultural, scientific, educational* and *recreational* values. (emphasis added)

The desert lands described in this passage seem wholly excavated. Listed, separated, and classified, their "values" grow dusty in the museum like mined artifacts.

The subject of every clause in the "Findings/Policy" section of the CDPA, Congress declares itself the juridical, scientific, and economic proprietor of these lands. Even more grandiose words like "extraordinary" and "inestimable" refer not to the desert itself but to the extractable resources that exist within it. These various rhetorical expressions of possession, resource commodification, and empirical understanding in the CDPA reverberate with William Cronon's views on the effect of property ownership in the age of capitalism: "To define property is thus to represent boundaries between people; equally, it is to articulate at least one set of conscious ecological boundaries between people and things."[77]

As a "federally owned" tract of land, a space with distinct "public and natural values" preserved within its boundaries, this desert property hardly seems to offer much in the way of intimacy between bodies and things. By pointing out some of these tensions in the CDPA's language, I do not mean to wholly denigrate efforts of federal land management. After all, it is difficult to imagine what a lack of federal involvement could mean for the United States' wild spaces. And I hardly think that replacing a word like "ecological" with a McTeaguean "something" in the CDPA would necessarily restore "poetic complexity" to our conception of national park spaces. With Bears Ears National Monument, the Alaska National Wildlife Refuge, and other public lands managed by both the Departments of Agriculture and the Interior facing threats of downsizing and drilling, many environmental humanists would be hard-pressed to argue that what we need now is *less* federal protection.

But how could exploring the "experiential quality" of elements and ecologies, to use Austin's description, that exist beyond, or perhaps in the shadows of, the dominant rhetorics of the nation-state open up alternative modes of affiliation within the boundaries of the nation's parklands? Could these "experiential" efforts offer more than passing moments of personal pleasure—and is it possible they could operate as yet another tool for manifesting new and resilient ecological futures? If, as Bruno Latour suggests in *The Politics of Nature*, human and nonhuman actors "appear first of all as troublemakers" who, acting as a collective, "get in the way of domination," then we must consider how our radical commingling with both the elements *and* each other can engender alternative modes of managing in and with the world.[78]

Environmental policymaking codes and shapes the future of human-wilderness interactions, and as Erickson and others have pointed out, such policies and futures often appear fixed and rhetorically sure of themselves. But even in the seemingly lifeless language that reduces the wilderness to a "cohesive unit," "life survives." Even more than that, the desert flourishes with a half-dead "something" that cannot be harnessed or naturalized by the codes of policy. Queer ecology gives us a way to push against—or, better yet, to play within—the language of environmental policymaking in an effort to disturb the masculinist attitude of environmental mastery that insists that Nature (with a capital N) is separate from and, therefore, immune to people. Even in spaces that are heavily marked by ideological and physical imprints of the nation, such as our national parks and monuments, innumerable experiential possibilities exist. Calling attention to sensual human interactions with the environment in literature can help us to better understand and develop nonnormative modes of citizenship because if we view environmental materialities not as distant entities to be controlled but as participants in a near infinite variety of human and nonhuman assemblages, our current oppositional management methods might begin to feel incompatible with the always-interactive ontology.

• • •

In the strange, interactive setting of Norris's Death Valley, McTeague fails to find a way out. His own hands—always desiring, always reaching forward away from the body—never direct him back to familiar ground. In the deepest sense, McTeague, the brute, gives in to matter, as the final scene shows him covered in alkali dust, handcuffed to a dead man, and soon to be buried in the sand like so much discarded desert waste. If desert hikers were to stumble upon this strange exposed grave one hundred years later, they might find a few scattered bones, a few scraps of preserved clothing. With more likelihood, the hikers would probably discover the "gilt" birdcage and the handcuffs, items that, due to their durable materiality, refuse easy corrosion and, thus, stick around as litter. McTeague's metallic, diuturnal trash objects, symbols of human and animal imprisonment, remain long after the human and animal bodies they once held have perished. Sand might chisel at the surface of these deserted items, wearing them down slowly, but they linger largely intact. While the connection might at first seem strange, today's toxic (and even radioactive) desert waste materials exhibit ontologies similar to the soon-to-be-trash that imprisons and then reduces life to "half-life" in *McTeague*.

The sections that follow attempt to chart a relationship between mobile sand in Austin's nature writing and uranium, an all-too-common radioactive element in the American Southwest that adds various dimensions to terms like "waste" and "elemental interaction." Even though turn-of-the-century vanadium miners cast uranium into waste piles, or "tailings," to get to the chemical element of their choice, the eventual mining of the valuable ore in the mid-twentieth century contributed to what Traci Brynne Voyles refers to as "wastelanding," or the corporate disregard for the peoples and ecologies of the Southwest.[79] In a work like *The Land of Little Rain*, the desert winds and sand of Southern California appear as lively—and maybe living—forces with their own temporal structures and managerial tendencies. While Austin's animated portrait of the American Southwest might overly romanticize the region and, as some critics have pointed out, participate in Indigenous erasure and essentializing, I argue that despite these evident shortcomings her conception of vital, energetic elements that emotionally and physically *do* something to bodies provides us with a set of tools that can help (critically) handle the disturbing, intra-active "waste" material that is uranium.[80] Similar to Austin's ever-moving sand, today's uranium dust travels through space and into bodies, linking both region and bodies with radioactivity.

"NOT THE LAW, BUT THE LAND SETS THE LIMIT"

According to Mary Austin, who wrote extensively about the arid wild space that surrounded her San Joaquin Valley homestead in the late 1800s, the desert existed as the "shadow side" of the wild, a description that resonates with McTeague's recurrent "I don' know."[81] The desert landscape—or nature's unmanageable and inaccessible "shadow side"—exhibits a queer kind of logic in Austin's work, one that "trick[s] the sense of time"; even when Austin's desert scorches and parches, it also "seduces" (Austin, *Land,* 9). Lawrence Buell has noted that Austin, "the desertwise speaker," "relishes the tricksiness of this intractable region" and, in her writing, "approaches the environment on its own terms."[82] In the remaining sections of this chapter, I pursue what it might mean, from a management standpoint, to "approach the environment on its own terms," especially when the environment in question is perceived as a near insurmountable problem. Many of the land managers I cite in this chapter read human-environmental relations in desert spaces in hierarchical terms, with war-ready humans at the top. Often, these managers use words like "conquest" and "battle" to describe their attitudes toward unruly arid regions. For others, the turn-of-the-century desert existed not as an enemy but as "a release valve, or safety hatch," offering California's coastal city dwellers the comfort of knowing that wild, supposedly untouched spaces still existed a few miles beyond the borders of the metropolis.[83] Regardless of whether Progressives viewed deserts as adversaries or abstract otherworlds, most agreed that humans could not easily manage in these sandy locales.

Turn-of-the-century Americans often favored a more restorative (and, hence, reformative) version of nature than what the so-called uncultivated desert could provide. For example, in *California: For Health, Pleasure, and Residence,* published in 1873, Charles Nordhoff says that the "worthless" deserts of Southern California need only "skillful treatment to become valuable," and he suggests that the joint tools of "culture and irrigation" hold the potential to reclaim these "vast tracts."[84] Austin, however, finds appeal in what Nordhoff perceives as waste—regions "squeezed up out of chaos" that make no promises to improve (3).

However, when Austin writes about "desertness" in her collection of essays *The Land of Little Rain,* she deploys a language rich in desirous contradiction, similar to the "something—something or other" language Norris uses to describe Death Valley. However, unlike McTeague, who battles furiously against desert heat, wind, and sand in hopes of overcoming its insolvability, Austin exhibits a management style rooted in this idea: "the land sets the limit" (3). Austin's land-oriented management style does not mean that she, the writer-manager, relinquishes all agency. On the contrary, she is very much present in *Land,* as exemplified by the frequent use of first-person pronouns and claims to her own passionate kinship with arid California. In fact, the very first sentence in *Land* begins with "I confess," a phrase that marks her collection of nature essays as an experiment in intimate disclosure.[85]

While Austin's romantic ode to the desert in *Land* largely disregards the many instances of violence Americans "perpetrated against Indigenous peoples and others in the Southwest, as many critics have keenly noted, her enthusiastic interest in the nonhuman, the minuscule, and what I refer to as the *slow present* of ecological attunement mark her as a different kind of land manager than those endorsed by Gifford Pinchot and other notable Progressives. Though Austin's environmental views grew complicated later in her life—for example, she publicly sided with ranchers during the California water wars, leading her to promote irrigation in the region—her exploration of sand's liveliness in *Land* demonstrates how human-environmental intimacy with so-called elemental waste can decelerate and destabilize what I have described as the anxious rush of managerial time.

Describing herself as one who is attuned to the liveliness of desert elements, Austin views nature writing as a vehicle for slow contemplation of one's surroundings. In other words, when Austin pauses to contemplate the world around her, she provides readers with an unhurried space within which they can imagine how management might operate when freed from the politics of improvement. So, what would management look like without the future tense? If it recognized the "presence" of the earth, to use Austin's language, how would it be organized—and what would it do?[86] And is there a way to be "present" without upholding commonly fetishized concepts such as "place" and "the local"?[87] In her work on "desertness," Austin seems interested in pursuing such questions.

As a California transplant whose brother was a dry farmer and husband was a Stanford-trained engineer, Austin would have been familiar with scientific land management's devotion to linear time, as well as its fixation on organizing productive futures. Austin's presence in the land of little rain has everything to do with management, in fact. Her brother's dream of becoming a dry farmer is what brought her to California in the first place, and after marriage she and her husband, Stafford Wallace Austin, moved to Inyo, California, where he would oversee the development of an irrigation project. Critics of Western literature often think of Austin as a preservationist nature writer in the key of John Muir and Wallace Stegner.[88] However, despite Austin's pleas for "environmental protection and limits to growth" in *The Land of Little Rain*, David Cassuto calls attention to the fact that she later became a convert to irrigation in the West, believing that "the [Owens Valley's] expanding agricultural aspirations were both natural and salubrious to the region's ecology even if they did not jibe with her overall vision of land use."[89] Her 1917 novel, *The Ford*, explores these struggles during the California water wars, and in that work she takes the side of ranchers who depended on diverted water for their livelihoods. While these views hardly make Austin seem like a radical environmental thinker, her choice to support ranchers over urban growth may have appeared the lesser of the two evils at the time, especially since she viewed Los Angeles's ever-expanding boundaries as a threat to her inland desert enclave. All around her, managerial negotiations with water, sand, and other elements were (re)shaping the political and environmental landscapes, so it's no wonder Austin ruminates on the animacy of these elements in her nature writing.

Austin alludes to her own Progressive impulses in her autobiographical work, *Earth Horizon*, which was published nearly thirty years after *The Land of Little Rain*. Writing about herself in the third person, as she does throughout the memoir, she states,

> Always she had been deeply aware that there was something that could be done about everything if not at once, then later, when you had learned this or that, mastered one or another intervening technique. It was the root of all her religious conviction of every sort that life is essentially remedial, undefeatable; the thing was to discover the how of it. (268)

Austin's belief that "something . . . could be done about everything" aligns with the Progressive Era's administrative ethos whereby problems were perceived as opportunities for remediation. As Cecilia Tichi notes, the turn-of-the-century manager held fast to "the belief that redesign is possible," meaning he or she viewed the world as a series of indefinite problems requiring solutions.[90] And similar to the manager's persistent focus on productive, always-improving futures, Austin also holds faith in the inevitability of progress "if not at once, then later." Though seemingly dedicated to a preservationist environmentalism in *The Land of Little Rain*—she praises the desert for its absence of people, and decries modern America's "greedy, vulgarizing hand"—Austin gradually grew more devoted to a politics of improvement later in life, as this passage reveals.[91]

To what extent, then, can we read Austin's desert as an "undomesticated" space that "exceeds and resists mastery," as critic Stacy Alaimo suggests?[92] Even though the region Austin describes as wilderness appears to be unruly and illegible to *some* humans, she positions herself as a veritable knower of its secrets—or, better yet, as a translator of a different kind of management style than that practiced by the Progressive Era's "management culture." In *Land*, Austin portrays herself as a more compassionate kind of Progressive manager—one in touch with the liveliness of the minuscule, the nonhuman, the granular, the non-Anglo. Even though she frequently "pulls the whole territory away from prior Anglo claims to it," which would seem to exemplify a rejection of Progressive management, Austin's desert is not a blank space, as many turn-of-the-century Americans figured it.[93] Instead, Austin's animated portrayal of the desert thrives with a multitude of queer temporalities and *eco-logics* that she, the writer-manager, attempts to communicate to readers, even when she cannot understand them entirely.

Austin's ecocentric approach to desert writing—in particular, her emphasis on the liveliness of desert *actants* like sand and wind—reflects a nuanced management style that remains open and alert to environmental "tricksiness" and ontological difference. To that end, in the first chapter of *Land* she states, "Desert is a loose term to indicate land that supports no man" (3). However, in the very next sentence she counters the assumption that the desert is altogether lifeless by affirming, "Void of life it never is, however dry the air and villainous the soil" (3). For Austin, "life" is not synonymous with "human life," and the West is not merely a passive landscape that "awaits settlement and development," as irrigationist William E. Smythe described it in 1900.[94] In other words, just because fewer humans occupy the nineteenth-century American desert than they do greener regions of the country does not mean that other forms of life (and liveliness)—animals, xerophilic biota, and grains of sand—fail to *matter* there. In fact, when she describes the soil as "villainous," she grants the element a kind of trickstery agency, inferring that its rejection of eastern agriculture is a choice and not a sign of "voided life."

To substantiate these life-claims, Austin "gets down to the eye level of rat and squirrel kind" to observe mouse trails, wild oats, and "the efflorescence of alkaline deposits" (11, 4). In repositioning the narrative eye from human height to rodent level, she invites readers to shift their attention to desert beings and phenomena that might go unnoticed by less observant passersby. Additionally, in the act of telling us that she, the "desertwise" manager, makes a deliberate point to kneel and observe, she attempts to position herself as a more attuned desert-lover, one whose knees and hands press into the sand as she lowers her head to listen. Austin's proximity to the desert floor in this scene communicates to readers that she is one who knows—and she knows by sight, sound, and touch. In her introductory chapter, her willingness to observe close up leads her to write an entire paragraph detailing the mysterious nature of "saline traces" that oddly shimmer in the interstices of roving sand dunes, a description that imbues the desert with a queer energy that at once moves her and moves *through* her, pleasurably and unmanageably so (4). Not only does Austin press into the desert on hands and knees, but its force presses back—and, unlike resistant McTeague, she seems to take pleasure in becoming-sand.

Time and again, Austin appears captivated by the transmutable potential of the desert, describing it as "a lurking, evasive Something"—reminiscent of Norris's agential "something or other"—that has the power to "come leaping out at me in odd contradictions of the accepted way of waking intelligence" (*Earth Horizon*, 187). Instead of turning away from the desert's unpredictable energy, or of struggling to prevent the desertifying elements from invading her body, Austin expresses fascination with sand's ability to vampirically "fasten" onto her "vitals" and take her in. Managers and environments engage in ongoing material exchanges, and in *Land* Austin seems open to exploring the possibilities of that mutual "fastening."

DESERT TIME AND SANDY LOGIC

In *Land*, the "land that supports no man" transforms into a "blossoming, radiant, and seductive" zone that flourishes both with life and with a peculiar form of desirability, allowing Austin to experiment with an approach to desert management that accommodates alternative, nonhuman temporalities, in addition to unusual pleasures:

> [Deserts] trick the sense of time, so that once inhabiting there you always mean to go away without quite realizing that you have not done it. Men who have lived there, miners and cattlemen, will tell you this, not so fluently, but emphatically, cursing the land and going back to it. (8)

Speaking in second person to a disoriented "you," Austin suggests that time is somehow different in the desert, and she explores how that difference serves ecological ends over economic ones. Time gets away from a person, inhibits their ability to escape. According to this passage, the "tricky" time is a manipulative force, and individuals seem to have little control in such an environment. They may "emphatically" scream and curse, but desert-time prevents them from moving on—or out. An environment that affords no remedy or escape ("you always mean to go away"), Austin's bewildering desert contrasts starkly with the healing, "virginal" reserves celebrated by John Muir and endorsed by Theodore Roosevelt.[95] These inviting green spaces at the turn of the twentieth century strengthened the aims of administrative time. Time spent in lush landscapes was said to regenerate the bodies of busy men so they could return to the city with "clean clocks." In *Our National Parks*, Muir suggests that the modern city exhibits its own corrosive temporality. "Few in these hot, dim, strenuous times are quite sane or free," he says, but beyond the city one can "rejoice in deep, long-drawn breaths of pure wildness."[96] While city-time smothers and wears the body out, turning men into "clocks full of dust," time expands in wild spaces, Muir suggests—and those *with the time* and the means should head West and shake off the dust.

However, Austin's "villainous" desert is not the regenerative environment Muir had in mind in his park manifesto. If one takes a "deep, long-drawn breath" in the windy desert, one is likely to inhale a mouthful of dust. So much for a clean clock! Instead, *Land* celebrates arid environments as places that both command and bend human time, "tricking" individuals into thinking they will one day escape its wayward logic. It is worth placing Austin's views on desert-time in the context of scientific management, which tended to operate on a more future-oriented temporal register. When faced with disobedient nature, most Progressives were determined to convert it into "directed energy," which is how Samuel Ball describes the aims of scientific management.[97] According to Ball, who at the turn of the century writes of Americans' duty to conserve "wasteful" and "extravagant" nature, the "human mind possesses the property of foresight and the ability to economize time and to make the forces of nature serve definite ends"—meaning humans, in their ability to design and execute efficient management strategies, are at once superior and "directly opposed" to wily, *untimely* nature.[98] In contrast, Austin's insistence that desert environments produce their own particular temporal auras—auras that, as she sees them, are capable of channeling human energy in the direction of "musky sweet" moments of pause and pleasure—stands in sexy opposition to Ball's call for linear and economical manager-time (57). In Austin's writing, the desert is an ongoing experience, and in its sensory dimensionality—its diverse flavors and tingling textures—time slows and complicates rather than economizes. The atmosphere of Austin's desert weighs heavy with "bitter dust" (23), and within that dust-cloud time decelerates, expands, and frequently arouses.

Multiple temporalities overlap within Austin's "tricky" desert-time, such as "seed-time" (53), "linnet time" (54), "blossom time" (57), and "mating time" (59); men, she says, "also have their season on the mesa," underscoring the diverse ways that plants, animals, *and* humans experience *being-in* the same place at once (61). These diverse temporalities do not compete with one another or exist hierarchically as they might when viewed through the eyes of a scientific manager. For example, when Ball aligns the aims of scientific management with "economical time," he deems that everything should operate in service to futurity: humans and "the processes of nature" they enact must be directed to an always-unfolding time-that-never-arrives. To read time in economic terms infers that time, itself, will be *wasted* if one fails to effectively manage it.[99] In this light, the environment emerges as the mute stage upon which human time and energy are "spent." Therefore, when Austin gets lost in desert's "golden dust" for entire paragraphs and reads into the deep time of desert geology, she indulges in more than mere narrative fancy. Instead, these detailed passages slow time and, in consequence, present readers with an alternative temporal logic, one that enlivens matter rather than "directing" it toward productive ends. In one moment, she observes that "the sculpture of the hills here is more wind than water work, though the quick storms do sometimes scar them," and thus invites readers to contemplate the slow, unintentional interactions between wind and rock that, over time, have given shape to the region. Such passages encourage readers to look back into the deep past—to be with the hill as it forms over the course of millennia—before arriving, once again, at the past-infused present. Rebecca McWilliams Evans argues, "[T]o criticize 'progress' is necessarily both a narrative and temporal action," and I read Austin's attunement to sand and other geologic materialities as a kind of environmentalist stance, one that attempts to challenge a politics of improvement.[100]

Although useful for guiding management in national park spaces, critical land management manuals, such as National Park Service (NPS) foundation documents, tend to represent land as imperfect future-spaces. Such manuals view land as a problem, one that *might* be corrected if the manager drafts and executes the right plan. According to NPS, foundation documents "provide basic guidance for planning and management decisions," and managers at each national park in the United States are charged with adhering to the directives outlined by these documents. The word "planning," which casts our attention to the perfectible future, appears several times in NPS's description of foundation documents. In just one sentence, the agency uses the word four times: "The foundation document . . . includes special mandates and administrative commitments, an assessment of planning and data needs that identifies planning issues, planning products to be developed, and the associated studies and data required for park planning."[101] The repetition of the word "planning" highlights the Park Service's relationship with land-in-future-tense. Each time that management gestures toward the future, it carves out a space for itself and justifies its surveilling presence. The document's recurrent references to futurity and vigilance fuel the notion that management is at once inevitable and necessary. After all, *someone* will need to do all that assessing; the raw data will not interpret itself. Data accumulate indefinitely in those moments yet to come, and there never seems to be enough of it. Management's "data needs," its alignment of the future with interminable trails of desirous information, reveal that "one is entangled with the data one is studying," as Morton suggests.[102] In other words, management is not separate from the thing it's after; instead, it interacts and tangles with the data—and with the loamy, dirty things the data represent.

Austin's suggestion that all who enter the desert become "saturated with the elements" underscores her refusal to read ecological materials as data that inertly dwell beyond the body. To that end, in her writing she animates sand, wind, and other vital materials in the region surrounding her home east of Los Angeles. In doing so, she stalls management's steady temporal progression. For her, sand operates as a substance that gives the surveilling manager-observer pause, making her reflect on the animacy of regulated matter. In several scenes, sand emerges as an agential force, testing the manager's belief that "there are only active humans encountering passive matter."[103] Dust devils "dance, whirling up into a wide, pale sky" (4); airborne sand "moves along the backs of the crawling cattle" (19); "dust-heavy winds" "wrestle" during a storm (28); "blown sand fills and fills about the lower branches" of a mesquite (34); and "little flakes of whiteness flutter" and cloud Austin's vision (57). Never quite still, sand trespasses into private property and personal space, touching the bodies that reside there both emotionally and physically. Austin's sand operates as a collective body, each grain coordinating with all the others to elicit amazement and irritation in human (and animal) bystanders.

In *Earth Horizon*, Austin recalls the blinding, sometimes deadly potential of the elemental granules during a sandstorm. "All vision blotted out in the sand and the long steady push of the wind. I have known flocks [of sheep] to be smothered by them: nothing to show but huddled lumps where they had been" (253). Providing the manager with the power to surveil and control nature, vision often allows one to convert "vibrant matter" into calculable resource.[104] However, this power to see and arrest matter with the eye fails in Austin's sandstorm—human vision cannot see through the swirling matter. Just as churning sand "blots out" perception, it also "blots out" life, "smothering" the animal-commodity and then hiding from vision the bodily remains. Instead of portraying sand as a pernicious roadblock to capitalism, one deserving of a villainous title (*murderous sand?*) to spur the Anglo-managerial regime into action, Austin's observation that a sandstorm can sometimes be lethal marks sand as one of the desert's most powerful actants. People (and sheep) may have their own agendas in these desert regions, but sand's agential *eco-logic* at times interferes with, and "smothers," these agendas. While Austin, the knowing manager-writer ("I have known") slightly sensationalizes sand's agency for her readers by calling attention to the "huddled lumps" that remained after the storm has passed, she offers no solution to what many might perceive as a "livestock production" problem. What readers are left with, then, is not the satisfaction of closure, but an open-ended deference to the desert as an elemental force. In its refusal to be a quaint and passive feature of the landscape, sand's mobility in Austin's recollections momentarily stalls the Anglo management apparatus and reveals a weakness in its operations.

A contemporary of Austin, J. Smeaton Chase, an English-born American author and photographer, traveled extensively through the desert lands of California at the turn of the twentieth century and describes sand as a "color agent."[105] Similar to Austin's attempts at describing the scattering eco-logics of desert sand, Chase is utterly captivated by sand's refusal to be just one monochromatic thing. In his 1919 travel narrative, *California Desert Trails*, he remarks on sand's remarkable renunciation of the logic of color:

> The geological simplicity of sand and rock does not result . . . in poverty of color. Sand, particularly, might seem to be capable of little change of hue. But, on the contrary, its reflecting power gives it special value as a color agent, a means of taking on varying effects from the everchanging sky. . . . From snow-white they have taken, often in rapid turn, all the hues of gray, of blue, of rose, of chrome, of brown, and purple, reaching even, under the gloom of storm, an approach to absolute black. Sand is actually as responsive as a chameleon, and I could never tire of the vagaries of these dunes.[106]

"Responsive as a chameleon," the sand, as both Chase and Austin describe it in their work, is not easy to see (or see through), let alone categorize. Chase marvels at sand's ability to change color "in rapid turn," a devious quality that at once tricks and pleases the eye. In an attempt to inventory all of the shades he has witnessed in the glittering dust, Chase adopts the manager's technique of listing: "of gray, of blue, of rose . . ." The momentum of his color list builds and builds, creating the impression that he cannot stop tracking the always-changing grains. Sand's generative unmanageability elicits perpetual pursuit on the part of Chase, and we doubt whether the manager will ever arrive at a pause or achieve some kind of totality.

Austin exhibits a similar kind of elemental awe when describing the qualities of a desert rainstorm as it builds in the distance and blows through a small town, sending a cloud of sand in the air that "shuts out the neighborhood" (*Land*, 99). Speaking to the reader in second person, Austin assumes her usual voice of experience and says, "But you have not known what force resides in the mindless things until you have known a desert wind" (99). By beginning the sentence with "But," a syntactical move she employs a few lines later as well, Austin's persona as the knowledgeable and rebellious desert sage shines through. "But," a conjunction intended to demonstrate a contrary view mid-thought, creates breathless momentum when it appears as the first word of a sentence. Its placement in this sentence signals the narrator's narrative authority; the story, like the looming storm, simply will not wait, she seems to say. She then proceeds to describe the elemental processes that contribute to the storm's force and periodically calls attention to the kind of work desert-weather does upon both human and animal bodies.

> The air begins to move fluently, blowing hot and cold between the ranges. Far south rises a murk of sand against the sky; it grows, the wind shakes itself, and has the smell of earth. The cloud of small dust takes on the color of gold and shuts out the neighborhood, the push of the wind is unsparing. Only man of all folk is foolish enough to stir abroad in it. But being in a house is much worse; no relief from the dust, and a great fear of the creaking timbers. (99–100)

Though the sentences in this passage are relatively long and contain multiple clauses, commas and semicolons work to contain and mediate that chaos. It is in this balance of structure and elemental disorder where Austin's unique management style shines through. Through the use of connective devices, such as the repetition of "and" and multiple semicolons, Austin communicates

the storm's elemental smearing while maintaining her position-
ality as one capable of seeing through the "murk." As the storm
builds and the passage continues, hyphens and listing emerge as
well, underscoring Austin's interactionist view of the desert environment. Weather-chaos reigns in this scene, but the author manages her way through the telling without resorting to McTeaguean
exclamations.

In the end, Austin compares her sensory-driven weather
summary to reports one might expect from the Weather Bureau,
a federal agency formed in 1870 whose job was to predict and
track weather systems in the United States. Rooted in "military
discipline," the bureau was placed under the War Department
in order "to secure the greatest promptness, regularity, and accu-
racy in the required observations," which is how Congressman
Halbert E. Paine described the agency.[107] Austin's tone is critical
when describing the bureau. The bureau's weather man, she says,
"taps the record on his instruments" and denies "the sense" of the
elemental "Spirit" he has just witnessed (95). She continues, "You
will find the proper names of these things in the reports of the
Weather Bureau—cirrus, cumulus, and the like—and charts that
will teach by study when to sow and take up crops. It is astonish-
ing the trouble men will be at to find out when to plant potatoes,
and gloze over the entire meaning of the skies" (100–101).

Whereas scientific management busies itself with "the proper
names of things," as Austin describes it, she views herself as a
keener, more sensitive manager. Her interactionist rendering of
the rainstorm functions as an alternative report, and in it she highlights the "electrified tense nerves" and "bite of the small sharp
sand" the storm produces (100). Management misses the mark,
she believes, in its fixation with the sky ("cirrus, cumulus, and the
like"). The real news, she believes, happens on the ground: in the
sand as it chisels the "exposed skin," and in the sound of "creak-
ing timbers" that enters the ear and fills the mind with momentary fear (100). For Austin, scientific management's inability to

account for human-environmental interaction is as much a temporal concern as it is a spatial and perspectival one. By framing her own account of the storm with references to the Weather Bureau, she demonstrates how the stylistic modes of realist nature writing—close observation, sensory details, and an emphasis on interrelatedness—might "demilitarize" and decelerate the thrust of Progressive management. In other words, Austin seems to be calling for a way of reading the natural sciences through a literary lens—what we might today refer to as the "slow scholarship" of the environmental humanities. The next section explores what Austin's slow, humanistic vision of management might look like in a contemporary desert context.

SLOW SAND, NUCLEAR SAND

Whether it clouds or distorts vision with its "windless blur" (Austin, *Land,* 62), or vibrates in queer "color-waves" (Chase, 5) across the vast expanse, the sand that these early Progressive writers marvel at in their writing "thwarts our desire for conceptual and practical mastery," to use the words of Jane Bennett, "and this refusal angers us, but it also offers us an ethical injunction."[108] The ethical injunction Bennett speaks of is an acknowledgment of the "thing-power" of the objects and substances that both surround and enter us, a recognition that environmental forces are engaged in a series of *doings.* Even though humans "use" materials such as sand for a variety of industrial purposes, which would seem to place humans at the top of a hierarchy of entities, the waste produced by these ongoing extractive practices often creates newer and bigger problems for management to tackle.[109] Nuclear waste—from both the front end (mining) and back end (spent fuel rods)—is but one example of management's inability to manage (in) its own aftermath. How, then, might a "slow focus" on sand in literary scholarship help shed some light on management's complicated, seemingly unending relationship with waste in contemporary desert spaces, especially since "the desert . . . is where they bury things"?[110] And what role can the humanities play in responding to waste—particularly radioactive waste? If, as Austin says, the desert "soil keeps the impression of any continuous treading, even after grass has overgrown it," what temporal strategies might environmental humanists employ in their scholarship to grapple with the longevity of that "impression" (11)?

Austin's *Land* can help us answer some of these questions. Sand and wind are particularly energetic in her collection of nature essays, and it is here where her writing holds the most relevance for environmental humanists, particularly those invested in issues related to the energy humanities, environmental justice, and "nuclear ontologies."[111] Just as Austin's sand "cakes in the nostrils" (37) and "drifts in the lee of every lost shrub" (57), so, too, do flecks of dangerous substances merge with and, in a sense, *become* sand in contemporary desert spaces. What exactly are we witnessing when we observe a sandstorm? The answer to this question might seem simple. But what we generically refer to as "sand," especially when seen from a distance, is actually an amalgamation of a whole host of particles that are both harmless and, at times, injurious: small bits of rock, crushed animal bones, pollen, rust from old cars, specks of house paint, desiccated fecal matter, human hair, dog fur, copper tailings, alkali dust, dried grass, insects, and so on. The definition of sand varies, and its composition depends on a location's geological, ecological, and cultural past. Composed largely of mineral particles, such as silica and calcium carbonate, sand is strange in that it combines and travels with small bits of other (eco)materials—even stirred-up specks of an environment's toxic signature, like glysophates and uranium dust. In *Gold Fame Citrus*, Watkins highlights the queer nature of contemporary desert sand in the Southwest when one of her characters observes a sand dune that "glowed radioactive with light" due to its toxic makeup, which included "fertilizer dust and saline particulate."[112] Even when these dustlike industrial particulates are managed and "contained," they hardly ever *lay waste*, but are perpetually exposed by erosion and stirred up by the winds, entering the mouths, ears, and pores of all who enter the region.

While Austin does not directly refer to toxic materiality in *Land*, her understanding of the way sand moves *through* bodies and time offers a paradigm through which we can think more creatively (and narratively) about the agential waste materials populating what some call "the tainted desert."[113] After all, the longer some of these materials, like uranium, hang around, the more we become them, which has the effect of transforming time into a precariously embodied experience. Between 1944 and 1986, mining companies extracted close to three hundred tons of uranium ore under leases with the Navajo Nation, and according to the Environmental Protection Agency, five hundred abandoned uranium mines exist on the reservation alone. Managing the cleanup and containment of those mines—particularly if they were open-pit operations—is no easy task. Often, the uranium tailings leach into springs and drinking water, or get churned up by wind, leaving many who live in the region at risk of exposure. The half-life of uranium, which refers to the estimated time it takes for its isotopes to decay and become less radioactive, ranges from twenty-five thousand to 4.5 billion years. Quick-fix, progress-oriented management narratives struggle to encapsulate that pernicious-and-lingering *hereness* that is uranium waste. Radioactive contamination leaks into deep futures and, as such, appears insolvable. Evans argues that long-term environmental crises ask us "to think across new scales of time. In other words, responding to environmental crisis requires the ability to reckon with slow, deep, and cyclical forms of nonhuman time."[114]

In its commitment to detailing the minuscule, as well as its attunement to temporal layering ("desert time") and cyclical life cycles, Austin's unhurried nature writing makes us think about the role slow narratives can play in "thinking across new scales of time" to address what Rob Nixon refers to as "slow violence," or the attritional impacts of environmental crises, like climate change, on the poor. Through both theme and structure, Austin advocates for slow time in *Land*, and in doing so she reveals how writers might employ decelerated temporalities as a political tool in their work. Management's "directed" spatiotemporal logic leaves little room for reflection, Austin argues. In its rush toward remediable futures, administrative time refuses to pause long enough for us to contemplate the temporal drag that defines climate change, nuclear contamination, and other lingering and evolving ecological crises. Austin's description of a sinister "something" that lurks under the soil reminds us that long-buried things, such as nuclear waste, have a way of bubbling to the surface and exerting their strange agency when we least expect them. In one passage, she says,

> A hidden force works mischief, mole-like, under the crust of the earth. Whatever agency is at work in that neighborhood, and it is popularly supposed to be the devil, it changes means and direction without time or season. It creeps up whole hillsides with insidious heat, unguessed until one notes the pine woods dying at the top. (29)

While Austin's devilish, "mole-like" something that "creeps" around in the earth, waiting for its moment to emerge and destroy, represents a "natural" force that takes on strange life in the desert, this weird energy resonates with the insidious nature of nuclear waste that dwells in and around abandoned mines and tailings piles in parts of the Southwest.

The kinds of temporal frameworks that we, as humanities scholars, create and engage with when examining environmental themes in literature matter as well. In "Mapping Common Ground," ten environmental humanists from diverse fields outline what they describe as a slow approach to scholarship. They arrive at the conclusion that humanities scholarship is, by its very nature, "slow to progress," and they view this unrushed methodology as a benefit to environmental scholarship:

> This emphasis on reflection and interpretation means that the humanities are, by their very nature, slow to progress—perhaps even

incompatible with the very idea of "progress." The skills of narration and of careful reading demand that we pay attention to texts and contexts until we can reveal their deeper implications, ambiguities, and blind spots.[115]

This call to embrace "slow scholarship" in the environmental humanities does not mean we must dismiss all appeals to "urgent action," nor does it require us to read "progress" in purely oppositional terms. Instead, it simply reminds us to "bring the human dimension into view," and, in the case of Austin's writing, the human dimension is inextricably meshed with the elemental. Reading sand in *Land* in other words is also reading the human-that-is-sand.

A focus on "slow sand" in works by desert writers like Austin, Vaye, and others provides us with opportunities to avoid what some are calling uranium's "comeback" in the regions surrounding Bears Ears National Monument in Utah. Just as individuals in Austin's *The Land of Little Rain* stroll "ankle-deep in shifty sands," unable to extricate themselves from the sticky element, so, too, are we up to our heads in the toxic *things* of our industrial culture. Additionally, what we call "industrial sand" touches our lives in very literal ways—from our cell phones to concrete—and we find ourselves more than "ankle-deep" in its materiality regardless of where we live. By remaining focused on the trails of material operations that link "wasteland" elements to our homes, our daily habits, and our bodies, environmental humanists will be able to communicate the intimate proximity of desert spaces to all of us, thus further eroding the myth that what happens "out there," away from us, is not also happening within us. Austin's call for readers to observe, experience, and, to a degree, relinquish the hope of *total* control over sand gives visibility to today's circuits of unmanageable "managed matter," allowing readers to think through new ways of living and managing in uncertain environments.

CHAPTER 3

"UNDER THE DITCH"

MANAGING BODIES (OF WATER) IN WESTERN AMERICAN LITERATURE

But no matter how rationalized the river became, how closely linked with human labor and its products, it remained a natural system with a logic of its own.

—RICHARD WHITE (1996)[1]

Looking out from the summit across the Salton Sea it was difficult to realize that the old traveled trail across the desert lay ten fathoms deep under water, where before not a drop could be found.

—W. P. BLAKE (1915)[2]

I am almost dead for water.

—SARAH WINNEMUCCA (1883)[3]

THE MATERIAL DRAMA OF WATER INFRASTRUCTURE

Considering the ongoing water crises in the American West and elsewhere, a focus on water-as-resource is paramount in the environmental humanities. The rhetoric of turn-of-the-century land managers, engineers, and developers insisted that humans and their environments remained separate, thus affording humans the ability to control both water and land from a safe distance. However, the works I examine in this chapter demonstrate that even thoroughly regulated waterscapes remain lively, desired, and hence beyond total control. To that end, this chapter investigates how turn-of-the-century attitudes regarding water management, as they are depicted in Progressive Era literature set in the arid and semiarid regions of the western United States, inform water policy to this day, especially as such policy attempts to reckon with infrastructural failure, Indigenous water rights, and ecological contamination. From deteriorating dams and toxic wastewater spills, to aging oil pipelines that threaten to leak into aquifers and sacred waterways, water at once emerges as a powerful and vulnerable element in our present political and ecological moment.[4] As Stephanie LeMenager reminds us in *Living Oil*, "[T]he ecological histories of modernity [are] evolving beneath my feet, in my house, my water," and she calls on environmental humanists "to make material or represent" these elements via acts of narrative conjuring.[5]

Ditch digging, dam building, civil engineering, and, in general, human relations with water captivated the minds of many American writers at the turn of the twentieth century, especially writers who resided in the West. Over the past decade, many ecocritics have offered compelling arguments detailing the ways that settler-colonial, imperialist, or capitalist ideologies negatively impact environments, especially in arid environments where water is in short supply.[6] In this chapter, I hope to shed a critical light on moments of intense intimacy between humans and so-called harsh ecologies in the realm of water management. The language of management often reduces land and water to its mere value as economic or national resource, but such language, I argue, also reflects the generative power that these elements hold over and with humans. In other words, when humans make contact with water, even when they wish to control it, they engage with the element as emergent co-actants, meaning one is always becoming (made and transformed by) the other in a range of ways.

The first third of this chapter offers a brief history of water development in the western United States and complicates what historian Kevin Starr has called "the irrigation novel," or Progressive Era literature that focuses on a hierarchical human relationship with diverted water in the post-Reclamation era.[7] While it at first seems as though the managerial imperative of the irrigation novel underscores the modern ascendency of humans over their environments—thus quelling water's unruly, animated potential—here I assert that even "managed water" induces both anxiety and longing in the manager and thus retains a near agential hold on him. In other words, the irrigation novel shows that water is not merely acted upon, as the name of the genre seems to imply; instead, the works I explore in this chapter demonstrate that water demands our attention, foments desire, disobeys, and ultimately acts with and upon humans as an energetic subject. Nowhere is this elemental animacy more palpable than in Ednah Aiken's little-known journalistic novel *The River* (1914), which I briefly explore as an example in the first section.

While that section investigates literature that takes water engineering and management as its central focus, the remaining sections investigate two very different Progressive Era works—a Western novel and an Indigenous memoir—where water management seems, at first, to exist as mere backdrop. In Owen Wister's *The Virginian* (1901) and Sarah Winnemucca's *Life among the Piutes: Their Wrongs and Claims* (1883), irrigation ditches, reservoirs, and water tanks pervade the Western landscape, and by highlighting their charged existence I argue that they initiate various forms of attraction and stimulate human drama. The prevalence of these built artifacts in the arid and semiarid bioregions of the West, as Wister and Winnemucca depict them, impact the social, cultural, and biological lives of humans and nonhumans alike and force readers to reckon with water's vibrant capacity to shape national and international economies at the turn of the century.

In addition to focusing on humans' shifting relations with water—and, moreover, with waterlessness—in late nineteenth- and early twentieth-century American literature, this chapter also focuses on the question of labor in the context of Western water development. Unlike Wister, who both obscures the labor involved in ditch digging and celebrates ditch technology as a symbol of national progress, Winnemucca frequently reminds readers that Indigenous laborers worked to construct many of the federal water projects that Americans so admire. Just who engages in water labor, and how do American writers depict the hard work of digging ditches, erecting dams, and maintaining these various infrastructures? And, ultimately, what does it mean if we can't see the straining backs and sweating brows as they construct the vast network of national flow technologies? The (in)visibility of water labor in the literary works I examine in this chapter offers critical insight into Progressive views of racial and ethnic belonging in the context of American expansionism.

It might seem odd to pay so much attention to the supposed "non-place" of water infrastructure in literary studies, especially since we so often fail to *see* the various human and mechanical apparatuses that divert, sanitize, store, and then deliver water to us in our daily lives. Even more invisible, perhaps, are the mechanisms that allow us to drain and flush "used" water from our homes into an unthinkable *out there*. Envirotech historian Etienne Benson argues that this failure to hold infrastructure in both sight and mind happens in spite of the hypervisibility and ubiquitous nature of these structures.[8] The presence of these human-engineered water systems and the modes of ecological and social relations they organize in works like *The River, The Virginian,* and *Life among the Piutes* make visible and tactile an elemental/material drama, one that significantly impacts the lives of those who believe they are separate from or managing over controllable flows. What would happen, then, if we were to direct our attention to the ditch, the reservoir, or the dam? This chapter's analysis of water management in three works that span very different genres—by authors who, at least on the surface, seem to have little in common other than the time in which they happened to be writing—attempts to challenge the human-centered rhetoric of Progressive Era resource management to uncover the animated or otherwise alluring life of the element.[9]

At the same time, however, I acknowledge that water is never *really* separate from the human; instead, the element trickles in and out of human lives, bodies, economies, and imaginations. Even when the element is scarce or absent, as happens frequently in the works explored in this chapter, the unending desire for it makes water's hold on human actors even more potent. Ultimately, this chapter asks what kind of contemporary environmental ethics, if any, can be born from directing our focus to the actively unimagined or naturalized water projects upon which so many human and nonhuman lives depend.

REFORMING ARIDITY IN IRRIGATION LITERATURE

In Ednah Aiken's *The River,* a novel that details the reclamation of California's Imperial Valley, strong men "struggle against Destiny and Time," as a 1916 review in the *Book News Monthly* put it, to tame the wild waters of the Colorado River.[10] The novel begins not with arduous work at the river but with a job interview in an office, the locus of bureaucratic power. Considering the Progressive Era's aim to "fulfill its destiny through bureaucratic means," this setting should not surprise readers.[11] Here we witness

Tod Marshall, "president of a half-dozen railroads" and "the controlling hand" of regional politics, offering the engineer-hero, Casey Rickard, the position of general manager of the Imperial Valley water project.[12] Though hesitant to become an administrator—Rickard prefers physical labor over paperwork, after all—Marshall entices the young engineer by framing management as an adventurous "war with the elements" (9). In a later scene, we are told that the Imperial Valley would soon be "reclaimed" as a well-watered Eden due to "the sort of men who had settled here, the men of the irrigation type. . . . The desert offers a man special advantages, social, industrial, and agricultural. . . . It is no accident that you find a certain sort of man here" (32). Aiken's novel vigorously celebrates this "certain sort of man" who devotes himself to water development—the visionary engineer, the steadfast manager, "the progressive man, the man with ideas"—over those who would prefer to sit and wait for "old-fashioned rain" (32, 222). This shift from *waiting for rain* to *making it rain* signals that humans, especially "the real soldier" of the Progressive Era, held both the power and training to subdue water, the wiliest of elements (385). After all, according to a Harvard-educated irrigation scientist in Aiken's novel, "The desert is a condition, not a fact," a statement that reflects the turn-of-the-century sentiment that environments could be crafted—or, in the language of progressivism, re-*formed*—to meet human/economic demands (30).

The River frames the engineer as a cultural hero of sorts, as his strength seems to lie in his ability to make the environment do what he wants it to—"in spite of the desert" (30). While characters throughout *The River* contend that a special kind of man holds the capacity to alter the "condition" of water's tremendous physical, cultural, and ecological power, Aiken's novel reveals that turn-of-the-twentieth-century land management acknowledges the liveliness and unending animacy of water at the same time that it attempts to suppress it. In other words, so long as humans engage in the act of managing—an ongoing, often monotonous process with no seeming end—the thing they are managing remains lively, beyond total control; otherwise, management would cease. A critical focus on land management, then, offers a way of reading the captivating vibrancy of "instrumentalized" matter.[13] Instead of merely managing these elements, or of reducing them to the one-dimensionality of "waste" or "resource," new possibilities open up when elements make contact with humans.

Despite the fact that management demands and desires clear demarcations between bodies, machines, environments, and people, on the ground these distinctions become messy and difficult to uphold. Instead, water management results in liquid engagements, or relations that prevent humans from gaining complete supremacy over the elemental. *The River* and other irrigation novels demonstrate that scientific land management actually writes agency into the bodies (of water) it strives to contain. The lives of the men in Aiken's novel orbit obsessively around the idea of water—they build their homes around it, map its boundaries, plot its future courses, relax at its banks after a hard day of wrangling it, desire its constancy, and, at times, even die in its undertow. As environmental historian Richard White notes in *The Organic Machine*, "The boundaries between the human and the natural have existed only to be crossed on the river," and even though the characters in *The River* may deny these fluid intersections for the sake of maintaining control, humans and water appear inextricably linked in the novel.[14]

While White insists that the boundary between humans and the natural world remains porous at best, the Progressive language of resource conservation held to the idea that water and other resources existed as "possessions"; in other words, the human-elemental relationship was vertical, with humans—especially land managers and engineers—existing at the top of the chain. A democratic appeal for patriotic unity often undergirded the urgent calls for resource management, as exemplified in work by leading conservationists such as Gifford Pinchot. In the first chapter of *The Fight for Conservation* (1910), for example, Pinchot exclaims, "We, the American people, have come into possession of nearly four million square miles of the richest portion of the earth. It is ours to use and conserve for ourselves and our descendants, or to *destroy*."[15] For Pinchot, first chief of the US Forest Service and a leading advocate for the American conservation movement, a vulnerable hesitation, represented by a comma, stands between the prospect of long-term, sustainable yields of natural resources and imprudent overuse (or "destruction"). Were the American people unwilling to implement and enforce scientifically driven environmental policy, one could unintentionally stumble over that thin barrier and risk exhausting the land's rich potential, Pinchot and other conservationists believed. Writing in the midst of the Progressive Era, a period devoted to widespread social improvement, technological advancement, managerial efficiency, and other reformist ideals, Pinchot's brief but charged recognition that such a vast "possession" could so easily be squandered shakes the bridge between resource conservation and the nation's desire for development and economic prosperity.

Historians of the American West have held varying points of view regarding the success of the "businesslike approach" to water resource management that originated in the Progressive Era.[16] Through critiques of rational management, capitalism and power, the human-nature divide, regional exceptionalism, Indigenous water rights, and top-down policy narratives—to name just a few grounds of the Western water history debate—historians from the 1950s to the first decades of the twenty-first century have demonstrated that water is a generative substance with which to think through American history and culture.[17] Since the late 1990s, literary scholars and ecocritics, including Mark Seltzer, David Cassuto, Paul A. Formisano, and Holly Jean Richard have also begun turning their attention to water development in American literature.[18] However, the imbrication of labor, race and ethnicity, and water's materiality in the West has often gone underexplored in both history and literary studies. According to Pinchot and other scientific managers, Progressive conservation promised that "every American [could] get his fair share of benefit from these resources, now and hereafter."[19] However, Winnemucca's *Life among the Piutes* questions the so-called democratic potency of water-as-resource in a number of ways. For example, when Winnemucca asserts, "The white people are using the ditch which my people made to irrigate their land" (77), the conservationist promise that everyone could "get his fair share" evaporates like the dry lake that, today, bears Winnemucca's name.[20]

The literary works examined in this chapter span the formative years of federal water policy in the American West. From the state and territorial laws of prior appropriation beginning in the 1850s, to John Wesley Powell's expedition down the Colorado River in 1869, and finally to the first major waterworks projects erected by the US Reclamation Service in the 1910s, American water development in the West underwent a number of critical transformations at the turn of the twentieth century. Within this time frame, a whole host of federal land and water management policies were instituted to support or override state, local, and individual land laws. Among the most notable of these policies were the Desert Land Act of 1877, the Carey Act of 1894, and the Newlands Reclamation Act of 1902. On paper, these policies aimed to catalyze settlement, transform arid "wastelands" into viable grazing lands for cattle, mitigate the impacts of hydraulic mining, regulate industry and speculative purchasing, and, among other purposes, encourage economic growth in the developing region. State, local, and private entities increasingly struggled to manage the complicated web of land and water rights in the West, and undertaking the construction of major waterworks projects required more capital than these entities could sometimes bear. Marc Reisner summarizes this dilemma in *Cadillac Desert*: "Everything had been tried—cheap land, free land, private initiative, local initiative, state subsidy—and everything, with a few notable exceptions, had failed."[21] As a response to these perceived managerial failures, the federal government began to intervene in the administration of western lands with more intensity by the end of the 1890s.

The development of the US Reclamation Service in 1902, known today as the Bureau of Reclamation (hereafter Reclamation), emerged from these calls for enhanced oversight. As the managing body of water supply, irrigation, hydropower, and other water development projects, Reclamation becomes a key player in Progressive Era irrigation literature, most notably in *The River*. While it is easy to read Reclamation as the nefarious political arm of an all-consuming imperial power, as historian Donald Worster does, more recent scholarship in environmental history, such as Patricia Nelson Limerick's *A Ditch in Time* (2012), argues that municipal and state agencies, as well as citizens' own water demands, have held more sway over water development, especially in places like the interior West. She contends that water histories devoted to narratives of a "power-hoarding elite," while provocative, may obscure our own resource demands and ignore local and regional exceptions.[22] Limerick's localized approach to water history reveals water development as a "tangled story of maneuverings, negotiations, initiatives, and counterinitiatives," and therefore resists framing resource management in reductive, purely oppositional terms.[23] In *Dripping Dry*, Cassuto urges us to consider the power of water's own agency in the context of American expansionism. "Where there was water, there could be food, and people, and all the concomitant changes they brought," he says. "In [Owens Valley], *water also carried the power* to decide who would work the land and how" (emphasis added).[24]

Any scholar embarking on a literary examination of water management in the American West at the turn of the twentieth century, regardless of the particular frameworks of their projects, will encounter a complicated web of public, private, and individual interests; competing policies and management strategies;

blurred boundaries between social and natural entities; and, much to the chagrin of administrators and engineers, "natural system[s] with a logic of their own."[25] Additionally, as White reveals in *The Organic Machine*, today's examinations must also absorb strange new actants, such as toxic waste, heavy metals, and radionuclides. As an indeterminate substance, water at once moves through, shapes, and is shaped by a number of agents, including terrain, human and animal bodies, climate, values, and ideologies, to name just a few.

Looking back from the present moment, it is hard not to be cynical about the Progressive Era's faith in modern hydraulic engineering and regulatory efficiency, especially when water historians such as Worster and Reisner define the era as the origin of supreme ecological, social, and political failure. However, by surveying the vulnerable moments in American literature where humans attempt to manage the environment and find themselves becoming it instead, we might be able to articulate a new way of managing *in*—an act that admits our immanent entanglements with all life—what Timothy Morton has called the "dark ecologies" of the twenty-first century.[26] Questions of power, agency, and energy pervade Western irrigation literature, and in this chapter I argue that *thinking with and in water*, as a scholarly undertaking, might provide us with the interdisciplinary tools necessary to not only forge new pathways in environmental justice activism, but to reconsider our relationships with managed lands.

TRACING THE EDENIC FLOWS IN WISTER'S WEST

Water management, as both a material practice and an ideal, fueled the Progressive dream of large-scale environmental management. At the same time, however, it threatened the notion that the West existed as a "country for men."[27] After all, ditches and dams, which enabled development, inevitably led to an exodus of land-seeking, westward-moving settlers—including entire families—at the turn of the twentieth century. This relationship between the commodification of water as resource and the modernization of the West is sharply evident in Owen Wister's 1902 work, *The Virginian*. This bestselling novel, regarded as one of the first Westerns, takes place on the precipice of Wyoming's infamous cattle wars in the late 1880s, and Wister's Progressive fascination with the control of water is apparent throughout. Despite *The Virginian*'s preoccupation with water-as-resource, the theme of water development has gone unexamined in the novel, especially as it relates to shifting gender roles at the turn of the twentieth century.

To counter what were perceived as the feminizing forces of modernity, Wister's narrator frequently *naturalizes* human-engineered waterways—or defines and experiences them as uncultivated elements of an untouched, edenic landscape—via a method that I call *narrative rewilding*.[28] Narrative rewilding absorbs human-engineered landscape features, such as irrigation ditches and reservoirs, almost wholly into the category of "the natural," making faint, if not altogether invisible, the traces of human impacts on the environment. For example, as a narrative device, rewilding may encourage readers to see a megadam as part of a mountain, or a canal as a naturally occurring stream, thus insisting on a mythical vision of the West as rugged and undeveloped. When Wister's narrator subverts the manmade nature of modern water infrastructure and hides water labor from view, he is attempting to preserve the West's reputation as an eminently *manly* realm, thus igniting a sense of soldierly purpose in the Anglo men who identify as tamers of the land.[29] In contrast to the flowing, diverted streams that course in and out of the narrator's frame of vision, still water, such as the water reserved in the tank in Wister's depiction of Medicine Bow, Wyoming, fails to be rewilded and remains utterly unnatural; its presence, as the narrator describes it, threatens to contaminate the region with a toxic eastern ethos. By shifting our attention to the artifacts of water development in *The Virginian*, we gain a unique way of understanding how Progressive Era engineering undergirds a white masculinist vision of both regional and national belonging in the United States. In the arid and semiarid environments that dominate Wyoming, thirst for water unsettles communities and social relations, burgeoning industries, and, as the narrator quickly discovers, human bodies. Wister seems fixated, as were many at the time, on both the economic and social potentialities of irrigation in the West.

Water's potential to *reform* the semiarid, "unproductive" high plains region of Wyoming is alive and well in the mind of Wister's narrator, known only as "the tenderfoot." When this wet-behind-the-ears visitor from the Northeast reminisces on his days spent visiting Wyoming's cattle country, his mind frequently turns to water. This is not surprising given the necessity of having access to water in the arid and semiarid American West, particularly if one's livelihood depends on the cattle industry. "In the afternoon on many days of the summer which I spent at the Sunk Creek Ranch," he says,

> I would go shooting, or ride up toward the entrance of the cañon and watch the men working on the irrigation ditches. Pleasant systems of water running in channels were being led through the soil, and there was a sound of rippling here and there among the yellow grain; the green thick alfalfa grass waved almost, it seemed, of its own accord, for the wind never blew. (44)

Water, in this serene moment of reflection, at once nominalizes place (Sunk Creek Ranch), stimulates the growth of agriculture with seeming effortlessness, and calms the narrator with its tranquil "sound of rippling." The "pleasant system" of this constructed waterway is a thing of both natural and economic wonder for the narrator, as he remarks on the channel's supreme ability to animate the grain and alfalfa that keep the cattle—and, in turn, the cattle industry—alive. Diverted water imbues this plant-life with a strange kind of liveliness, as the narrator tells us the grass "waved almost . . . of its own accord." What is perhaps most interesting about this reflection, however, is that the narrator calls forth an image of the men who dig the irrigation ditches. Their labor, though not described in high resolution, manufactures the "natural," verdant setting that the narrator so enjoys. Soon after the workers' bodies are referenced, they disappear into the background, granting both water and plant-life the appearance of agentive movement.

Water infrastructure, as this scene reveals, elicits a series of powerful social, ecological, and economic *presences* in Wister's work, making *The Virginian* an ideal novel for critically analyzing the diverse ties between men and diverted water.[30] Even when the narrator does not directly conjure water, its potent animacy can be registered in nearly every scene. From the pastoral descriptions of the "plentiful and tall" grass around Sunk Creek Ranch (43), to depictions of the "wretched husk of squalor" that is human settlement in Medicine Bow (10), water keeps humans, plants, animals, towns, entire industries, and the relations between these entities alive in the novel. Wister occasionally offers readers brief but charged glimpses of irrigation ditches, diverted streams, water storage containers, and other artifacts of civil engineering that, when combined, deliver water from distant, unseen sources into lives, bodies, and economies. Even though Indigenous and migrant laborers worked to construct many of the water projects Americans so admire, Wister obscures the labor involved in ditch digging and instead celebrates ditch technology as "natural" symbols of national, masculine progress.[31] If we are willing to wade into Wister's natural-but-engineered ditches and streams, we might discover to what extent managed water drives national, gendered, and racial narratives in the United States.

Prior to the popularization of large-scale irrigation in the late 1890s and the explosion of federal waterworks projects under the direction of the newly formed US Reclamation Service in 1902, individual farmers, communities, and local and state governments in the arid and semiarid West often hired pluviculturalists,

or so-called rainmakers, who, many believed, could induce rainfall via a variety of "scientific" methods. Rainmaking practices
were diverse and ranged from releasing clouds of chemical gases
into the air from metal funnels positioned on the ground, to
directing "heavy discharges" of cannon fire in the direction of
moisture-laden clouds.[32] As a science that gained much popularity
in the 1890s, pluviculture was rooted in the belief that "the agency
of man" could—and, moreover, should—harness and redirect
atmospheric energies for "useful," economic ends.[33] To not make
use of the moisture reserved in the clouds would be deemed wasteful. According to the ethos of rainmaking, one no longer had to
depend on the unpredictability of rain or snowfall for agricultural
survival; instead, humans would be liberated from aridity, freed
from the bonds of drought.

A key proponent of pluvicultural theory, Edward Powers,
rejected comparisons between Native American rain dancing and
what he termed "scientific rainmaking," insisting that good science trumps "superstition" any day: "Aside from its connection
with the superstitions of certain savage tribes, . . . [scientific rain-
making] is confined principally to those who are accustomed to
draw conclusions only from adequate premises."[34] For Powers, as
for other rainmaking advocates of the day, to pray or dance for rain
was to admit human subordination to weather's will. Rainmakers
would not wait for the weather to change in their favor: they
would engineer it into existence. When natural forces "fail to
act," or where rainfall was deemed "insufficient," science offered
a solution, adherents to pluviculture believed.[35] For farmers and
ranchers hoping to make a living on the public domain lands of
the American West, lands that constituted over one-third of the
entire area of the United States near the end of the nineteenth
century, scientific rainmaking seemed a less labor-intensive, more
economic enterprise than, say, digging irrigation ditches.[36]

In Powers's *War and the Weather*, published in 1890, he asserts
that loud noises, such as heavy cannon fire during battle, could

shock moisture-heavy clouds into producing rainfall. Throughout the book, which reads, in part, like a rainmaking manifesto, Powers documents various nineteenth-century battles in both the United States and Europe that purportedly led to precipitation. He attributes the often intense weather events that followed battle to the effects of "human agency" and argues that if the nation fails to take scientific rainmaking seriously, it would risk squandering its economic potential.[37] Great wealth, he asserted, was but a gunshot away! The book ends with a sense of patriotic urgency: if Americans do not act now to solve the nation's aridity problem, other countries might beat us to the clouds.

> We have the powder, and we have the guns and the men to serve them, and we ought not to leave other nations nor to after-ages the task of solving the great question as to whether the control of the weather is not, to a useful extent, within the reach of man.[38]

This call to action reads like a battle cry, and Powers assures readers that America's rainmaking regiments are weapon-ready and prepared to take on "the task." Not only does Powers deploy the rhetoric of war when describing human-environmental relations in this passage, but by claiming that rain-on-demand is within "the reach of man," he situates the environment as an antagonistic force that exists beyond the body. The environment, for Powers, taunts humans from the other side of the skirmish line. According to Powers's aspirational views on rainmaking—a management practice that today's geoengineers refer to as "precipitation enhancement," "climate control," or "weather modification"—"human agency" has the power to manage desert landscapes out of a state of perpetual, unproductive aridity.[39] Aridity was, and is, seen as a problem; for disobedient "waste," science had the duty to "break" such environments into submission. Scientific rainmakers, land managers, and civil engineers frequently used the language of justifiable violence to describe the work of managing water. For example, John Melbourne, a pluviculturalist who went by the moniker "Rain Wizard," even promised that there existed "no part of the United States east of Oregon not subject to *destructive drought*, which *I can break*" (emphasis added).[40] In order to mitigate future destruction, humans had no choice but to develop better battle tactics.

By the end of the 1890s, innovations in irrigation technology in the arid and semiarid West led to the gradual phasing out of scientific rainmaking. Despite its early appeal, pluviculture came to be viewed as an unreliable weather modification method, and enthusiasm for irrigation as a more practicable solution to aridity spread quickly among farmers and ranchers alike. While different in both structure and method from the scientific rainmaking that preceded it, irrigation was fueled by a similar faith in human agency. Federal investment in the development of dams, reservoirs, and ditches via the Newlands Reclamation Act, which culminated in the development of the US Reclamation Service, worked to expand, standardize, and provide administrative guidance over these more intensive water diversion projects in the West. As cultural critic Mark Seltzer notes in *Bodies and Machines*, the Progressive Era witnessed the rise of the civil engineer as a cultural hero, and an intense interest developed around the "culture-work of channeling, bridge-building, and canalization."[41] Both pluviculture and irrigation, as well as twentieth-century innovations in dam-building and hydroelectric power systems, depended on the idea that rational management tactics could effectively redirect environmental elements to human/economic ends and thereby eliminate, or at least reduce, "wasted," unused energies.

Published the same year as the passing of the Reclamation Act, *The Virginian* expresses various infrastructural impulses that seem to anticipate the large-scale water development projects of the 1900s. For example, even though we never see his body engaged in water labor, we are told that the Virginian makes his living in the summer months digging ditches. Moreover, intense human drama, including violence and romantic love, materializes from the region's waterways in *The Virginian*, demonstrating both the economic *and* social potentialities of water-as-resource. More generally, characters frequently converge around water and water infrastructure throughout the novel. According to Progressives like Wister, dams and ditches have the potential to bring together entire communities—and, perhaps, even a sprawling nation—into a single, connected network.

DRY REALITIES AND WET DREAMS

Throughout *The Virginian*, the narrator perceives Wyoming's arid landscape as both a thrilling spectacle and a problem that only water can cure. Just as Melbourne and Powers deploy the rhetoric of viciousness ("destructive drought") and deficiency to promulgate their diverse precipitation agendas, so, too, does Wister align Wyoming's "unending gulf of space" with overwhelming lack (7). Water may appear in the names of towns—Bear Creek, Sunk Creek, Westfalls, Willo' Creek, Stinkin' Water, etc.—but it rarely materializes in the region's vast rangelands. Oddly, the most turbulent waterway in the novel cuts through the town of Drybone, a name that announces the nonexistence of water. The overwhelming presence of water in Drybone underscores the often unpredictable and contradictory nature of water in the region.

The narrator comments on the absence of Wyoming water as soon as he steps off the train. "Where in this unfeatured wilderness is Sunk Creek? No creek or any water at all flowed here that I could perceive" (7). Absence emerges in various forms in this passage, from the prefix of "*un*featured," to the tenderfoot's claim that "no creek or any water" exists. References to resource shortage and environmental desiccation such as these predominate the tenderfoot's observations of the novel's arid spaces, and he seems to find refuge only when near flowing bodies of water. Wyoming immediately emerges as a vexing problem, causing the narrator to define its environment not by what it contains, but by what it fails to provide.

Cultural theorist and historian Daniel Belgrad views humans' concerns with ecological uncertainty as a way of reading agency in the environment, an agency that instigates a variety of responses in the bodies of individuals who interact with it. "[U]ncertainty about rainfall and its effects on the condition of the range could generate anxiety among ranchers," he states, "contributing to the tensions over range use that erupted into violence."[42] In addition to the anxiety that unpredictable nature-spaces provoke in bodies, Belgrad imbues water—or *waterlessness*—with the power to engender violence. For Belgrad, lively, arid absences stimulate movement and, in general, force bodies to respond, sometimes in terrifying ways. However, in addition to inciting unease and civil unrest, waterlessness propels humans to develop various methods of conjuring water, or of managing it into existence.

Both Wister and other turn-of-the-century Western writers depend on rhetorical negation to spur excitement about development in the region. For example, in John Cowan's 1906 article on arid agricultural methods, he describes the "absolute desert" as "unimproved," "uncultivated," "unoccupied," "inhospitable," "worthless," and with other terms denoting ecological insufficiency.[43] For Cowan, as for Wister's tenderfoot, calling attention to everything the desert was not was meant to stimulate interest in the "problematic" region and prompt men into action. The concept of dry farming—of producing yields out of "waste"—energizes Cowan, and he cannot help but imagine hundreds of farmers tilling "every acre of arable land . . . to the utmost limit of its productiveness."[44] Similarly, the tenderfoot's energized response to "the alkali of No Man's Land" (194) causes him to perpetually scan its topography and "[take] its dimensions" (10) into his body for future contemplation.

Though neither man is a water engineer—Cowan even openly admits his disdain for irrigation's "inefficiencies"—their fascination with aridity as an unresolved problem underscores the era's engineering ethos. Both exhibit a deep, almost ecstatic desire to conjure flowing water where it is in short supply, which demonstrates water's vibrant materiality even (and maybe especially) when it is meager or altogether absent. In several scenes, the tenderfoot almost imagines water into being, allowing the idea of it to well up in his mind when it fails to appear in reality. "All things merged in my thoughts in a huge, delicious indifference. It was like swimming slowly at random in an ocean that was smooth, and neither too cool nor too warm" (32). His watery imaginings—or *wet dreams*—are then interrupted by the arrival of a train "coming as if from shores forgotten" (32). The tenderfoot's water-thoughts express the regulatory logic of water development, in that he tames the waves ("an ocean that was smooth") and controls the temperature ("neither too cool nor too warm") at will. What is more, the wild body of the ocean transforms into a recreational space for this dreamer, as he imagines himself "swimming slowly" without a care. The Progressive dream of regulated flows—the same dream that culminated in megadams and transregional and transnational irrigation networks—is alive and well in the mind of the narrator, even though he does not have the expertise to realize his vision on the ground.

Beyond the narrator's dreams of a perfectly regulated water world, *real* water seems to disappear at will in the novel, imbuing the element with a power over men who depend on its constancy. When a "young cowboy" purchases two cans of tomatoes so that he can drink the juice, the proprietor of the dry goods shop asks, "Meadow Creek dry already?" The boy responds, "Been dry ten days" (30). The narrator then offers readers additional information about the state of the waterless creek, noting that "water would not be reached until sundown, because this Meadow Creek had ceased to run" (30). The proprietor's shock that the creek was "already" dry calls attention to the unpredictable, seemingly defiant nature of water in the region. Flows of water, if left unmanaged, might simply refuse or "cease" to run, as if by their own will, leaving men to quench their thirst (and deplete their wallets) with juice from a can. At the other extreme, when flows of water build, rush, and exceed infrastructural capacity, bodies and machines risk losing control, as when the river "came sucking through the upper spokes" of Molly's carriage, taking it under—and nearly taking her down with it. The potent animacy of flowing water, from its absence to its hyperabundance, reveals just how permeable the boundary is between humans and ecologies. Geographer Karen Bakker reflects on this idea when she says,

> water is a resource upon whose constancy (of both quality and quantity) we depend; and yet, water engenders attempts to regulate its inherent variability in time and space—which are in turn frustrated by ecological, technological, and economic barriers to human control.[45]

Arid environments, as these scenes in the novel demonstrate, represent complex locations of possibility for characters in *The Virginian*. Despite the attempts made by Powers, Melbourne, Cowan, and Wister's narrator to refuse human-environmental enmeshment by positioning the elements on the other side of the skirmish line, their inability to wholly manage water reveals that intimacy with the elements is unavoidable. Their attempts to manage water, to both channel it and imagine it into existence, demonstrate an unending responsiveness in the element they wish to control. While Donald Worster in *Rivers of Empire* conceives of American imperial power as a coercive net that covers everything, resulting in what he calls "a hydraulic society" that began in the West, the rebelliousness of managed matter pervades water history and literature. So long as the men are merely managing, even if their management materializes into vast architecture that delivers water hundreds of miles from its source, the "vibrant matter" that is flowing water keeps their bodies always at the alert.

THE HARD LOGIC OF THIRST IN THE WESTERN

Even though the novel equates the presence of irrigation technologies with white masculine ascendance in the semiarid West, Wister almost paradoxically views the (male) body's ability to withstand thirst as an emblem of masculine endurance. In other words, the less water one's body requires, the more likely he will emerge as a true man of the West. To be a man meant to inhabit an efficient, resilient body. As soon as the narrator steps foot in Wyoming, thirst begins to overtake his body, which calls attention to the dryness and harshness of the territory. Much to the tenderfoot's dismay, water is in short supply in this "planet of treeless dust" (17), and surviving in such an environment will require self-discipline and a roughening of both form and spirit. This acknowledgment of human-environmental relationality in the arid West represents the hard logic of the novel, the drive to make tough and resilient the bodies of men.

Many men who wrote about Western farming techniques at the turn of the twentieth century, such as Cowan, arrived at these same conclusions about the ideal body. As a practitioner of "dry farming," or what was also called "scientific soil culture," Cowan argues that only a *certain* kind of modern, male body would be able to prosper in the arid and semiarid West. Unlike the eastern farmer who has the luxury of consistent rainfall, the dry farmer, Cowan says, "knows no season of rest or idleness. He knows that eternal diligence is the price he must pay for good crops."[46] For Cowan, land management in arid environments requires industry, a dedication to efficiency, and "eternal" attentiveness; without these necessary inputs, the farmer will be left with "lands that are now waste," or property without economic purpose.[47] Instead of succumbing to arid "waste" and admitting defeat, Cowan urges newly arrived farmers in the West to experiment with hardy, drought-resistant crop varieties and "natural" tilling methods that would reserve water in the under-soil. The western farmer could convert desert waste into wealth if, and only if, he could resist the temptation of merely transplanting the familiar farming practices from "humid America" to the dry regions of the West.[48] Cowan believed that irrigation was a lame (and costly) attempt at mimicking eastern environmental conditions. He therefore encouraged western farmers to get out from "under the ditch" and adapt to aridity. As both Cowan and the Virginian contend, men had to learn to live with the western climate—to become as resistant to drought as the durum wheat that thrived there.[49]

Dryness in *The Virginian* calls upon bodies to become more efficient, and the rustlers seem proud of their ability to withstand a world where water is in short supply. For example, while waiting for the narrator's lost luggage to arrive, Steve and the Virginian emphasize Wyoming's extreme climate to great effect. Both men claim that an ability to stave off thirst in the region's alkali expanse is central to being a man. Wyoming "makes a man thirsty," says Steve to the tenderfoot. The Virginian adds, "Yes . . . thirsty while a man's soft yet. You'll harden" (17). The process of hardening in this social and ecological context is as physical as it is psychological. In other words, to become a *true* man of the West, one must not only learn to live with little water but also to train away any thought of thirst. "And if yu' keep a-thinkin' about it," says the Virginian, "it'll seem like days and days" (17). To desire a remedy for thirst when no remedy exists exhibits a lack of restraint, according to the Virginian; he claims that one wastes both time and energy if the desire lingers for too long. Wasted thoughts do not align with the Progressive values of efficiency and self-control. Steve and the Virginian continue to build on each other's claims of climatic intensity. As their talk continues, the environment becomes so startling dry—and, in consequence, their bodies so apparently resilient to its harshness—that even a "drop of wetness" in their depiction of Wyoming would seem out of place (17). Their speech, like the wringing out of an already-dry cloth, stands as testament to their ability to withstand a landscape that makes human survival difficult.

In spite of the tenderfoot's early claims that much of Wyoming was an arid "No Man's Land," water-rich environments frequently emerge in the novel, startling both characters and readers alike with their unlikely presences. With the exception of the Virginian's private stream where he goes "to leave behind all noise and mechanisms," many of the novel's watery environments seem

to impede mobility and, thus, interfere with white masculine
ascendance (375). Periodic glimpses of soft, watery landscapes—
such as quicksand, crumbling banks, and standing pools—bubble forth as problematic ecologies, and a man must learn to bypass
such terrain without losing his footing. Softscapes evoke the textural give of swamps and bogs, and, according to Wister's *hard
logic*, too much give could result in both unproductive landscapes
and sluggish, unmanly bodies.[50] Soft, liquid environments suc-
tion bodies in place and threaten to *waste them away*.

As an example, the narrator, whose newly arrived eastern body
seems incompatible with the range's extreme climate, falls into or
misidentifies wet environmental substances throughout the novel.
He stumbles and drops his luggage in the river, mistakes quicksand
for a ford, and emerges from a pond as a "spectacle of mud" (46).
The "slippery," "weltering heap" that is the tender body of the tenderfoot demands regulation and a harder, more resilient corporeal
architecture in order to direct and contain what seems an endless
seepage (46). Thus, the project of hardening the bodies of men and
building water infrastructure reach toward what Seltzer perceives
as a common goal: "a channeling of natural floods into orderly
movements."[51] As a "spectacle of mud," distinct environmental
elements—mud and water—become muddled on the tenderfoot's
body. Irrigation ditches, which transport water from a source to a
destination via channels carved out of the earth, hold separate—at
least ideally—the liquid energy from the earthy conduit. When
he falls into the mud and emerges with the substance sticking to
his body, the narrator gets presented as a management problem.
He is unable to separate the liquid from the solid, the vital energy
from its infrastructure. Frequently wet, mired, and hindered by
his "Eastern helplessness," Wister's tenderfoot is never fully a man,
the novel's logic suggests (376).

While *The Virginian*'s tenderfoot frequently perceives aridity
as a problematic agent that assaults bodies and renders environments sterile, water development may pose even greater threats in

the novel. For one, water infrastructure facilitates the arrival of women and children in what was formerly considered an all-male space. What is more, land deemed arable via irrigation was, at the time, referred to as "under the ditch," a phrase that places man under the agency and weight of water infrastructure—and, subsequently, under the hand of civilizing and feminizing forces. Land "under the ditch" is land that is ostensibly reclaimed, regulated, and "brought to a high state of productiveness," to use Cowan's optimistic language.[52]

If the novel idealizes hard (male) bodies and landscapes, and outlines steps for how masculine toughness may be achieved, it also suggests that the reform-oriented, regulatory practices of Progressivism might interrupt the hardening processes in the West. For example, Wister's depiction of the sickly "engineer's woman" in Medicine Bow offers a troubling vision of the potential effects of the region's water infrastructure. Readers are told that "there was a woman—an engineer's woman down by the water-tank—very sick" (28). Here, the narrator aligns the water-tank, a structure that facilitates the settlement of Medicine Bow, with the image of a failing, unproductive woman's body. The storage tank is the first example of water infrastructure we witness in the novel, and it is worth considering how Wister distinguishes between tanks, ditches, and "natural" waterways. For example, structures meant to contain and reserve water for future use, such as the sickly woman's water tank, fail to receive the same kind of admiration as irrigation ditches and other "flow technologies."[53] The fact that this woman is "the engineer's woman" points to the possible pitfalls of water development in the region: while channeling the flow of water requires hard bodies, the eventual containment of water would seem to domesticate and, in effect, sicken them. The woman's *stilled* body has a taming effect on the town, one that seems to contaminate it with a disquieting, unmanly calm. The narrator tells us, "she brought a hush over Medicine Bow's rioting" (31). Even though we never see the woman, her presence hangs heavy "over" the town, drowning it with a feminizing "hush." A town that exists "under the ditch" seems to be under the woman as well, in other words. Unable to regulate the flows of his wife's body, the engineer's work stalls, leaving the town in a state of veritable stagnation.

Life becomes pastoral—it settles, slows, softens, and loses its generative impulse—around built waterways, as evidenced by both the human and animal communities that converge around them. Just as Medicine Bow "hush[es]" at the arrival of the engineer's wife (and her representative tank), so, too, do Wyoming's ranching communities mellow out along the muddy banks of streams and ditches. Though these moving bodies of water are not deemed as threatening as the still waters of Medicine Bow, the lush landscapes they engender pose significant risks to (re)production. "The placid regiments of cattle lay in the cool of the cotton-woods by the water," we are told, and the narrator, a man capable of performing labor, spends many leisurely afternoons lounging at their side (43). Likewise, Emily, a chicken driven mad by her inability to reproduce, tends to her "changelings" near the edges of an irrigation ditch (50). During one of her more intense episodes, she "cross[es] the ditch" to join a flock of wild turkeys, an act that marks the dry ditch with a trace of the unnatural (50). More than anything, the novel depicts irrigation as a question, one that, despite its economic promises, threatens the health and vitality of bodies. Molly's interest in irrigation delights the Virginian, and it is worth examining what it means when women take an interest in water management. After all, we are told that Molly's "mind was alive to Western questions: irrigation, the Indians, the forests" (322). Unlike the mired body of the engineer's wife, Molly's reform-minded, analytical outlook on the West—much like Irene, a woman with managerial interests in Aiken's *The River*—allows her to maintain a critical distance from the muddying effects of *too much water*. The engineering ethos stimulates Molly's curiosity, thus opening the masculinist project of water development to women—or at least to the women who "have always wanted to be a man," as Wister puts it (85).

Seltzer's insightful examination of the rise of civil engineering and the dream of the "directed nonstop flow of water" in Progressive Era American culture points to the gendered nature of water development in Wister's novel. Seltzer's alignment of water management with a "transcendence of female/nature" is compelling, especially when we pair nineteenth-century water diversion projects in Wyoming and other regions of the arid and semiarid American West with the concurrent drainage of swamps and wetlands in the South and Midwest.[54] What Seltzer overlooks in his focus on masculine "transcendence" in the context of water development is how drainage, storage, and diversion efforts resulted in domesticated landscapes—landscapes that enabled settlement and assisted the so-called civilizing project. In other words, nineteenth-century civil engineering defines "manliness" at the same time that it places that category at risk. While the labor involved in controlling / channeling the flow of water might, at first, seem like "man's work," the result, as *The Virginian* seems to argue, facilitates the migration and settlement of women, children, and families, thus disrupting "the playground of young men" celebrated by Wister (44).

To mitigate these effects in the novel, and to preserve the West as a manly zone, Wister rewilds human-engineered waterways, or blurs the lines between "natural" and "artificial." Just as it is often difficult to discern "natural" from the "manmade" waterways in our daily lives, the novel frequently fails to tell readers whether a water source is naturally occurring or engineered by human labor. Terms like "natural" and "manmade" begin to lose their distinct meanings in the context of damming and irrigation. After all, is a manmade reservoir altogether unnatural? Do such distinctions matter to the algae that develop there, the fish that populate it, or the humans who fish from its shores?

At times, Wister goes out of his way to emphasize the supposed naturalness of "virgin" bodies of water, such as rivers, springs, natural pools, and brooks. These references to "natural" water sources, such as Yellowstone's "swift ripples," the "heavy-eddied Missouri," and the edenic pool "that had come to seem his own," usually exist in the "unsurveyed" regions off the grid (112, 99, 295, 484). The novel assures us that despite the encroachment of "new-scraped water ditches" and fences, the West is still large enough to harbor wild bodies (of water). However, the Virginian's private "island"—the secluded place where he occasionally escapes to daydream, languorously swim, and ride his "hot, wet" horse— is no wild, raging river (484). Located in what the novel describes as a lush, "virgin wilderness," the peaceful island emerges at the convergence of two gently flowing streams. One can easily forget the semiarid environment that surrounds the refuge on every side, and the narrator even informs us that "lakes of warmth flowed into the air," flooding the atmosphere with moist fecundity (490).

Contrary to what we might expect given Wister's views on manliness and saturated landscapes, the island poses little threat to the Virginian's hard masculinity. Instead, the "murmuring" waters regenerate the cowboy by hardening him in new, more intimate ways. When the Virginian's unbridled horse begins to roll in the island's tall, dewy grass, for example, we are told that "his master would roll also, and stretch, and take the grass in his two hands, and so draw his body along, limbering his muscles after a long ride" (484). This description of the naked Virginian (he had "thrown his own clothes off" a few lines earlier) writhing and flexing his body in damp vegetation reads like a moment of sexual pleasure. Just as he clenches the grass and, thus, tightens the body, his muscles go "limber," signaling the sweet release of bodily tension. Readers might assume that the act of relaxing the body in such a fluid ecology would put the Virginian at risk of absorbing water and, hence, of softening up. However, I argue that since he interacts with this humid environment—a "virgin" environment at that—by "taking" it in his hands and fucking it—allows him to remain a manly man, according to Wister's red-blooded vision of masculinity. The Virginian loosens up, but he does so by *getting hard*, and any water his body soaks up in this damp microclimate inevitably returns to the land as ejaculate. Essentially, our young cowboy wrings himself dry.

In a strange twist at the end of the novel, the cowboy marries Molly, and for their honeymoon he takes her to his secret island—now referred to as "the bridal camp"—so that she, too, can experience the water's healing "ripples." The happy "western" couple then relocates to Vermont to start a family, leaving the wild lands of Wyoming behind them. However, the narrator explains that Molly and the Virginian return to the island year after year to camp and reconnect with their old, more adventurous selves. Miraculously, the secluded corner of Wyoming remains untouched and "shut away" from civilization during the many years they are absent, reflecting the "reserved and withdrawn" status of the country's newly established national parklands.[55] Wister never directly refers to his private paradise as a national park and instead remarks that, for the Virginian, the tucked-away spot "had come to seem his own" (484). However, as a "sheltered" place from which "the world was far," the unpeopled refuge resonates with the preservationist mission of the nineteenth-century national parks movement, which culminated in the country's first federal "pleasuring-ground" in northwestern Wyoming. A frequent visitor of Yellowstone National Park and the Teton Range, Wister would have been very familiar with middle- and upper-class Americans' desires "to mix and enrich their own little ongoings with those of Nature," as John Muir put it in *Our National Parks*, and reflected those exclusionary desires in the Virginian's managed fantasyscape.[56]

Unspoiled by developers and, even more surprisingly, absent of Indigenous communities, the Virginian's island functions as a white utopian space in the novel wherein whiteness, like water, could seep into the land and thereby manage it by "mixing" with it. For example, when the Virginian voices to Molly that he wishes to "become the ground, become the water, become the trees, mix with the whole thing . . . never unmix again," he weds himself to what Carolyn Finney calls "a legacy of Eurocentrism and the linkage of wilderness to whiteness, wherein both become naturalized and universalized."[57] By imagining a *liquid whiteness*—a racial materiality that floods, percolates, and mixes with "the whole thing" of wilderness—the Virginian attempts to "naturalize" his claim to the land by envisioning it as an extension of his own white, (supposedly) heterosexual body. Herein lies the paradox of the management project in the West as *The Virginian* depicts it: if the Virginian wishes to lay hold of this little patch of wild land, his white, manly body must open, leak, and blend with the elements, an affiliative process that highlights the role of tenderness and vulnerability in what, for much of the novel, Wister defines as hard management. While these moments when management fails—or when the manager's body intimately engages with vibrant ecologies—often strengthen white ties to the land, as Wister's novel seems to argue, the next sections asks how human-environmental "mixing" often produces relations with the land that swerve away from top-down, Eurocentric management models. To that end, the remaining sections of this chapter investigate nineteenth-century Indigenous autobiography as environmental justice literature, paying specific attention to the interactions between American expansionism on Indigenous environments and bodies in Winnemucca's *Life among the Piutes: Their Wrongs and Claims*.

THE HUMAN ELEMENT: ENVIRONMENTAL JUSTICE AND ELEMENTAL INTRA-ACTION IN *LIFE AMONG THE PIUTES*

Due to the large-scale nature of water development in the West, maps were integral tools for surveyors and engineers. For irrigation companies and speculators, project-planning maps also came to represent topographies of white wealth and possibility. In "A Map of Wyoming with Special Reference to Shoshone Irrigation Company's Lands and the City of Cody" (1900), political boundaries, such as state and county lines, intersect with the blue lines of proposed ditches and canals, revealing, in visual form, the complex relations that water engenders between governments, individuals, and private enterprises.[58] The Big Horn Basin, from which all irrigation lines on the map originate, dominates the map, and in the center of the basin one can see the boundary lines of the Wind River Indian Reservation, a reserve for the Shoshone and Arapaho tribes established in 1868. The blue ink that represents the basin shades the names of towns and leaks over the borders of counties and reservations. The Shoshone Irrigation map informs us that the Big Horn Basin is a landscape feature of great significance; after all, geysers, mountains, hot springs, rivers, and other landforms are represented as faint black outlines, and unless we examine the map closely, these muted features easily fade into background. Wealth is water, the map tells us, and as the irrigation lines thread outward from the sky-blue source, the social and economic potentialities multiply—as do the risks. For the Indigenous inhabitants of the Wind River Reservation, whom Wister never mentions, the risks associated with water development and mining loom large, especially as we move through the twentieth century. As Wyoming's Shoshone and Arapaho residents continue to battle the Environmental Protection Agency and Department of Energy over uranium-contaminated water—water that, as recently as 2010, spiked to one hundred times the legal maximum contaminant levels—water's liveliness becomes far more nefarious than what we witness in Wister's novel.[59]

While *The Virginian* shows us that water infrastructure holds many meanings in the American West, Wister in his novel makes largely invisible the lives and communities of Native Americans and, instead, focuses on Anglo futurities in the region, contributing to a vision of Wyoming as a "sparsely peopled wilderness," to use the language of a popular irrigation enthusiast of the day (xvii). The absence of Indigenous voices in his work highlights the racial/ethnic subjugation that often results from American expansionism in general and water policy more specifically.[60]

Paiute translator, speaker, writer, and Indian rights activist Sarah Winnemucca offers a very different take on human-elemental relations in the context of water development in her provocative memoir, *Life among the Piutes: Their Wrongs and Claims* (1883). In what is often considered the first autobiography written by an American Indian woman, *Life among the Piutes* chronicles several transformative moments in Winnemucca's life, beginning with "the first coming" of white settlers into the tribal communities of northern Nevada and continuing through multiple land wars, forced relocations, sexual assaults of Native women perpetrated by white settlers, and other hardships resulting from American expansion in the West.[61]

Among her many aims, Winnemucca wrote *Life among the Piutes* as a direct appeal to the US Congress to honor native rights to treaty lands, and the memoir ends with a petition "to restore to [the Paiutes] said Malheur Reservation," a "well watered and timbered" territory from which the federal government removed her people (247). As this and many other passages reveal, it is difficult to separate the ecological from the political in Winnemucca's work, as Indigenous rights to land, water, and biotic resources remained central to her fight. What's more, she urges her readers to view water as foundational for Paiute cultural identity, such as when she declares, "We Piutes have *always* lived on the river," a claim that challenges American water policy, especially the doctrine of prior appropriation (76, emphasis added). Enforced by individual states and territories, prior appropriation commodified water as a resource in the mid-nineteenth century and asserted that the first (non-Native) person to claim water for "beneficial" purposes held a priority right to that water. In addition to monetizing water, Devon G. Peña notes, "An unfortunate and ill-conceived aspect of [the prior appropriation doctrine] is that water can be severed from the land," thus allowing "land owners to convey water rights to others, even if that means one moves water over mountains toward money."[62] Peña reads Anglo water policy as an unnatural violence ("severed") whereby certain humans reduce the liquid element from a lively, emergent "member-actant" to a fixed resource valued on the basis of utility.[63]

Ironically, prior appropriation rights did not extend to the *prior* inhabitants of the West, those who "were living there and fishing, as they had always done" (Winnemucca, 77). According to Daniel McCool in *Native Waters*, "the prior appropriation doctrine was designed to meet the needs of the leading political forces in the American West, primarily mining, ranching, and agricultural interests."[64] In a West where land and resource managers stood among those "leading political forces," American Indians were deemed a "disordering element," to use Martha Banta's term, and their mere presence "disrupt[ed] the hope of installing efficient management systems."[65] In other words, to the progress-oriented engineer or developer, "irrational forces"—those individuals making cultural, historical, and biological claims to valuable land and water—needed to be contained.[66] What this means is that in addition to the management of natural resources in the West, American soldiers, settlers, and developers also had to contend with *the human element*, whose presence could be found nearly everywhere in the region. In turn-of-the-century irrigation manifestos, such as William E. Smythe's *The Conquest of Arid America* (1900), American Indians were often described as "the common enemy and an obstacle to settlement and development," even when their laboring bodies aided in said development.[67] If progress were to prevail, men would need to develop methods of overcoming such "obstacles"; these methods often went unnamed in irrigation project proposals, however. For example, when referring to the establishment of the Colorado Territory, Smythe says that settlers were then "able *to deal more effectively* with the Indian," a euphemism that guards his eastern readers from the brutality of conquest.[68] "To deal with"—a verb phrase that abbreviates a complicated set of actions and turns a messy human problem into a precise and knowable object ("the Indian")—becomes a rallying cry for Progressive management. However, in *Life among the Piutes,* Winnemucca reminds us that conquest is not such an easy endeavor, even when one comes armed with blueprints and (other) weapons. Just as streams and rivers frequently dry up or overflow, threatening those who depend on their constancy, so, too, is the human element often difficult "to deal with," especially when their waters, lands, and lives are at risk.

While federal agents and developers would continue to frame American Indians as a management problem throughout the nineteenth century, Winnemucca instead sheds light on the corruption, maladministration, and gross negligence of Anglo military men, engineers, and bureaucrats assigned to manage American interests—including the human element—in the West. In their unpredictable, often reckless treatment of both Indigenous peoples and Western ecologies, Anglo-Americans suffer from a failure to manage, Winnemucca asserts. She suggests that their managerial tactics become more violent and erratic when they feel *out of their element.* At the same time, however, any historical or literary analysis of Winnemucca must acknowledge her work as a translator for the Office of Indian Affairs, a position that, despite her better wishes, surely aided American water development in the West. By pointing to these moments when environmental elements and settler-colonial oppression coalesce, Winnemucca develops an early narrative of environmental injustice in her work, one where a national thirst for resources, including water, puts Native bodies at risk. Reading *Life among the Piutes* with an eye toward water-as-resource, then, allows us to contemplate the immanent entwinement of ecomaterials and racial/ethnic subjugation in the history of American expansionism. In critic Stacy Alaimo's words, "social justice is inseparable from physical environments."[69]

Despite Winnemucca's persistent claims to land and water during what she calls "the greatest emigration" (14) of settlers, critics have been hesitant to read *Life among the Piutes* as an example of environmental justice literature.[70] Water is many things to Winnemucca, and she views American usurpation of Western water as a loss on many fronts, including biological; after all, the human body depends on the intake of water for its literal survival. In this part of the chapter, I call attention to particular moments in *Life among the Piutes* where the elements—namely water—emerge as lively cultural and physiological actants for Winnemucca and other American Indians in the nineteenth century. For example, when combined with dirt, water provided entertainment for children "modelling in mud" (57); for Paiute men, rivers and lakes held vast reserves of fish and migratory ducks, both of which were critical components of a traditional diet; and for adolescent girls, water was a sacred element, as "attendants take [them] to a river to bathe" after their first period (48).

In addition to documenting Paiute relations with water that existed before "the best land [was] taken from them," Winnemucca's memoir also shines a light on Indigenous laborers who engaged in ditch and dam work for various water projects in the West, both on and off reservation land (122). Not only does an emphasis on labor reveal shifting relations between American Indians and water during the expansionist period, but it also highlights the mismanagement of the Office of Indian Affairs, the federal agency under the Department of War assigned to oversee infrastructure projects on the newly forming reservation lands.[71] Ultimately, if we follow the streams of water in Winnemucca's work, paying close attention to the bodies, economies, and ecologies those waters animate, a more peopled vision of the West will emerge, one that runs counter to romanticized depictions of an unpeopled wasteland promoted by irrigation enthusiasts, settlers, and white regional writers like Wister (Smythe, xvii).[72] By reading *Life among the Piutes* alongside more nationalistic, Anglo-authored works like *The Virginian* or *The River*, alternative water epistemologies begin to bubble to the surface, thus challenging the common Progressive Era claim that water development in the West would strengthen and unite an anxious country.

NARRATING THE UNSETTLED DUST AND POISONED WATER

Andrew S. McClure notes that Winnemucca is sometimes perceived by literary critics as being "overly assimilated and sympathetic with the dominant culture," especially given her work as an interpreter for Indian agent Samuel B. Parrish, and as a translator and messenger with the US Army during the Bannock War of 1878.[73] However, he contends that *Life among the Piutes* "is an important autobiography both in terms of giving an account of the complexity of tribal identity as represented through the bi-cultural medium of the autobiography and through its power as a detailed exposé of U.S. hypocrisy in dealing with natives in the nineteenth century."[74] As this section argues, in addition to offering a critique of early US Indian policy in the West, Winnemucca sheds light on settler-colonial environmental degradation, land expropriation, and the necessity of water to Paiute cultural and physiological survival, themes that literary scholars have not yet considered when exploring her work. What would happen, then, if we approached *Life among the Piutes* from an ecocritical perspective, paying special attention to human relations with water? Additionally, what do we gain by reframing Indigenous autobiography, such as *Life among the Piutes*, as environmental justice literature? As an author who vehemently denounces what today's scholars would term environmental racism, Winnemucca shows how a focus on human-elemental affiliations can offer a more particular and immediate story of Manifest Destiny, a story whose traces exist to this day in both bodies and environments. As Devon

Peña notes, "[W]hen I talk about environmental degradation, I am talking about the degradation of our bodies, as well, because our bodies are in the environment and they are a microecosystem in themselves."[75]

Using the language of environmental elements, Winnemucca tells of "the greatest emigration" of white settlers who seemingly storm into Paiute lands, and in doing so she aligns American expansionism with both cultural and ecological disruption (14). "[W]e were all afraid of them," she says. "Every dust that we could see blowing in the valleys we would say it was the white people" (11). With the arrival of soldiers and settlers in what is now western Nevada, Winnemucca begins to read clouds of stirred-up sand, or dust devils, as signals of white presence. Though often naturally occurring, dust devils take on new meaning for the author in the context of American expansionism, and now she must remain vigilant of "every dust" that becomes unsettled. The westward migration of homesteaders, military men, miners, and others seeking to occupy the West issues in a new era for Winnemucca and her people, one where even the once innocuous desert sand becomes suspect. Winnemucca furthers the association of environmental animacy with Anglo settlement when she cites a dream her father narrated to her:

> He said, "I dreamt this same thing three nights,—the very same. I saw the greatest emigration that has yet been through our country. I looked North and South and East and West, and saw nothing but dust, and I heard a great weeping. I saw women crying, and I saw my men shot down by the white people." (14)

For Winnemucca and her father, the hyper-mobile bodies of American men stir up the surface of the arid Nevada desert, culminating in frenzied whirlwinds and sandstorms that sweep across the vast panorama. In her father's recurring dream, distinct, white bodies remain largely invisible, as dust, now kicked up from the desert floor, swirls into chaos and disorients the Paiute witnesses. Haboobs, or intense dust storms, obscure the forms of those who commit the violence, leading Winnemucca's father to note, "I . . . saw nothing but dust." Despite the sharp visibility and aurality of pain and trauma in most of the dream—"*I saw* women crying," her father says, "and *I heard* a great weeping"—the roving perpetrators remain obscured in cloaks of sand (14, emphasis added). The cloud of dust, ever on the move and growing in strength, becomes a metonym for the white, interloping bodies of the settlers. In this scene, and throughout *Life among the Piutes*, Winnemucca stresses that the intensive settler-colonial impacts on the environment equate to physical and emotional disruptions in cultures, bodies, and memories. However, the Paiutes' watery emotionality in the dream, as expressed via their "crying" and "weeping," aligns them with an insubmissive kind of moisture; even amid the swirls of desiccating dust, the Paiutes continue to mourn, refuse to dry up.

According to Stacy Alaimo, who explores the material interchanges between bodies and ecologies in her work *Bodily Natures*,

> one could rewrite the entire expanse of the history of the United States from an environmental justice perspective, rethinking the grand narratives of manifest destiny and noting that many of the forms of violence toward and subordination of Native Americans, African Americans, and Mexican Americans, in particular, could be understood as environmental justice issues.[76]

She continues by noting that "the slaughter of the buffalo and the genocide or 'removal' of Indians from the environments essential for their cultural and physical survival" constitute heinous acts of injustice that impact both humans and nonhumans alike.[77] Alaimo introduces the concept of *transcorporeal materialism* as a method of reading these injustices *in* actual bodies. Through a transcorporeal lens, human bodies and nonhuman materialities encounter one another as emergent, "mediating membranes," and as they relay matter back and forth, the composition of both changes, transforms.[78] Transcorporeal materialism, she suggests, provides scholars with a new method of reading Indigenous and minority histories in the United States because it undoes the notion that human bodies are discrete, isolated, and separate from (toxic) environments. This radically intimate, intra-actionist conception of materiality can shine new light on nineteenth-century expansionist narratives, allowing us to see the material traces of conquest in bodies and ecologies.

Environmental justice movements, Alaimo says, "epitomize a trans-corporeal materiality, a conception of the body that is neither essentialist, nor genetically determined, nor firmly bounded, but rather a body in which social power and material/geographic agencies intra-act."[79] For example, when Winnemucca questions whether a poisoned water supply (probably by cholera) might be the cause of a mass "die off" in her community, conquest manifests as an imbibable materiality, one that disturbingly exemplifies "the ever-emergent interrelations of race and place."[80] Winnemucca depends on witness testimony and a cause-and-effect structure throughout the poisoned water passage to reveal white culpability for the Paiute deaths. She states that one of her tribe "said that the white men had poisoned the Humboldt River, and our people had drank the water and died off" (41). Later in that same scene, she tells readers that *One and all said* that the river must have been poisoned by the white people, because . . . our spirit-doctors had tried to cure the sick; they too died while they were trying to cure them" (42, emphasis added). Winnemucca argues that all Paiutes present are in accord with the theory that "white men" are to blame for poisoning the river, and her insistence that Humboldt water led to the widespread deaths rhetorically animates the liquid resource. Water becomes more than water in this scene, as its dangerous agency now holds the potential to terminate, rather than sustain, life. Tainted water emerges as an imperialistic tool in this chilling scene, allowing Anglos to "deal with" Native Americans from a safe distance. For the Paiutes, a culture that defines itself, in large part, by water, the realization that water could be toxic—and, worse yet, that its toxicity could be wielded as a colonial weapon—must have come as an epic shock.

While the intentionality of the "poisoning" remains unclear—Winnemucca's grandfather, for example, does not believe "my white brothers would do such a thing"—the equation of water with white violence remains real for those who witness and emotionally absorb the mounting deaths (42). As the stories about the poisoned water continue to grow, it becomes evident that the contaminated element impacted more than just the sick and deceased. As Winnemucca tells us, "Every one of them was in mourning" (42). A wave of disbelief and grief overtakes the community, initiating the flow of a very different kind of liquid: tears.

> We heard [the mourners] as they came nearer and nearer; they were all crying, and then we cried too, and as they got off their horses they fell into each other's arms, like so many little children, and cried as if their hearts would break, and told what they had suffered since we went away, and how our people had died off. (42)

In this scene, Winnemucca writes wateriness onto Indigenous bodies by referring to the act of crying three times in just one sentence. According to psychologists, crying is "a key attachment behavior" that is "intended to elicit care and comfort from close others throughout life."[81] Researchers have even found that human tears express distinct chemical signals that others unknowingly respond to.[82] In other words, water, as a bodily element, can invite bonding, security, and even the sharing of grief when secreted in the form of tears. The Paiutes' tears, a consequence of white encroachment onto Indigenous lands, reinforce Winnemucca's plea to her eastern readers by aligning expansionism with desiccation and environmental destruction.

Though not an overtly sentimental work, *Life among the Piutes* combines Winnemucca's matter-of-fact, autobiographical observations with brief moments of intense emotionality. This melding of nineteenth-century literary classifications resonates with essays by Sioux writer Zitkála-Šá who, according to Susan Bernardin, "drew from sentimental and autobiographical genres for a pre-dominantly non-Indian readership. This strategy encouraged her to claim and reshape the narrative and moral authority associated with the two literary forms."[83] Similar to Zitkála-Šá's "methodol-ogy for speaking to her readers' sensibility and in drawing their attention to the concerns of Indian country," Winnemucca also relies on this early nineteenth-century mode to reveal the "slow violence" of American expansionism; in other words, water con-tamination is violence that doesn't look like violence.[84] The perpe-trator exists in another time and place, and culpability is therefore hard to trace.

Structurally, these teary, emotional scenes in *Life among the Piutes* leak, drop by drop, into what is otherwise a realist mem-oir, water-logging the work with evidence of white violence. Time slows, almost grinds to a halt in this and other emotional scenes, forcing readers to face the Paiutes' grief before return-ing to Winnemucca's progressive chronology. Furthermore, this moment of shared grief reveals that no one in the community is immune to the contamination. Even if the noxious element fails to invade the body, fear and anguish will surely find a way in, caus-ing individuals' legs to fail ("they fell into each other's arms") and "hearts [to] break" (42). Winnemucca's emphasis on the way that grief penetrates and makes vulnerable the human form reveals the affective nature of environmental toxicity on a community's men-tal health. In other words, a substance need not enter one's skin, digestive tract, or bloodstream to impact the body; its near mate-rial presence in their minds is enough to wreak havoc, as many contemporary examples have shown us.

For example, the Paiutes' grief in this scene, wrought by an invisible contagion and an unseen source of the contagion, mir-rors the "long-term psychological consequences" of those dealing with the effects of the lead-contaminated water in Flint, Michigan and elsewhere.[85] In a *New York Times* article published two years after the traces of lead had been discovered in the Flint water supply, journalists Abby Goodnough and Scott Atkinson state that "Health care workers are scrambling to help people here cope with what many fear will be chronic consequences of the city's water contamination crisis: profound stress, worry, and depression." The authors cite "uncertainty about [the residents'] own health and the health of their children, the open-ended nature of the crisis, and the raw anger over the government's role" in the crisis as the roots of the citizens' enduring psychological unease and bodily harm.

Despite the difference in time, place, and lives affected, Winnemucca's story of the poisoned river shares many similarities with stories coming out of Flint and other cities across the United States. In both, contaminated water does more than just physically intra-act with—and, thereby, chemically and biologically alter—human bodies; the mental impacts also lace into bodies in ways that *feel* tangible, material. Just as the Paiutes fall into each other's arms in the midst of the crisis, so too do the residents of Flint experience the chronic stress in their own bodies. For example, when speaking of the emotional trauma associated with the contamination event, one resident of Flint says, "It never leaves you. At some point you just want to jump up and down and yell and scream." The indeterminate "it"—the water, the anger, the apprehension—imbeds itself in bodies, urging those bodies to "jump up and down" and vocalize their trauma. As an unwanted resident of the body, "it" settles in, multiplies, and seems almost unmanageable at times. In a way, Winnemucca's documentation of the poisoned water becomes a way to manage all that grief, to both contain and rhetorically concentrate the powerful event for her readers. Just as "everything was recorded" in Flint by federal administrators in an effort to write order into disorderly circumstances, so too does Winnemucca detail the poisoned river episode in an attempt to channel immense grief into a discernible argument against white violence (Winnemucca, 92). Though the poisoned river passage takes up only one page, variations of the word "die" ("die," "died off," "dead") appear eight times, and "cry" ("cry," "crying") appears four times, reminding us of the force of contamination on those still living.

DIGGING DITCHES: FLOWS OF BODIES AND LABOR

In addition to detailing the impact of Anglo settlement on extant water sources, Winnemucca describes how Indigenous labor contributed to a variety of federal water development projects, particularly ditch and diversion work in the arid West. Undertaking water development at any level—local, regional, national, or transnational—involves more than just extensive blueprints and capital. Workers are also a critical component of water "control work," since ditch diggers, dam builders, dredgers, brush cutters, and others actually *make* infrastructure happen.[86] According to recent work in the growing field of "maintenance studies," the unending upkeep that follows innovation remains largely unseen and undervalued: "Maintenance and repair, the building of infrastructures, the mundane labour that goes into sustaining functioning and efficient infrastructures, simply has more impact on people's daily lives than the vast majority of technological innovations."[87] H. T. Cory, a turn-of-the-century civil and mechanical engineer with the California Development Company, and the figure upon whom Aiken's Casey Rickard is based, understood the ongoing-ness of water maintenance when he wrote, "The Lower Colorado is not merely a problem of yesterday, presenting a vague general moral. It is a vital problem of to-day and tomorrow and of years to come."[88] Despite our fleeting recognition that maintenance, though unsexy, is "a vital problem," water history and ecocriticism have, until recently, privileged the innovators—the engineers, politicians, and financiers—over the maintainers in their work. In such writing, dams and ditches seem to materialize from sheer desire alone.

As so-called feats of engineering, dams and ditches often overshadow the tedious labor that contributed to their making and maintenance, leaving admirers to believe that infrastructure, like empires, just happens naturally. Patricia Limerick's 2013 case study of Denver Water, *A Ditch in Time*, however, takes readers into the often hidden processes of both building and maintaining water infrastructure. Included alongside Limerick's vivid descriptions of communities of labor are photographs of early dam construction sites, allowing readers to glimpse development-in-process. To see workers scaling and dangling from the edges of a half-built dam is to understand the communities that converge around (and in many ways develop from) sites of labor. Despite Limerick's unique insistence that labor and materiality play integral roles in water history, her work does not examine the significant contributions of Indigenous workers to water development in the West. In fact, the literature on Native water labor is relatively scant, making this a ripe topic for environmental humanists to explore. *Life among the Piutes*, as well as turn-of-the-century technical papers and irrigation manifestos, reveal that Indigenous water workers existed as the backbone of Western water development as we know it, especially when it came to ditch and diversion work.

Life among the Piutes shines a light on the near compulsory Indian labor that contributed to various state-sponsored water projects and thus documents the often troubling modes of engagement between Native Americans and water-as-resource during the first treaty era.[89] Not only does Winnemucca offer a more close-up, humanized view of water labor than we get in nineteenth-century irrigation pamphlets and manifestos, but her depiction of water development as a largely mismanaged enterprise stands in contrast to the "able and honest management" style that engineers, administrators, and irrigation boosters extolled in their writings.[90] For example, in her memoir Winnemucca cites a relatively small water project on the Pyramid Lake Reservation—a three-mile ditch—that has remained unfinished for nearly twenty-three years due to administrative incompetence and a high turnover rate of Indian agents: "There have been twelve different agents there during that time, who taught [the workers] nothing" (109). In contrast to these more ineffectual agents, Winnemucca frequently praises US Indian agent Samuel Parrish, for whom she worked as a translator. Characterized as more sympathetic than the agents who "look out for their own pockets," Parrish, she says, is determined to "improve" the Northern Paiute's Malheur Reservation via the modern tool of irrigation (136). A strong work ethic is paramount to Parrish, and as Winnemucca explains, he tries to instill this Progressive value into the Paiute water workers during his first meeting with them. Winnemucca quotes Parrish:

> I have come to show you how to work, and work we must. I am not like the man who has just left you. I can't kneel down and pray for sugar and flour and potatoes to rain down, as he did. . . . The first thing I want you to do is to make a dam and then dig a ditch. That is to irrigate the land. Some of you can dig the ditch, some can build the dam, some can go to the woods and cut rails to build fences. I want you to all work while the government is helping us, for the government is not always going to help us. (106)

In an attempt to distinguish himself from the Christian agent whom he has just replaced, Parrish urges his listeners to see him as a more practical and enterprising figure, one who prefers to engineer water into existence rather than waiting and praying for water to fall from the sky. To motivate the Paiutes, Parrish frames the moment of his arrival as an opportunity, one that must not be wasted.

In this scene, the concept of waste—wasted water, a wasted opportunity, wasted time—becomes, in Cecilia Tichi's words, "a summons, not a dire threat."[91] According to Parrish's scientific logic, concerted labor will enable the Paiutes to take advantage of new, future-directed flows of diverted water. Similar to Aiken, who in *The River* divides Indian labor by tribal affiliation due to the belief that certain tasks were performed better by different tribes, Winnemucca also calls attention to the division of labor that Parrish introduces to the community.[92] His relegation of three tasks—digging ditches, building dams, and cutting rails—sounds almost machinelike in its quick delivery. While "some of you can dig the ditch," "some" others, he notes, can build the dam or construct the fence. In just one sentence, a desert landscape is remade, sparkling with the glints of newly flowing water. What is more, this tidy, concise sentence redefines individual Paiutes by the work they fulfill. The repetition of the unspecified "some," when combined with the particularized tasks to be performed, blots out the laborer while revealing in sharper relief the products of his labor (ditches, dams, and fences). Who these workers are becomes less important than the work they do; to put it another way, when Parrish anonymizes Indigenous labor, water infrastructure is allowed to transform into monuments of national, economic, and Anglo futurity. Similar to Parrish's elevation of the product over its creator, Wister's *The Virginian* praises the extensive networks of "new-scraped water ditches" while hiding from view the men who do the scraping. Even though the Virginian is, himself, a seasonal ditch digger, we never see him engage in such work.

When not referring to labor in the abstract ("the element of human labor"), promoters of Western irrigation at the turn of the century would often refer to water laborers in either condescending or heroic terms, depending on the race or ethnicity of those doing the work.[93] For example, Cory described Mexican and Indian water workers as "a motley crew" of "gipsies" whose work camps required strict policing, despite "the loyal support [these workers] commanded" in California's Imperial Valley project.[94] Similarly, in Helen Hunt Jackson's sentimental novel *Ramona*, American government officials frequently refer to hard-working Indigenous characters as "Indian beggars" and other terms that associate Indigeneity with laziness.[95] This ethnic stereotype is alive and well in *Life among the Piutes*, as when Parrish says to Winnemucca, "your other agent told me that you would not work, that you were lazy," and he therefore seems surprised that the Paiutes were "so willing to work" when he first arrived at

Malheur (109). Anglo water workers, on the other hand, are often cast in a much different light, as evidenced in Smythe's irrigation manifesto, *The Conquest of Arid America*. When describing white, westward-moving farmers, Smythe renders their work a Progressive endeavor; he celebrates the "industrious settlers" who act as "the creative force which alone gives value to any form of security."[96] Indians, he concedes, "are useful laborers in the simpler agricultural tasks," but he does not believe they can be trusted to undertake more large-scale projects.[97] Smythe downplays the role of Indigenous labor in the history of Western water development, muting their contributions in an effort to amplify the "creative force" of white labor. Additionally, Smythe's rendering of labor as a disembodied "soul" dematerializes labor and shields from view the real bodies that dig, sweat, strain, desire, piss, and sometimes die along the edge of the ditch.

Wister's Virginian participates in ditch digging and other types of strenuous, physical labor on the Wyoming ranch as a proud expression of his masculine national identity. To dig into the newly acquired soil in an effort to aid the flow of water (and capital) would seem the ultimate path to becoming both an American and, perhaps more importantly, a "man of the West." This romanticized, somewhat mythical view of labor is rooted in the American ideal of property ownership: that working to improve one's own land—even, and maybe especially, when such work taxes the body—reinforces one's connection to the land. Ditch work, which requires both hard work at the onset and persistent upkeep, would seem the ultimate expression of one's right to the land—that is, if one owns the land upon which he works. In his environmental history *A Land Made of Water*, Robert Crifasi expounds on the relation between ditch digging and settlers' "tie to the land and water":

> It is no wonder that farmers remain so possessive toward their water. Once the backbreaking process of digging ditches and establishing their homestead was completed, the experience was seared into their psyche, and the labor they expended served as proof enough of their

right to use their water and control their ditch. Building the ditch and the labor expended during many subsequent years of maintaining and upgrading it reinforced the farmers' and ranchers' tie to the land and water and renewed the ownership they feel toward that water and the lifestyle it enables.[98]

Crifasi's use of corporeal words like "backbreaking" and "seared" to describe labor's effects on the body emphasize the intense intra-actions between humans and the elements with which they work.

Labor enabled settlers to bond with their soil, Crifasi notes, reflecting, in perhaps more romantic terms, Richard White's notion of the "organic machine."[99] White argues that through labor, humans come to know nature—or rather, their bodies and social realities become entangled with it in a kind of shared "energy" system. White calls this messy, lively system an "organic machine," a term that blurs the borders between so-called natural and mechanical entities. In works like *The Virginian*, it seems that only certain men are capable of sharing "energy" with or embodying the Western landscape; this becomes especially true for the Virginian, a seasonal ditch worker who, despite his name, exudes a Western aura from head to toe, from the "weather-beaten bloom of his face" to his dust-covered boots (5). Readers never see the Virginian engaging in water labor, however. The sweat and strain and monotony of water work remains obscured in the novel, and we are only left with the oblique idea that (white) men work hard somewhere—*out there, in the wild periphery*—to make irrigation possible. What's more, *The Virginian* favors the creation/ construction of infrastructure over the tedium of maintenance. After all, Wister never mentions the amount of labor it takes to keep water flowing—dredging, debris removal, erosion repair, slope maintenance, and so on—once the initial ditches have been carved. By preventing readers from seeing ditch work up close, Wister epitomizes the Virginian as a man of the West without particularizing him as a laborer. As a character in *The River* notes, "Perspiring men are not inspiring men," a sentiment that pits labor against the dry skin of civilization (354). Although ditch work, according to Crifasi, reinforces a connection to place, the truth is that the work was hard, monotonous, and unglamorous—and it is hard to imagine the reliably entertaining Virginian involved in such tedious work. Armed with shovels, hoes, and draft animals (if they were lucky), diggers had to move a lot of earth, often for miles without end. Crifasi asserts that "the soil was hard, and [ditch diggers] had to continually lift out cobbles that were often one or two feet across."[100] This is the work that readers fail to see in the novel, despite the fact that "newly scraped ditches" shimmer on every horizon.

In contrast with the out-of-sight water labor in *The Virginian*, *Life among the Piutes* offers glimpses of Indian labor on the ground. Reading water work in late nineteenth-century Indigenous literature forces us to ponder Crifasi's claim that interacting with the elements via labor strengthens one's "tie to the land." To put it quite simply, the Indian laborers Winnemucca documents in her autobiography can no longer claim sovereignty over the (home) land upon which they work, and so their labor likely holds a different value. As one Indian agent says to Winnemucca, "Nothing here is yours. It is all the government's," a statement that aligns expansionism with Indigenous dispossession (133). On the newly forming reservation lands, the Paiutes are required to work to receive basic necessities and, sometimes, money. The ditch diggers in *Life among the Piutes* often compare their work to forced labor, and unlike the Virginian, they rarely reap the benefits of their efforts. For example, with a half a mile left to dig on the Malheur Reservation ditch project, Winnemucca says that Parrish received a letter from the "Big Father in Washington" informing him that a white man wished to purchase a portion of the now-irrigated reservation. "[Parrish] told us that we had two hundred and ninety-two enemies in Canyon City. He said the name of the captain of these men was Judge Curry. This man wanted the west end of our reservation, and our Big Father in Washington wanted to know what we thought about it" (115). Winnemucca then quotes Parrish directly: "'These white men,' he said, 'have talked to your Father in Washington, saying that you are lazy, and will not work'" (115). Despite their intimate contact with land, water, and water infrastructure, the Paiutes are left *without* water—and without much land and compensation, despite the many promises made by the Office of Indian Affairs. The threat of land and water loss in this passage, especially since the threat comes directly from the ultimate seat of power—the president of the United States—underscores the vital role that natural resources play in settler-colonial conquest.

Winnemucca frequently reminds readers that Indian laborers worked to construct many of the water projects that Americans so admire:

> The first work that my people did on the reservation was to dig a ditch, to put up a grist-mill and saw-mill. . . . My people do not own any timber land now. The white people are using the ditch which my people made to irrigate their land. This is the way we are treated by our white brothers. (76–77)

Ultimately, the reservation fails to absorb the energies expended by the Paiutes' working bodies; instead, the product of their labor flows outward, trickles over the ever-shifting borders of Pyramid Lakes, and funnels into the bodies and economies of the Paiutes' "white brothers." This waterlessness is further emphasized by the prevalence of the word "water" in Winnemucca's memoir, which appears thirty-nine times. Despite the word's frequent occurrence, it often appears in the context of "no water." Waterlessness, or the fear thereof, permeates other Indigenous writers of the era, such as when Zitkála-Šá recalls her mother's fear of the "paleface" who "takes away from us the river we drink."[101] As *Life among the Piutes* and other autobiographical works by Indigenous authors demonstrate, race, class, and gender mediate one's access to and contact with water-as-resource. Through an analysis of the "poisoned" river episode and descriptions of Native Americans' participation in the construction of early federal water projects, Winnemucca's work stands as an example of environmental justice literature, one that demonstrates the entwinement of social justice with ecological realities.

Near the end of her autobiography, Winnemucca passionately speaks out against the recurrent threats of expropriation using a chilling water metaphor. Speaking directly to Christians who "rise from . . . bended knees" and claim ownership over Indigenous lands, she says, "your so-called civilization sweeps inland from the ocean wave; but, oh, my God! leaving its pathway marked by crimson lines of blood, and strewed by the bones of two races, the inheritor and the invader; and I am crying out to you for justice" (207). Winnemucca's use of the oceanic wave as a conveyer of Anglo-American expansionism aligns the "so-called civilization" of the "invader" with cultural and environmental desiccation that verges on apocalypse. After all, even after the unmanageable wave recedes, its salty residue will remain, she argues, choking out life for years to come. According to Winnemucca, white Americans can hardly control the tsunami upon which they ride, and its lethal effects for both "the invader" and "the inheritor" seem far from mitigable. Similar to the foreboding sandstorms that wreak havoc in her father's dreams, the image of the desiccating wave of whiteness leads Winnemucca to "cry out . . . for justice," or to fight water with water.

Winnemucca's likening of white violence to an "ocean wave" remains a vital metaphor for today's Indigenous water protectors and allies, particularly those who fought against the completion of Energy Transfer Partners' Dakota Access Pipeline. During 2016 and 2017, thousands of peaceful protesters converged near the Standing Rock Sioux Reservation in North Dakota and were forced to engage in multiple standoffs with local police, state, and federal law enforcement, private security guards, and even the National Guard. Several news organizations, Twitter users, and bloggers covering the news coming out of Standing Rock used the phrase "wave of violence" to describe the often brutal tactics law enforcement used when responding to those protecting the Ogallala Aquifer from potential crude oil contamination.[102] At times, the "wave of violence" transformed from metaphor to materiality, such as when police pelted water protectors with high-velocity water cannons in an attempt to disperse the crowd.

Even though the water protectors were ultimately unable to prevent DAPL's completion, Indigenous-led movements such as what we witnessed at Standing Rock offer new paradigms for managing and protecting water's collective value, as Chief Arvol Looking Horse considers it.[103] "Standing Rock is everywhere," he says, meaning the varied threats posed to clean water in the Dakotas exist on a global scale—and, if we fail to continue acting on the goals articulated at the Standing Rock encampment, we risk losing the life (meaning *our* life) that water fosters. In more ways than we can count, water and mass infrastructure intersect with pressing ecological, social, cultural, and biological concerns. In our efforts to map and manage water, we must admit that our fate precariously flows in its currents.

CHAPTER 4

THE SALT CURE

BRINING SOFT BODIES IN THE "WILD WASTE" OF THE PACIFIC OCEAN

The Salt Cure, popularly so termed, is a system according to which hypodermic injections of substances to reinvigorate the nervous system are administered to patients whose vitality may apparently be exhausted, and whose reserve store of nerve energy may thus be stimulated and increased. It is therefore only because it prolongs the life of the individual that the so-called Salt Cure may be termed the elixir of life.

—CLAIRE DE PRATZ (1901)[1]

[W]hen I could hold my breath no longer, I breathed the stinging salt water into my lungs.

—JACK LONDON (2007[1904])[2]

The sea is not a metaphor. Figurative language has its place in analyses of the maritime world, certainly, but oceanic studies could be more invested in the uses, and problems, of what is literal in the face of the sea's abyss of representation.

—HESTER BLUM (2010)[3]

BODIES OF WATER

This chapter goes west of "the American West" to examine how turn-of-the-century seal hunters, neurasthenics, Japanese immigrants, and other oceangoing individuals navigated, with varying degrees of success, what Jack London calls "the new and elemental environment" of the Pacific Ocean (30). Often understood in *fin-de-siècle* American literature as an "illimitable," unpredictable, and highly inhospitable environment, the briny Pacific figures as a risky realm of potentiality for many Progressives, particularly those working and writing in California.[4] Unlike the semiarid high plains and arid desert spaces discussed earlier in this book, the Pacific Ocean is, of course, not an exclusively American space. While its salty waters lap upon the shores of the continental United States, Alaska, Hawaii, and ten American territories, the largest and deepest of the Earth's oceans also touches five of the seven continents, making it an international and transnational space. What's more, for the Indigenous peoples of Oceania and Pacific coastal regions, the ocean exists as a veritable homeland that sustains their biological needs and engenders their diverse cosmological orientations. Throughout the nineteenth century and well into the twentieth, the United States began expanding its territorial vision ever westward by claiming Pacific land masses and oceanic resources as "possessions," which led many to believe that the country had "a strong foothold" in the watery expanse.[5] A 1908 *National Tribune* article even says of the Pacific, "We Will Make It an American Lake," extending the Progressive Era's land-based management ethos into what the author describes as "The World's Wildest Waste of Waters."[6] Despite these claims of political ownership and administrative might, today's blue humanists inform us that the *world ocean* has always been a highly mobile, "de-territorial" space, meaning "human beings cannot live for extended periods of time" in the deep sea—not that this has stopped them from trying.[7]

The strenuous process of trying to manage the sea, and manage *at* sea, even when oceanic materialities ravage the hair, burn the skin, sicken the belly, dampen the clothes, and parch the mouth, is at the heart of this chapter, which examines works by Jack London and Yonejirō (Yone) Noguchi, both of whom crossed the Pacific at various points in their lives and wrote of its allure from the California coast. When the main characters in London's *The Sea-Wolf* (1904) and Noguchi's *The American Diary of a Japanese Girl* (1902) attempt to manage life at sea, salt—existing in the form of seawater, "briny air," and even canned meat—roughens and messes their so-called delicate features, coarsening their bodies for their eventual arrival on American soil. Progressive Era literature set in the Pacific's rough waters communicates the idea that these radical exposures to saltwater—the substance meant to facilitate new contacts on the world stage—though risky for some (gendered and raced) bodies, might help to energize the next generation of global managers. However, "the salt cure," the term I use to describe how turn-of-the-century seafaring tested and transformed the bodies of culturally and economically privileged white men, often renders unintended results. Additionally, when women and immigrants take to the salty sea, as we witness in Noguchi's work, saltwater appears no less permeative and instructive, thus destabilizing the masculinist assertion that only Anglo men can endure and gain strength from its turbulent waters.

The Sea-Wolf and *American Diary* demonstrate that when individuals make contact with Pacific saltwater, they struggle to adequately regulate the borders of their porous bodies. While these ongoing failures to manage in the open ocean promise to build and, to use a salty metaphor, *preserve* strong men for the hard work of trans-Pacific empire-building, London and Noguchi show that life at and with sea occasionally produces unanticipated and even queer modes of social and ecological belonging. I argue that these new relational orientations might be capable of challenging the nation-state's sprawling and inflexible management regimes, which tend to perceive oceanic spaces through economic goggles.

It might seem odd to pair London and Noguchi in a chapter on American literary criticism in the Pacific, especially since Noguchi, who was born in Japan and only spent eleven years in the United States, never attempted to become a naturalized citizen. Moreover, other than a general geographical focus on coastal California and the Pacific in their writings, the themes and styles that London and Noguchi pursue could not be more dissimilar. This might be why literary critics have never thought to examine their fiction in the same project. Considered a "savage realist" who writes of rugged men in extreme, "manly" environments, London's devotion to the gritty naturalist tradition comes through like a foghorn in *The Sea-Wolf*.[8] The novel's celebration of violence and its exploration of Darwinian evolutionary philosophy seems a far cry from Noguchi's little-known *Diary*, a work of fiction narrated in the voice of an aristocratic Japanese woman who has journeyed across the Pacific to write nature poems.[9] When not commenting on Americans' misconceptions of Japanese culture or lounging comfortably on the beach with a close friend, Noguchi's narrator speaks adoringly of the natural world, often sounding like the Romantic authors she so admires. Despite these significant differences in both style and genre, both works find anchor in the authors' autobiographical experiences and feature first-person narrators trying to adapt to the literal and cultural tides of the Pacific world.

Though I have found no archival evidence proving that London and Noguchi ever met in person, it seems their paths must have crossed at some point given their connection to the Bay Area Bohemian group, led by Joaquin Miller, and their close friendship with Charles Warren Stoddard, author of several works based on his Polynesian travels. London and Noguchi even rented studios at the Monkey Block, a low-rent building in San Francisco that nurtured the region's community of artists and writers. Of interest to this project, both authors shared an intense awareness of the growing ties (and tensions) between Japan and the United States and, through their fiction and essays, expressed concerns over the future of the Pacific world. London himself had visited Japan on more than one occasion, most notably as a war correspondent commissioned by William Hearst during the Russo-Japanese War, where some say he was not well received due to his open loathing of the Japanese.[10] As an expounder of the Yellow Peril ideology, London viewed East Asians as cultural and economic threats to the United States.

From 1909 to 1910, London and Noguchi communicated with one another on the subject of the Yellow Peril via essays in *Sunset Magazine*, a periodical published in California that largely featured the work of West Coast writers. In London's "If Japan Awakens China," published in December 1909, he expresses fear over Japan joining forces with China to engage in a "race-adventure" against "the branches of the white race."[11] Noguchi's response to London, written after he had returned to Japan, appeared seven months later, wherein he argues that Americans' fear of the Chinese is unreasoned. In "No Yellow Peril in China," he writes, "If there exists a Yellow Peril, I dare say it is nowhere else but in the Western mind which created it herself; we are almost inclined to say that we Easterners are much afraid of the White Peril."[12] Noguchi's bold public response to London's xenophobic rhetoric reveals the high stakes of Pacific mobility at the turn of the century—that oceanic spaces function as a conduit for anxiety and possibility for all parties involved.

Given that characters in *The Sea-Wolf* and *Diary* cross the waters of the Pacific, with both Japan *and* California acting as destinations in each work, London and Noguchi experiment with using saltwater as a literal *solution* for managing race and gender in the context of American expansionism. Reading their works side by side illustrates that elemental forces played a central role in transforming national bodies into imperial (London) or transnational

(Noguchi) bodies. As an unmanageable substance in these works, Pacific saltwater quite literally exfoliates vulnerable national skin to encourage the production of resilient modern bodies.

To better understand the idea of the Pacific in the minds of turn-of-the-century Americans, it is important to consider what Helen Rozwadowski calls "a twin scientific and cultural awakening to the deep sea" that began in the mid-nineteenth century.[13] In addition to biological surveys of oceanic plants and wildlife inspired by Charles Darwin's travels in the *Beagle*, not to mention the birth of oceanography as a field of study, the late nineteenth-century's burgeoning outdoor movement prompted an interest in beach vacationing and yachting, meaning that for those classes with ample leisure time the ocean became a destination and not merely a byway.[14] In addition to this growing interest in *going to the sea* for scientific and recreational purposes, American business began to question more intensely how to turn the "trackless waste" of the Pacific into profit.[15] Though geographically and materially distant from the arid environments populating the western United States, the salty Pacific, similar to the continental "wastelands," had until the late nineteenth century largely remained an economic desert for the United States, save for a few fledgling maritime industries. Regarded by the "older generation" as a watery void "dotted with savage isles and crossed by only an occasional trader," the biggest and deepest of the earth's ocean systems began to figure not as waste but as opportunity, as it linked the Americas with Asia, thus opening new avenues for trade.[16]

Further enabling these trans-Pacific relations, turn-of-the-century innovations in oceanic transportation, such as steam-powered liners with steel hulls, bridged the broad divide between the United States and East Asia, spurring trade, international tourism, and immigration. For example, if conditions were amenable, in 1894 it would take approximately sixteen days for both the Pacific Mail and the Occidental and Oriental steamers to reach Yokohama from San Francisco, "or 18 days if

Honolulu be touched at."[17] In the mid-1800s, this same trip might have taken thirty days or more. As a result of this opening up of the Pacific to more efficient travel and trade, historian Thomas J. Osborne suggests that the US federal government became much more interested in bringing the West Coast into the national fold. "Asiatic commerce," he says, operated "as the driving motive for American annexation of both Oregon and California" in the middle of the nineteenth century.[18] The Pacific was no longer deemed the unmanageable sibling to the well-trafficked Atlantic; in fact, many viewed it as an economic "rival" to America's eastern ocean.[19] According to an 1899 *Anaconda Standard* article, "the boy of to-day sees . . . a body of water with English and American communities at every strategic point and *coigne* of vantage, law and order prevailing, in every isle and with every port the scene of a commerce that is destined soon to rival the older harbors and havens of the Atlantic."[20] At long last, it appeared as though the United States had arrived at "every" corner of the Pacific, and the "boy of to-day," equipped with a sharp mind and a hard body, seemed ready to manage its tempestuous waves—if the currents would only be still, that is.

In early twentieth-century American literature, including the two works explored in this chapter, trans-Pacific travel exposes the fomenting cultural, economic, and ecological relations between the United States and the Pacific world, East Asia in particular. For even though London and Noguchi regard the winds and waters of the Pacific as violent, inherently disobedient elements— as forces that "sting," "pound," sicken, and "crush" men to smithereens—they also depict the ocean as a modern arena populated by engineers, Japanese poets, machinists, diplomats, mail steamers, health-seeking tourists, immigrants, ship paths, "herds" of marine wildlife, capitalists, canned beef tongue, biologists, war correspondents, pollution, and even women. For them, the Pacific Basin operates as a location of cross-cultural and, at least for London, trans-species encounter. Characters in both works engage in various social relations at sea, painting the Pacific as a bustling arena, much like the thriving port city of San Francisco.

Though certainly still a trying environment for humans, as evidenced by the numerous ailments and even deaths that occur in their works, the Pacific also emerges as an active interstate. In fact, a *National Tribune* article written in celebration of America's increasing military presence on the Pacific describes the "stretch of waters" between the United States and East Asia as the "world's greatest ocean highway," "The Main Commercial Highway of the Future," and "The World's Greatest Thorofare" [*sic*], imbuing the agential hydroscape with cartographical and infrastructural promise.[21] To envision the deep waters of the Pacific as an economic "highway" born from American blueprints is to consider it an extension of the nation—or, at the very least, a vehicle for national profit. Given that America's earliest continental highways crossed the country from east to west, often originating in Washington, DC, or New York City, the author's description of the ocean-as-thoroughfare connects once-distant markets to the nation's political and financial centers. No longer out of reach, East Asia becomes a manageable journey down the liquid road, thanks, at least in part, to modern oceanic transport. Stressing the potential of these new economic highways, the author of the *National Tribune* article waxes poetic about what enhanced trade relations with Asia could mean for the global legacy of the United States:

> Instead of China, Japan and Hindustan being 15,000 miles away from the world's business center, they are only 7,000 miles across the deep blue sea from our western coast. The trade which in the past raised to splendor Ninevah, Babylon, Tyre, Athens, Rome, Venice and Genoa is now to flow across the Pacific under the American flag into our western seaports.

In this author's eyes, the Pacific Ocean is a promising future-space that links the United States, still a relatively young nation, to former oceanic empires.

But what of the elemental liveliness of the ocean itself? What role did saltwater play in both strengthening and possibly debilitating these imperio-managerial gestures? Even though the *National Tribune* article suggests that all the riches of the Pacific will "belong to the United States sooner or later," can the ocean really *belong* in a territorial sense? These are some of the questions we might ask of salt as it works its way into the so-called self-contained bodies of the turn of the century, forcing them to seek out ways to survive in dynamic times and "huge scales of measurement," as Noguchi describes the United States.[22]

THE SALT CURE

Given this chapter's focus on the animacy of salt(water) in the context of Progressive Era management regimes, it is important to consider the role that salt has played in shaping American economies and bodies, particularly as it moved from east to west in the decades leading up to the so-called closing of the frontier in the 1890s.[23] According to Mark Kurlansky, salt was one of the first industries in the United States, and its power as both an economic and ecological agent cannot be overestimated.[24] By 1860, American per-capita consumption of salt had surpassed that of Europeans, with major domestic saltworks operations existing in New York, Louisiana, and Virginia.

While salt in the western United States was plentiful, especially in the Great Salt Lake region where "the most spectacular salt strike in North America" could be found, it was often considered of lower culinary quality than that of New York or Liverpool salt. Even though mining companies would often proclaim that their salt—which covered "the ground like an immense incrustation of diamonds," as one company put it—rivaled "the best imported English salt" in terms of taste, many Westerners continued to ship their table salt from either the East or Britain throughout the nineteenth century.[25]

Given salt's use in the process of purifying ore, however, Western salt extraction and production were in high demand during the silver boom.[26] Located a convenient distance from several California silver strikes, the marshlands of the southern San Francisco Bay provided the perfect environment for producing evaporated sea salt, and Kurlansky notes that over a dozen salt companies operated in that region in the nineteenth century. The story of American salt production does not end in California, however. The Pacific Basin also played a vital role in the salt trade, and California imports of salt from China, Hawaii, and South America helped to build economic relations between the American West and the rest of the Pacific Basin. For example, Gregory Rosenthal, who examines the vast amount of labor involved in producing salt in Hawaii in the early twentieth century, notes that the salt trade "connected Hawaii with every corner of the Pacific world," solidifying deep and enduring ties among the United States, Polynesia, and East Asia, among other regional and governmental bodies.[27] Considering that processed salt traveled on saltwater as an imported and exported good—and that, aboard ship, various forms of the element would be used for cooking, fish and pelt preservation, as ballast, and even as a kind of currency among the crew—its manifold role as a good at sea helped to shape relations among Pacific Rim nations, revealing its agency as both energetic element and commodity.

While our critical inclination might be to overlook these embodied relations with salt(water), given salt's ubiquity in the Pacific world, historian Timothy LeCain argues that a scholarly focus on material "vitality" can be a radical act in that it enables scholars to wrest matter from a purely economic way of reading environments. Historians often dismiss the material environment, he says, "as little more than a passive reservoir of 'raw materials' or 'natural resources,'" an act that suppresses their vitality in the name of human primacy.[28] Given salt's wide circulation in human economies, it would be easy to reduce processed salt to a "good" or saltwater to an "economic highway," thus diluting what Jane Bennett refers to as the "thing-power" of the nonhuman world.[29]

However, as a pervasive actant in the Pacific, salt was never mere cargo or foodstuff, or an inert element of the landscape.[30] In fact, LeCain reminds us that "humans come alive or live *through*" matter in ways that sustain them or, at times, threaten the body's well-being (130).

For example, salt's invasive quality would certainly impact the individuals who engaged in salt labor throughout the Pacific world, including the Chinese salt workers in California who "wore wide sandals to avoid sinking into the thick layers of white crystal."[31] Recent research in occupational health alerts us to the ways that salt penetrates the bodies of salt workers, highlighting the fact that their frequent exposure to sodium chloride often leads to skin lesions and high blood pressure, among other issues.[32] Salt's "transcorporeal" nature poses a real threat to human bodies in its ability to dehydrate, weaken, and sometimes kill, depending on the intensity and duration of contact. Aboard the trans-Pacific steamer, Noguchi's Miss Morning Glory even compares her body to a paper bag being blown into a tempest, rendering the human body too weak a fortress to stave off the briny infiltration. However, in the late nineteenth century, many understood salt's strange ability to worm into the "jelly-like life" of humans, as London puts it, to be not only corrosive but also potentially restorative for both physiological and mental health—that is, if the dosage is correct and the right (white) body receives the *cure*.[33] London frequently emphasizes the whiteness of those like Van Weyden and Larsen who are capable of enduring the rough seas, ignoring almost completely the Native American, Chinese, and Eastern European crewmen who often worked aboard American sealing ships.[34]

The "salt cure," as it was so termed by certain turn-of-the-century medical professionals, emerged as a fad wherein patients suffering from ailments as diverse as neurasthenia, tuberculosis, gastroenteritis, and certain skin diseases could find relief via hypodermic injections of saltwater. In some dispensaries, "very pure sea water" "free from sediment and organic matter" was sterilized and injected into patients over the course of several sessions, the idea being that "salt water is the base of all organic life. All organisms exist originally in the sea, and blood is itself nothing but a modified sea water."[35] Therefore, adding seawater to the ocean-depleted bloodstream could revitalize one's health, practitioners believed. This procedure, which literally involved shooting small doses of the ocean into one's veins, parallels the powerful ways that salt enters and transforms the bodies of white men in London's writing, as the following section reveals. Similar to London, who believed the absorption, ingestion, and inhalation of saltwater might be reparative for "sissy" men like his narrator, Van Weyden, promoters of the salt cure also alleged that frequent saline injections could "stimulate and reinvigorate" the "sluggish nerve centres."[36] "The pure air of the sea and high mountains has a similar action through its bracing qualities," says Claire de Pratz in an article promoting the salt cure, comparing the effect of the injections to the influence of wild, stereotypically manly environments, such as the hydroscapes we see in *The Sea-Wolf*.[37] Noting that the body is "brought into training" by routine shots of saline, de Pratz argues that "weak" and "flabby" vascular systems are to blame for both mental and physical exhaustion; what the blood needs is a salty "flick of the whip," a violent metaphor that reflects how oceanic elements were meant to discipline and "restore" hard, manly, and utterly American bodies in the context of feminizing modernity.[38]

Dismissed as yet another health fad in an age of fads, the salt cure soon faded into the same obscurity as the sun-bath cure, the blue-glass cure, the rabbit cure, and various forms of hydrotherapy that involved everything from drinking copious amounts of water and wearing wet sheets to "taking the waters" at Saratoga Springs. (Even Darwin, who suffered from various afflictions with no known cause, was a water-cure devotee.) Health care professionals were quick to note that the French, who started performing saltwater injections before Americans, "are dying off at the usual rate, salt cure or no salt cure."[39] In its seeming failure to soldier up the body so that it may do battle with modernity, the salt cure, then, becomes an apt way of describing the often disappointing process of manager-making in the "bracing" environment of London's Pacific Ocean. Van Weyden's ultimate failure to remain a manly man at sea—after all, at the end of the novel he couples up with Maud Brewster and heads for the safety of land—reveals that London's salt cure is no less a letdown than the clinical version.

TENDERIZING MEN IN LONDON'S *THE SEA-WOLF*

William Dean Howells said that one of the aims of American literary realism was "to make us know people."[40] While Howells and other realists of the period developed diverse and descriptive ways of depicting regions and the characters who inhabited them, naturalist authors like London seemed less invested in "people" than in bodies. Despite both realism's and naturalism's focus on characters' struggles within "the social field," Jennifer Fleissner argues that naturalism, much more so than realism, "includes the body and sex in what it seems to order and classify."[41] In *Women, Compulsion, Modernity,* Fleissner notes that naturalist meditations on bodies and bodily processes were subjects from which their "genteel realist predecessors tended to shy away" (6). This is especially true for a novel like *The Sea-Wolf,* a work that paints a bloody, oily, and yeasty depiction of bodies, particularly ascendant *white* bodies, at sea. For the narrator, developing and maintaining a self-contained body requires hard work and vigilance, and this section explores how Pacific salt(water) simultaneously aids and threatens to undo that work. More often than not, the fragile, aging, sick, "sissy," or leaky bodies in the novel fail to remain *under control,* and management becomes particularly trying in the "orbit vastness" of the Pacific Ocean.

To further challenge survival at sea, the characters must contend with Wolf Larsen, the captain of a seal-hunting schooner who is described as the unpredictable ocean in human form. Though a dangerous individual whose relationship with Van Weyden often feels sexually predatory, Larsen represents the ideal "manly man" whom Van Weyden admires and, at times, emulates. Quite often, London makes disturbing decisions about the kinds of individuals who will or should survive in the new century, relying on what I call *the saltwater cure* to bring untrained male bodies to their full gendered and racial potential for the difficult work that lies ahead of them. Even though the saltwater cure seems to fail at transforming Van Weyden into a man (and manager) among men, London's refusal to end the novel on land leaves the Pacific's potential open for debate. In other words, Van Weyden has yet to arrive in the final chapter, leaving readers to wonder how his new body and mindset will be put to use on land, if at all.

In addition to describing *The Sea-Wolf* as "a sea novel," London scholars have argued that the book aims to "topple" the captains of industry, promote Darwinian evolutionary philosophy, and either reflect or undo the Progressive norms of gender and sexuality.[42] While London certainly seems to probe all of these issues in this naturalist novel, the book never extricates itself from the Pacific brine. The novel's wateriness makes it a prime study for considering how immersion in the oceanic spaces of literary naturalism contributes to the making of managerial bodies.[43] Even though London wrote several works set in the Pacific Basin, such as *The Cruise of the Dazzler* (1902), *The Cruise of the Snark* (1911), and *South Sea Tales* (1911), none rose to the same popularity as *The Sea-Wolf,* which sold forty thousand copies before it was even printed.

Published eleven years after his own experience working on a seal-hunting schooner off the coast of Japan, the novel takes place almost entirely at sea. In fact, out of thirty-nine chapters, only eight occur on land, an undiscovered seal rookery in the Bering Sea. Even the rookery, where Van Weyden and his shipwrecked partner, Maud, live for several months, is described as "damp and soggy" and "always buffeted by storm winds and lashed by the sea," painting it as an altogether saturated landscape (215). Otherwise, the plot largely unfolds aboard various types of seafaring vessels, some more modern than others: a ferry, Larsen's schooner, and a small seal-hunting boat. Numerous steam-powered ships also make an appearance, sometimes quite forcefully, as when a "Leviathan" strikes Van Weyden's ferry, sinking the vessel and sending everyone, including the erudite narrator, overboard. These moments of accidental immersion are not infrequent in *The Sea-Wolf*, marking the ocean as a highly dynamic, if not downright volatile, environment.

Despite Van Weyden's perpetual desires to reach land throughout the novel, be it the United States or Japan, the soggy tale both begins and ends at sea and thereby refuses to grant readers the security of steady ground. Even though Maud and Van Weyden, the happy couple, spy a US Revenue Cutter in the final scene and believe it will come to their aid, the novel ends before the rescue takes place, leaving them (and us) afloat in deep waters. All this water highlights "the dynamic forces of the sea as a sovereign and threatening environment to human agency and survival," says critic Regina Schober, who writes of nineteenth-century representations of oceanic spaces.[44] It is in these threatening international waters that London initiates Van Weyden's salt treatment.

Van Weyden's body falls short of naturalism's idealization of hard, toned physiques. Prior to his curing aboard the *Ghost*, his body was "small and soft" as a result of his "dusty existence in the city" (32, 1). "I was not strong," Van Weyden says.

> The doctors had always said that I had a remarkable constitution, but I had never developed it or my body through exercise. My muscles were small and soft, like a woman's, or so the doctors had said time and again in the course of their attempts to persuade me to go in for physical culture fads. But I had preferred to use my head, rather than my body; and here I was, in no fit condition for the rough life in prospect. (32)

What begins as a crisis of self-management, exemplified by Van Weyden's refusal to comply with his doctors' orders, develops into London's salty experiment. As a genteel character who "preferred to use my head" rather than work on his abs, Van Weyden's feminized body is in need of a violent remedy, the novel argues. Stranded on a ship in the middle of the Pacific, Van Weyden, whom Larsen renames Hump, is forced to encounter what Seltzer calls the "surrogate frontier" of his own body. "The closing of the frontier," Seltzer notes, "indicated a . . . relocation of the making of Americans: a relocation of the topography of masculinity to the surrogate frontier of the natural body."[45] Hump's untrained, wilderness-of-a-body requires taming—but, oddly, this "taming" is meant to make him into more of a man, according to the logic of the "surrogate frontier."

While this devotion to managerial domestication might seem like a paradox for an author so often associated with "the wild," London's heroes, I argue, are not so much wild themselves as they are capable of using their Progressive logic to survive *in* or adapt *to* the wild. Additionally, the taming or hardening process, as Seltzer attests, will make Van Weyden more wholly American. (The idealized Nordic body of Wolf Larsen, the ship's captain, is frequently described as a not-too-rugged, not-too-tamed mountainous geography, perhaps providing Van Weyden with a map for his own corporeal expedition.) Seltzer's alignment of solid, masculine bodies with citizenship injects a sense of patriotic duty into the human and environmental brutality Van Weyden experiences in the novel. To be an American man, one must endure, even when his own body seems too hard to handle.

Before his ferry collides with a ship in the Pacific's "desolate foaming waves" (26), Van Weyden observes how pleasant it is to *not* be a manager-type. Unlike captains and sailors who labor daily in the ocean's unending waves, Van Weyden rejoices in the "division of labor which made it unnecessary for me to study fogs, winds, tides, and navigation" (1). As a literary critic, or a man with a "book-congealed mind" who lives a "dusty existence in the city," Van Weyden believes he exists as a being far removed from the Pacific's elemental chaos; as a result, a close study of the ocean's particularities is not necessary for this nonmanager.[46]

Lost in poetic reverie aboard the ferry, he instead "fell to dwelling upon the romance of the fog," viewing the atmosphere not as an entity to bear, as literary naturalists would have it, but as a source of artistic inspiration (1). From the dry deck of the ferry, which should soon deliver Van Weyden, the Romantic, safe and sound to his home in San Francisco, the academic perceives the Pacific as an abstract thing, one that elicits a chain of fanciful metaphors and similes, such as when he describes the fog as "a gray shadow of infinite mystery, brooding over the whirling speck of earth" (3). The narrator's reimagining of Earth as a mere "whirling speck" emphasizes his distance from the planet and its murky elements; like a Google satellite, his narrative eye peers down at the globe from space, a perspective far different from Wolf Larsen's "sea eye."[47] Prior to his extended exposure to salt on Larsen's *Ghost*, the separate-though-stirring oceanic environment is always *like* something else for Van Weyden. He never has to make direct contact with it even though he lives in a coastal region and frequently travels across the San Francisco Bay by ferry to visit a friend. As both a hazy concept ("gray shadow of infinite mystery") and a "brooding," personified force, atmospheric matter momentarily inspires but does not touch the body of the narrator, keeping him at what seems a secure distance from the environment. In other words, the fog, the breeze, emerge not as *literal materialities* but as *literary material* that the narrator conjures from the elevated platform of the ferry's deck, and London seems critical of this supposed detachment from all things elemental. If *The Sea-Wolf*, as Lee Clark Mitchell argues, privileges "selfhood as a principle of action, not of contemplation," then Van-Weyden-the-intellectual exists as an incomplete figure in the opening chapters of the novel, according to London's hard, masculinist logic.[48]

However, the tide of the narrator's life shifts when he nearly drowns following the sinking of the ferry. This is a critical scene in the novel, as it catapults Van Weyden into not only the "stinging" waters but also the turbulent world of Wolf Larsen. In *Male Call*, Jonathan Auerbach compellingly claims that the narrator's drowning "clearly represents a birth trauma" that allows him to be reborn as a "man among men" on the *Ghost* ship.[49] However, given *The Sea-Wolf*'s ecomaterial preoccupations, as well as London's devotion to environmental exposure, one could also read the drowning as a literal kind of brining or tenderizing that fortifies Van Weyden's unfit body. As a youth, London actually worked long hours stuffing pickles into jars at a cannery and must have witnessed firsthand how briny solutions could warp and thicken the skin of factory workers.[50] While "tenderizing," at first, seems to imply a softening of the flesh, it also involves the taking-in of rock in liquid form. In other words, tenderized bodies are at once reinforced *and* made flexible, representing the ideal "natural" body of the Progressive Era manager: not too hard, which could develop into brutishness, and not too soft, which implies overcivilization.

In contrast to London's vision of a manly-but-malleable approach to management, the author often criticized China for what he considered its "set," "crystalized," and stifling managerial style, believing that the country's so-called obsession with preserving the past at all costs kept it from innovating and moving forward.[51] American management, on the other hand, should be more elastic, he believed, which would prevent it from suffering the same kind of stasis as did the Chinese. London's durable but radically transformable management ethos translates to the bodies we witness in the pages of *The Sea-Wolf*. When "soft," porous bodies like that of Van Weyden become saturated by the brine, salt begins to transform them from the inside out, strengthening their constitutions while also allowing them to amphibiously adapt to new territories, new futures. For example, nearly halfway through his adventure, Van Weyden observes that his "muscles are growing harder and increasing in size," while his hands "have a parboiled appearance" (79). Life at sea affords Van Weyden a firmer body and a thicker skin, making him more capable of weathering the real and metaphorical waters of the new century.

It might seem odd that liquid, which London and other naturalists often linked to the apparent sponginess of women's bodies, arises as a masculinizing agent in the novel.[52] Unlike bodies of fresh water, which are usually less abrasive to human bodies, the acridity and invasiveness of salt in oceanic water operates as an apt tool for London's bodybuilding project. Drownings and near drownings are common occurrences in the novel, be they accidental or purposeful acts of punishment, and on occasion the dead bodies of humans and animals are tossed into the sea to be embalmed. Van Weyden almost dies by drowning four times "by some freak of waters," but each time he makes it out alive—and more thoroughly cured (124). When he first "plunged into it," Van Weyden notes, "The water was cold—so cold that it was painful." The element's ability to inflict pain continues, nearly killing the man whose "small" body doctors liken to that of a woman:

> The pang . . . was as quick and sharp as that of fire. It bit to the marrow. It was like the grip of death. I gasped with the anguish and shock of it, filling my lungs before the life-preserver popped me to the surface. The taste of salt was strong in my mouth, and I was strangling with the acrid stuff in my throat and lungs.

Van Weyden's first plunge into saltwater initiates a series of dermatological openings, allowing the substance to enter his body and begin the transformation. He notes that the water "bites," "pangs," and burns, terms that denote violent acts of aggression that, with time, will seal the cracks of his skin, shaping him into a more buoyant, resilient form so that he may take on the forces of modernity without the need of a life-preserver. In addition to seeping into the skin, saltwater invades his mouth, throat, and lungs, radically flooding the body and momentarily overcoming the voice and breath. In fact, the narrator goes on to say that the waves "continually broke over me and into my mouth sending me off into more strangling paroxysms" (7). Depicted as an untamed frontier space, the Pacific does not merely tingle the surface of the narrator's American body; it enters the vital interior, thus changing Van Weyden by allowing him to embody a small dose of its wilds.

As these violent immersions continue and Van Weyden takes more water into his body, he seems to gain more control over the Pacific's immense power. For example, in the early drownings, the ocean exhibits almost complete agency at the level of the sentence even when its waves are "small," as the narrator describes them. Van Weyden stresses that the water relentlessly "breaks" and "strangles," and all the while the "soft" man, aided by a flotation device, bobs helplessly in its waves like an untethered buoy. While the ocean's force does not lessen in Van Weyden's later immersions— on the contrary, it seems to intensify, striking "stunning blows . . . nowhere in particular yet everywhere"—our manager-in-training becomes somewhat amphibious and more capable, thus allowing him to breathe underwater (124). "Crushed" under water during the third near-drowning, and unable to hold his breath, Van Weyden tells readers, "I breathed the stinging salt water into my lungs," an act that stresses his development as one who instinctively acts before he thinks (124). Even though the water "stings," reminding us of its salinity, Van Weyden *chooses* to take it in via breath. At this moment, we begin to observe saltwater inspiring the narrator in a managerial direction, for just as soon as he takes in the water, thoughts of progress flood his being: "But through it all I clung to the one idea—*I must get the jib backed over to windward*. I had no fear of death. I had no doubt but that I should come through somehow" (124).

Though still a ruthless substance, saltwater's corrective potential materializes in this scene, as Van Weyden, the maritime manager, concentrates on mechanical repair at the moment his body is taxed the most. Management, which understands itself as the vehicle of the future tense, must operate as though its own death were not possible. When Van Weyden assertively states, "I had no doubt but that I should come through somehow," he is already imagining himself in the future-Pacific, and his presence there grants him a kind of possession over the oceanic environment. Just as a writer of the *National Tribune* lays rhetorical claim to the Pacific when he says, "it is all destined to belong to the United States sooner or later," Van Weyden's confidence that he will "come through"—by which he means he will still be there, manly and undead—highlights his emergence as a man of action fit for the project of imperial expansion.

In addition to achieving transformation by drinking Pacific saltwater, Van Weyden had to shed his old, "flabby" skin to make way for a new, more durable shell. Skin exists as a problem in the novel, as it constantly threatens to erupt, erode, and reveal one's ranking in the Pacific world's racial hierarchy. London's own skin suffered badly from painful yaws while he was voyaging in the South Seas, and it was only when he returned to "the wholesome California climate, [that] my silvery skin vanished," he says.[53] For Van Weyden, exfoliation is a necessary step to attaining manly embodiment on the *Ghost*, and salt operates as the magic ingredient for such a procedure. Essentially, Van Weyden must slough off his outer layer of skin so that a newer—and whiter—form can emerge. After the *Ghost* rescues Van Weyden following the sinking of the ferry, the narrator awakens to the sensation of "being dragged over rasping sands": "The rasping, scorching sands were a man's hard hands chafing my naked chest," he says as a member of Larsen's crew attempts to revive him. "I squirmed under the pain of it. . . . My chest was raw and red, and I could see tiny blood globules starting through the torn and inflamed cuticle" (9). Unaccustomed to such roughness (which sounds strangely sexual), Van Weyden's salt-coated skin reddens and bleeds from the friction, and Mugridge even remarks that Johnson had "bloomin' well rubbed all the gent's skin orf" (9). For several pages following this initial skinning, Van Weyden references his "raw and bleeding" chest that "creeps and crawls" when he attempts to put on a shirt (10, 11). Much to the narrator's dismay, the only shirt available to wear smells sour from "being put aw'y wet" (11). Hardened by salt and reeking of mildew, the wool shirt operates as a host for lively oceanic elements—elements that will surely enter Van Weyden via his open sores, thus contributing to his curing. This radical encounter between the human body and salt demonstrates the mechanism by which Van Weyden's skin, as a "mediating membrane," takes in the world around him.[54] It is only a matter of time before Van Weyden's chest will scab, dry, and harden from the coarse treatment, providing him with a barrier to the feminizing effects of land-based modernity.

The use of salt to toughen manly skin was not uncommon at the turn of the century, particularly with athletes. In fact, when James J. Jeffries came out of retirement at London's urging to reclaim the heavyweight boxing title from Jack Johnson, he looked to salt for a physical and racial boost. Since Johnson was the first black heavyweight champion, the stakes were high for Jeffries, known in the boxing world as "The Great White Hope." According to Wayne Rozen, Jeffries, who had fallen out of shape in retirement, "soaked his hands and face in brine to toughen up the skin and refused showers because he thought they 'robbed oil food from the skin.'"[55] Jeffries's belief that his (white) skin was the gateway to his strength—or, moreover, that his skin *was* his strength—reflects a growing belief in the Progressive Era that one's body was "self-contained" rather than in mutual relation with the environment; more than just tissue, "skin protected a body from its surroundings," Progressives believed.[56] In *Inescapable Ecologies*, environmental historian Linda Nash says that "for the modern body, 'health' . . . implies both purity and the ability to fend off harmful organisms and substances," and that at the turn of the century medical professionals began to think about the body as "closed off," or in opposition, to the larger environment.[57] For both Jeffries and London, entering the athletic and oceanic arenas to face off with their racial "menaces" would elicit anxieties about the preservation of tough white skin.[58] If the skin is "more like a lydy's than any I know of," which is how Mugridge describes Van Weyden's uncured skin, then, according to the logic of Progressive management, contaminating forces might try to invade (11). In order to prevent the infiltration of so-called racial, gendered, and environmental hazards, Jeffries and Van Weyden paradoxically invite the radical absorption of salt into the body.

Achieving hardness, it seems, requires momentary sponginess so that (hopefully) beneficial substances may enter. If a man were not vigilant, however, harmful substances might find their way into the small, vulnerable openings. In other words, white preservation required strict self-regulation of one's own body, meaning a man had to be able to decipher the harmful from the helpful; otherwise, he could put himself at risk of losing both bodily and territorial governance. Before developing the keen eye of the manager, Van Weyden asks if he, too, was "being tainted by my environment," aligning the "callousness" of the nonwhite bodies aboard the *Ghost* with threatening environmental impurity (50). As the guardian of both health and cultural survival, skin carried a lot of responsibility at the turn of the century, and London viewed white skin as particularly vulnerable to invasive forces: "We of the white race are the survivors and the descendants of the thousands of generations of survivors in the war with the micro-organisms," he says in *The Cruise of the Snark*. "Whenever one of us was born with a constitution particularly receptive to these minute enemies, such a one promptly died."[59]

Since "The Great White" Jeffries lost to Johnson in the fifteenth round, it seems that salt, on its own, is not enough to safeguard white supremacy. Even if salted skin could not save Jeffries, however, the mineral *was* quite skillful at preserving the skins of seals aboard the *Ghost*. Ultimately, however, skinning and salting sealskins actually interferes with London's project of building rugged, capable men and does not seem to amplify the management project when we take the broad view. After all, Larsen tells us that after the skins are fully processed on land, they are then manufactured into handbags and other accessories for women in London. While the salting down of Van Weyden's body seems to elevate his status to what Gail Bederman refers to as the "natural man," a vision of turn-of-the-century masculinity that combined "racial supremacy with powerful manhood," the skinning and salting of seal bodies to be sold in the global marketplace carries civilizing potential.[60] Given the violence inherent in hunting and skinning, as depicted in *The Sea-Wolf*, it at first seems like sealing would enable masculine ascendance. It has all the ingredients:

> After a good day's killing I have seen our decks covered with hides and bodies, slippery with fat and blood, the scuppers running red; masts, ropes, and rails spattered with the sanguinary color; and the men, like butchers, plying their trade, naked and red of arm and hand, hard at work with ripping and flensing-knives, removing the skins from the pretty sea-creature they had killed. (117–18)

The narrator's thrill at recalling the men, all of whom are "*hard* at work" as one body skinning the agile sea creatures, shines through in this panting sentence. Unable to stop and catch his breath, Van Weyden uses two semicolons to stream together the bloody imagery, and the sentence both begins and ends with a reference to "killing." He does not want readers to forget that men—men on the Pacific, like him—slaughtered the "pretty" and, therefore, feminine animals.[61] But even the saltiest of men cannot manage their way out of capitalism's feminizing effects, as the hunting scenes suggest. This is especially true when we consider the devastating economic and environmental implications of exploiting the bodies of marine animals. At the turn of the century, overhunting in Pacific waters led to the near extinction of fur seals, not to mention the death of the so-called manly seal-hunting industry.[62] In other words, the better the hunters became at killing seals, the fewer seals there would be to hunt. Improvement, in the Progressive sense, did not always render lasting economic success, nor could it prevent ecological depredation in the Pacific, as elsewhere.

INESCAPABLE ATMOSPHERES

Near the end of the novel, after Hump and Maud make a break for land and wind up on a yet undiscovered seal rookery in the Bering Sea, the narrator emerges as a man with "executive ability" capable of managing in the "elemental strife" (122, 127). Broken-down boats, a lack of food, and tumultuous storms are no match for Hump, who had endured "prolonged soaking" in the Pacific's corrective waters (30). Faced with near insurmountable obstacles, such as how to repair the wrecked schooner still occupied by the increasingly enervating captain, Wolf Larsen, Van Weyden assumes the role of a Progressive Era manager, one whose investment in perpetual improvement will not allow him to rest until the job is done—and, as it is with management, the job is never quite done. For example, when Maud and Van Weyden realize that Wolf has destroyed the throat-halyards of their escape vessel with shears, Maud says to Van Weyden, "You will have to begin over again," to which he responds, "I shall do nothing but begin over again" (248).

The beached schooner, which is caught in a cycle of repair and disrepair in the final chapters, becomes Van Weyden's principal management problem. "Suffering from thirst," his lips "dry and cracked," and thoroughly salt-cured, he fixes the boat again, and again, and again, and with each fix he finds he has developed a new skill (253). The word "again," which is used twice in the conversation cited above, appears nearly 150 times throughout the novel, most frequently in the chapters set on the rookery, or what I refer to as the "management chapters." The narrator's reliance on the adverb "again" to modify action in these scenes is not insignificant, especially since recursiveness, trial and error, and other Progressive management ideals allow Van Weyden to "master" the "gray primordial vastness" of the Pacific (7). Since London's own "flawed" sailboat, the *Snark*, "broke down faster than she could be repaired," the author would be familiar with these slow, steady, and frequently disappointing engagements with technological improvements while at sea.[63] For him, when a man oversees management's ongoingness—especially when he experiences moments of success in the process, such as finally setting sail in a once broken boat—not only does he become more of a man, but he becomes a *white* man, one who is worth his salt. "Commend me on the white race when it comes to grit and surviving," London says after enduring many trials in the *Snark*.[64] Whiteness, for London, is a product not only of skin color but, more importantly, of one's propensity to endure in challenging environmental circumstances.

As soon as Van Weyden takes the proverbial reins of the newly repaired *Ghost*, he experiences not just bodily change but an atmospheric change as well. This shift in atmospheric pressure, I contend, reflects the material impact of American expansionism on oceanic environments. In the first half of the novel, the narrator describes the air as altogether salty, moist, and thick, and quite often it prevents men from being able to orient and collect themselves. "Briny wind" (134) burns Maud's face, "salt spray" (26) roughens Van Weyden's skin, "crystal globules" (197) of dew dampen one's hair, and fog "veils and hides us in its dense, wet gauze" (181). The *hyperobjective* Pacific Ocean does not end where the waves peak, that undulating surface; instead, oceanic materialities are always already airborne, preventing bodies from extricating themselves from their viscosity.[65] As Timothy Morton says of hyperobjects, be they deserts, oceans, or global warming, "we are inside them. Like Jonah in the Whale" (20). With perpetually wet hair, clothes, and skin, Van Weyden cannot get outside of the pervasive brine, which is everywhere—and yet nowhere in particular.

Change is not just in the air; change *is* the air, and as Maud's nostrils "quiver to the rush and bite of the fresh salt air," London's conception of the Pacific as a place for men to go and become men is challenged (273). After all, Maud is very much the manager-type, and she redirects the course of Van Weyden's life on the Pacific. Not only does Van Weyden's attraction for Maud hold sway over his emotions—"you managed me with your eyes, commanded me with them," he says—but Maud is also instrumental in helping Van Weyden fulfill various tasks necessary for their survival, including landing the boat on the rookery, rebuilding the schooner, clubbing seals for food, and finding shelter (158). What's more, while held captive on the *Ghost*, she "guides the conversation" and softens Larsen's rage with poetry, which dramatically attenuates the vessel's brutal, manly atmosphere (189). Maud's ability to control the climate aboard the *Ghost* sends Wolf "quite out of himself" and leaves Van Weyden in "a half-daze," almost as if the men were under the spell of a hallucinogenic vapor (189). At one point the narrator even notes that the crew struggled to "prevent the rescued woman from being spilled out," granting her a liquid agency similar to that of saltwater (134). Instead of reading Maud's palpable presence as a threat, Van Weyden, the newly made manager, comes to perceive his relationship with her as a "comradeship," meaning certain kinds of women—those willing to take on the "dirt and weather-beat" like a man—could both improve *and* find improvement in the briny atmosphere (272). This, of course, threatens London's all-male utopia, but perhaps Maud's ability to harden and endure—both of which are manly traits—make her a near-man among men, similar to Molly in *The Virginian* and Irene in *The River*. Unlike London's *The Call of the Wild*, wherein both women and female dogs routinely meet their death in the Northland's forbidding environment, *The Sea-Wolf* carves out a space for women like Maud who have both intelligence and muscle. London frequently sailed the Pacific with his wife, Charmian, and in *The Cruise of the Snark* he even notes that she fell ill far less than he, proving her ability to endure "manly" adventures. Even in the middle of the Pacific Ocean, whiteness can adapt, endure, and, with luck, reproduce, London seems to argue—and Maud's presence especially provides hope for the latter.

Together, Maud and Van Weyden's near-electric presence elicits atmospheric changes in the Pacific, especially when the pair are at their most energized and industrious. Thinking he has exerted a "mastery over matter," which is how the narrator refers to his technical achievements in the Pacific, Van Weyden transforms the air around his vessel from "briny" to "businesslike," representing the environmental impacts of Anglo-American imperialism even in landless, oceanic spaces. For example, prior to disembarking from the rookery on the newly mended *Ghost*, the narrator says, "We were very comfortable, and the inadequate shears, with the foremast suspended from them, gave a businesslike air to the schooner and a promise of departure" (259). The mere presence of the tool with which Van Weyden reconstructs the vessel alters the surrounding climate, revealing the material impacts of Progressivism on so-called frontier ecologies. Like weather, the schooner's "business-like atmosphere" spreads outward and floods the air with its economic "promises." In Noguchi's autobiography, *The Story of Yone Noguchi*, he similarly refers to "the smell of commerce" in the coastal United States and recalls its signature "odor" for readers: "The Americans carry their business atmosphere with them wherever they go. . . . In their footsteps always they leave behind the unagreeable smell of commerce; they are like ones who scatter around some ill odour."[66] For both London and Noguchi, the American economy pervades the air as a tangible vapor, and when humans breathe it in, it has the potential to either enliven (London) or, as the next section highlights, sicken (Noguchi).

Echoing these authors' comparisons of capitalism to an invasive atmospheric materiality, theorist Mark Fisher also describes capitalism's global reach as a "pervasive atmosphere," imbuing it with a humid *thinginess* similar to Pacific fog. Capitalist realism, he says, is "like a pervasive atmosphere, conditioning not only the production of culture but also the regulation of work and education, and acting as a kind of invisible barrier constraining thought and action."[67] Not only does capitalism's atmosphere "constrain," however, as Fisher suggests; for those at the top, like Van Weyden, it induces action and, when inhaled, enthuses. After all, the "businesslike atmosphere" spurs Van Weyden into a building frenzy, prompting him to engineer a way out of oceanic isolation. As a new member of the modern manager class, the narrator can weather capitalism's storm, so to speak—at least for now.

One might think that the final scenes in the novel reveal management's "mastery over matter"—that the happy couple, who disembark for Japan only to encounter a US revenue cutter, will soon be rescued and delivered to their country of origin. Now thoroughly cured, their hands will never be clean again, Maud says almost proudly, and one wonders what those hands will build, discipline, or, in general, transform once the pair reaches the so-called firm ground of California. However, Wolf Larsen— the brutal captain who tormented Van Weyden to the very end— does not yet seem quite dead, casting doubt on the longevity of the comrades' newfound power. Unmanageable Larsen is described throughout the novel in oceanic terms, and it seems possible that Van Weyden's final act of tossing Larsen's half-dead body into the sea could possibly revive the raging captain. Larsen, whose eyes were blue "as the sea" (73) and whose words, like saltwater, carried "a sting" (114), was "as contrary as air currents or water currents" (64), Van Weyden says. Even more remarkable is that saltwater frequently flows freely from Larsen's body. In one scene, we witness Larsen's "sinewy hand, dripping with water," grabbing at the rail of the schooner. "The sea-water was streaming from him," the narrator observes with a combination of awe and fright. "It made little audible gurgles which distracted me" (100). As a man who creates his own "air currents" and generates "squalls" when he is out to seek revenge, it comes as no surprise that Van Weyden struggles so completely to quell the salty, rebellious agent that is Wolf Larsen. Suspended in the brine as a pickle of a man, Wolf "still lives," Van Weyden tells us, revealing how naturalism preserves the dead bodies of the frontier for future cultural consumption. Never quite dead, Wolf continues agitating the managerial apparatus and, in doing so, keeps it alive.

In a 1904 *Guardian* review of *The Sea-Wolf,* W. Heinemann praises the "freshness and vivacity" of London's sea novel and offers a caution to the author in the final paragraph: *do not become too refined.*[68] What so pleases Heinemann about London's novel is its "vigour that overpowers distinction," meaning he appreciates that the work devotes itself to raw action over stylistic and technical precision. Were London to overthink the literariness of his craft rather than to merely draw from his "natural force" as both a man and a writer, he would achieve success and "safety," surely, but his work would lose its edge, Heinemann argues. In contrast to London's apparent refusal to play it safe in his writing, according to Heinemann, safety does arrive to Van Weyden and Maud in the form of the US revenue cutter, and the narrator appears reluctant to view the modern, governmental steamship as a rescue. "'We are saved,' I said soberly and solemnly. And then, in an exuberance of joy, 'I hardly know whether to be glad or not'" (277). He and Maud then kiss for the first time, after which they call each other "my man" and "my woman," representing the heteronormative pressures of the cutter's atmosphere on the managers' bodies. When the nation returns, comrades transmute into couples, ocean dissolves into sentimental backdrop, and all that is liquid and generative hardens into solid forms. With seeming gladness, Maud and Van Weyden—who, time and again throughout their journey, had rescued themselves—now wait to be rescued "from ourselves," marking the Pacific as the location of brief adventure. The cutter/nation seems to pull the two wayward bodies into its orbit, leaving Maud and Van Weyden with little else to manage— for now, at least. Everyone, after all, must return home sooner or later, the novel suggests, and perhaps their new skills will aid them when back on solid ground.

While London's sentimental conclusion seems contradictory to his naturalist aims, the final rescue also reveals the strange temporality of the management project. A man(ager) could not remain at sea for long lest he be preserved by saltwater. In other words, after one "masters" the Pacific, as Van Weyden believes he has done, what more is there to do there? What challenges would remain if one were to stay? If the salty quest toward mastery is what makes a man a man(ager), then it seems manliness cannot survive beyond "possession," be it individual or governmental. Van Weyden's oceanic adventure can only last for so long in the open sea before the nation comes looking for him, pulling him back to land, his familiar habits, and his former occupation: writing. After all, since *The Sea-Wolf* is written in the form of a first-person recollection of past events, the so-called wild Pacific is only accessible to him via the medium of his pen.

Mitchell also argues that "Hump is unable to manage a clear account of his time at sea," as evidenced by the odd shifts in tense and point of view that occur throughout the work, causing us to doubt whether Van Weyden was able to put his administrative skills to any use back on land.[69] His failure to control his own story emerges in other places as well. For example, after a lengthy and quite lusty description of Wolf's "intense and masculine" eyes, Van Weyden struggles to regain control of the storyline and, in haste, interjects the transitional phrase, "But to return . . ." (18). As if trying to collect himself, he then picks up where he left off. Whereas at sea Van Weyden's fruitful "agains" propelled the young manager into salty futurities, back on land he spends his time returning to the past—again, and again, and again—a reiterative and near compulsive act that works to preserve his body as a relic in the literary brine.

In *Resisting Regionalism: Gender and Naturalism in American Fiction, 1885–1915*, Donna Campbell says that local color authors celebrate "activities of preserving and storytelling" (41). Such activities might include canning food, holding on to family mementos, and other acts that "preserve the present for the future" (41). Even though London might cringe at the thought of being compared to local color authors, his character, Van Weyden, also writes to preserve the memory of his manly adventure at sea. Since salt is, itself, a preservative—even if it might dry the life and moisture out of the thing it is meant to save—his writing becomes a kind of salt substitute, but one that never quite tastes like the real thing.[70]

For London, Noguchi, Stoddard, and others who traversed the Pacific Ocean at the turn of the century, remaining at sea was never the ultimate aim. This is especially true for Noguchi, who, as the next section explores, was a "thorough sea-hater."[71] Land always beckons for both London and Noguchi, and characters in both authors' works can often be found yearningly peering back at the land from which they first set sail. While London spent much of his life on the Pacific as a sealer, oyster farmer, island hopper, journalist, and novelist, he always returned home to California. In *Jack London: A Writer's Fight for a Better America*, Cecilia Tichi even says that from his sailboat in "the middle of the Pacific," London drafted memos of ranch advice to mail to the caretakers of his ranch in Glen Ellen, a managerial act that connects his peregrinating body back to the land he loved so dearly.[72] These memos highlight that even when at sea, London was never landless—his mail, his thoughts, crossed the Pacific like bowlines, securing him to national ground. So to what end was all that curing? Even though Stoddard states that the experience of traveling in the South Seas "will, in all human probability, effect a permanent cure," he goes on to say that the cure becomes largely ineffectual once a man returns home. "You can then settle down and be as stupid as the great majority. I did it."[73]

• • •

To conclude this discussion of *The Sea-Wolf*, it is important to offer a brief reflection on the absence in it of Japanese characters—and to contemplate that absence in the context of turn-of-the-century American expansionism. After all, Noguchi's writing draws attention to the thriving Japanese community in California, as well as Americans' intense interest in Japanese literature, art, and landscaping in the 1910s. It would seem probable, then, that Van Weyden might run into Japanese oceangoers during his time at sea, especially since Japan plays such a central role in the novel—and in America's cultural and economic life in general. London's novel reads Japan as a distant resource. The sealers go to the Japanese coast to hunt, and before Larsen "captures" Maud, her intentions were to journey to Japan, by doctor's orders, to improve her health. As a destination for many characters, the Japanese coast is visible on the horizon on at least three occasions, but the plot never arrives there.[74] What's more, given the importance of sealing to Japan's economy at the turn of the century, Japanese hunters never materialize in *The Sea-Wolf*, painting the Pacific Ocean as a space wholly populated or possessed by Americans and Europeans of various social and economic classes.

Similarly, in *The Cruise of the Snark*, London relegates the Japanese to the hazy background despite the significant role at least two Japanese men played in making his journey happen. Wada and Nakata, who work as the cook and cabin-boy, respectively, comprise two of the ketch's five crew members, but London does not read their domestic work as equal to the hard, manly labor of keeping the boat afloat:

> There will be no crew. Or, rather, Charmian, Roscoe, and I are the crew. We are going to do the thing with our own hands. With our own hands we're going to circumnavigate the globe. . . . Of course there will be a cook and cabin-boy. Why should we stew over a stove, wash dishes, and set the table? We could stay on land if we wanted to do those things. Besides, we've got to stand watch and work the ship.[75]

London refuses to view Wada and Nakata as necessary crew members—or as crew members at all—despite the fact that they fulfill very important domestic roles on the *Snark*. By suggesting that he, his wife, Charmian, and Roscoe will "do the thing with our own hands," London defines the adventure as an experiment in white mastery, rendering nearly invisible the hands that wash his dishes, dress his wounds, and provide him with sustenance. While Noguchi's fictional diarist in *The American Diary of a Japanese Girl* is far from a servant—in fact, she is the wealthy, aristocratic niece of a Japanese mining executive—her presence in the Pacific, in addition to the numerous Japanese citizens and immigrants she meets in coastal California, reveals that the ocean *west of the West*, though vast, is far from the unpeopled frontier London imagines in his work.

"ON THE OPEN DECK, FACING JAPAN": NOGUCHI AS PACIFIC RIM WRITER

Written in English like most of his published works, Noguchi's *The American Diary of a Japanese Girl* is loosely based on the author's own experiences crossing the Pacific in 1893 to become a writer in the United States, which he also writes about nearly fifteen years later in his autobiographical work, *The Story of Yone Noguchi* (1915). Some critics contend that Noguchi transposed his own story onto a female protagonist in *Diary* to appeal to American curiosities during the rise of *Japonisme*, "a form of Orientalism that specifically focused on Japan as an aesthetic fetish."[76] While this interpretation is certainly persuasive, the remaining sections of this chapter argue that Noguchi's narrator does more than express "fantastic notions of Japanese femininity" for readers on the other side of the Pacific.[77] Instead, Miss Morning Glory—an upper-class, high-maintenance Nippon woman—offers Noguchi the opportunity to critique Western imperialism and Progressive Era management, especially given America's influence on the modernization of Japan at the turn of the century.[78] Due to Miss Morning Glory's social and economic status in Japan, she is at first intensely fixated on her appearance—and for good reason; early in the narrative she informs readers that cultural authorities regularly police women's hair and fashion in Japan, and so her body requires constant upkeep. Therefore, when Noguchi tells his transoceanic story through the voice of a carefully managed woman, it becomes all the more dramatic when the narrator *lets herself go* in the United States.

Similar to the transformations we witnessed in *The Sea-Wolf*, the Pacific Ocean initiates what I consider a productive loosening in Miss Morning Glory. But unlike Van Weyden, who seems to harden and achieve an industrious assertiveness when "cured" by saltwater, Noguchi's narrator becomes hopelessly seasick while at sea, ultimately providing her with an opportunity to manage (in) California's social and environmental landscape with an aimless though productive drift. In the final section, I argue that the diarist's "queasiness in the world," a queer, disorienting way of *being-in* modernism's managed life, permeates the structure of *Diary* and allows us to imagine modes of environmental management that are perhaps more liquid and affiliative than scientific management's strictures often permit.[79]

Considered both the first Japanese American novel "if we take a broad view of Japanese American literature" and "one of Asia America's earliest queer texts," *Diary* never achieved much success in the United States at the time of its publication.[80] Even though some critics credit Noguchi for helping to popularize the haiku in the West and suggest he may have prefigured the writers of the Beat Generation, Noguchi is not a household name in American literary criticism.[81] Nor is he American in the legal sense, which might be why scholars who focus on national literatures often struggle to incorporate Noguchi into their critical scope. Even though Noguchi lived and worked in the United States for over eleven years and wrote most of his poetry, essays, and fiction in English, including a collection of Romantic-styled poems inspired by Yosemite National Park, critics have been reluctant to read his work as American literature.[82] Turn-of-the-century Americans' disturbing views of the Japanese, who many believed "would always remain unassimilable" in their perceived racial difference, might be partly to blame for this hesitation to place Noguchi's works in an American canon.[83] Similarly, Edward Marx informs us that "Japanese critics, like their U.S. counterparts, tend to regard Noguchi as an essentially foreign writer," leaving him to float somewhere in undefined literary waters.

This challenge to classify Noguchi's writing as American or Japanese—or something else—makes him such a fitting figure for this project preoccupied with moments of managerial and categorical collapse. Unlike London, whom critics deem an American writer, a California writer, an Alaska writer, and even a Pacific Rim writer, Noguchi, who did the bulk of his writing in or about California and was heavily influenced by America's "New Woman" novel, usually falls outside of the register of both American literature and its regional subsets.[84] Commenting on Noguchi's "exclusion from the ranks of acclaimed Asian American writers" due, at least in part, to what was only his temporary stay in the United States, Amy Sueyoshi states that critics, not knowing where to place the writer, often describe him as a "traveling Japanese national rather than a Japanese American."[85] London, also an avid traveler, lays easy claim to diverse literary geographies as a white American author. Noguchi, on the other hand, remains untethered, drifting offshore.

In his historical overview of Noguchi's career, Marx chooses to define Noguchi as an "unsettling Japanese American," or one who "did not, in most cases, settle in America."[86] Works by writers in this cultural category "may help unsettle some restrictive conceptions of Japanese Americans created by subsequent generations," Marx adds.[87] The "unsettling Japanese American" operates as a useful category for reading Noguchi's work since it fuses his two national identities. However, the term's emphasis on national *land* tends to overlook the vast oceanic space that simultaneously connects and separates the two countries in question, obscuring the Pacific Ocean's deep impact on Noguchi as a writer and thinker.

Furthermore, since readers, particularly turn-of-the-century read-ers, in both Japan and the United States have read Noguchi as a "foreign" writer, it seems unfitting to build his literary identity around these two national categories only. Focusing on Noguchi as a Pacific Rim writer, I argue, reminds us that unlike London, who sailed confidently across the Pacific in a boat of his own mak-ing, Noguchi, who journeyed to the United States by steamer, was forced to travel in Chinese steerage, meaning that before he even left Japanese shores, his body was marked by its perceived alterity. Categorized by the American-owned steamer as Chinese—or, at the very least, Chinese-like—and subsequently "thrown in as if a little bundle of merchandise for America," Noguchi's transfor-mative, *felt* experience of voyaging across the Pacific Ocean must factor into the way critics theorize his work, even when his writing is not overtly about the ocean.[88]

If we read Noguchi as a Pacific Rim writer, as Jay Williams does for Jack London in the *Oxford Handbook of Jack London*, what can sometimes seem the limiting framework of national lit-erature opens up, revealing "American literature as world litera-ture," as Lawrence Buell and Wai Chi Dimock propose in *Shades of the Planet*.[89] Buell and Dimock argue for "conceiving the United States as connected to or impinging upon far-distant lands via its environmentality," an act that involves moving "from discrete entity to porous network."[90] In other words, when we perceive the Pacific Ocean as an ecological space where various nations, cul-tures, species, living and nonliving particles, and global materials swirl into and change one another, then it can become the loca-tion of immense possibility instead of a mere domain of political claim and desire.

The radical material agent that is salt(water) actively partici-pates in this commingling of liquid relations, and in the sections that follow I argue that the element physically and psychologically overcomes Noguchi's fictional diarist as she traverses the open ocean. As a shared materiality, salt interacts with *all* bodies that

cross the Pacific regardless of race, gender, class, or ethnicity; however, each individual responds to saltwater's liveliness in distinct,
intersectional, culturally mediated ways. At the same time, when
saltwater enters the body's thin membrane, the briny element
makes bodies "Pacific" at the physiological level. The concept of
"Pacific Rim writer" holds onto the idea of bodily porosity and
elemental intra-action, reminding us that "the Oceanic order
holds all together in a common but highly fluid space," as William
Boelhower suggests.[91] With that "fluid" ordering in mind, this
project allows both London and Noguchi to represent multiple
national and geographical identities at once while also defining
both men as Pacific Rim writers. As a prolific composer of letters,
poetry, and diaries, the fictional character who is Miss Morning
Glory also engages in the literary Pacific, and, as we discover, saltwater makes an indelible impact on both her writing and her body.

SEASICK AND LANDSICK: HOW TO MANAGE BY NOT MANAGING

Even before Miss Morning Glory's journey across the ocean
begins, and while she is still docked in Japan, the movements
and the materialities of the Pacific begin to invade her senses and
threaten her well-being, causing her to lament that "the human
being is a ridiculously small piece. Nature plays with it and kills
it when she pleases" (23). A few pages later, she refers to the ocean
as both a "nothing" space and an "eternal absence," viewing it
as an inconvenient blankness she must traverse to arrive at *someplace* (30). In contrast to London's thoroughly soaked sea novel,
where Van Weyden never finds refuge beyond "the wild tumbling
of water," Noguchi devotes only a single chapter, titled "On the
Ocean," to Miss Morning Glory's voyage from Japan to the United
States. According to Miss Morning Glory, the tormenting waters
of the open ocean are not deserving of great literature. Written in
the form of a travel journal, Noguchi's *Diary* includes large gaps
throughout, particularly in the ocean chapter. For example, Miss

Morning Glory includes only two sentences on November 7, the day of her departure:

> Good-night—native land!
> Farewell, beloved Empress of Dai Nippon! (23)

The next entry does not appear until November 12, leaving the first five days of her journey as blank as she considers the ocean to be. Moreover, Miss Morning Glory writes that she does not "expose myself on deck" until day six, choosing, instead, to rest off her seasickness below deck, where she also socializes with global diplomats, Yale graduates, and other notable passengers, including her uncle, a mining administrator (25). For Noguchi's fictional diarist, a young, single woman who adores Romantic nature poetry, the "monotone" Pacific is no match for the steamer's lively social scene.

Despite the narrator's decision to turn away from the "eternal absence" of the ocean, the water's "heavenly whiteness," as Miss Morning Glory calls it, finds its way into and onto her body via wind, thick fog, and the dizzying movement of the steamer cutting through the waves, leaving her utterly sick. "The tossing spectacle of the waters (also the hostile smell of the ship) put my head in a whirl," she writes after nearly a week of silence. "The last five days have been a nightmare. How many a time would I have preferred death!" (24). The "tossing" waves and "hostile" smells achieve terrifying animacy for Noguchi's narrator, and she half-seriously contemplates death as a way out of the oceanic "nightmare." Noting that waves and ill odors "put her head in a whirl," Miss Morning Glory grows confused, disoriented; the environment she perceives as waste leaves her once put-together form in a constant state of agitation.

Miss Morning Glory's seasickness might, at first, seem like more of a corporeal experience than a material encounter with the elemental, especially when we compare her secluded queasiness to Van Weyden's violent and prolonged saturation in briny waters.

To put it quite simply, Noguchi's narrator does not *become salted*, at least according to London's manly depiction of the process. However, Miss Morning Glory's overwhelming queasy disorientation "alerts us to the viscerality of being embodied and entangled in the swaying human and nonhuman nets of materiality and meaning," which is how Elspeth Probyn describes the strange state of being sick at sea.[92] In other words, seasickness is contingent upon and, moreover, an extension of the ocean's elemental forces. When combined with the flustering gusts of salty spray, fog, and hair-wrecking wind, saltwater imbues Miss Morning Glory in powerful ways, contributing to her eventual failure to manage. In the middle of her journey, she even exclaims that the Pacific is "the breaker of the world," and as the narrative progresses this environmental force persists in beleaguering the narrator (24).

To be seasick is to radically embody *and* reject saltwatery spaces, and its symptoms often involve disorientation, nausea, lack of hunger, dizziness, and vomiting. Probyn even describes it as a "moment of fundamental queasiness in the world," thus making it difficult for a person to productively engage with her environment. Though uncomfortable to say the least, seasickness represents the agential nature of water to agitate the smooth functioning of the body via the ears and eyes. After all, the malaise is brought on when the ear senses movement even when the eye does not. In other words, seasickness is the manifestation of a sensory discordance, acting on the body like a mind-altering drug—a *bad trip*, so to speak. Miss Morning Glory's seasickness continues to evolve in the short ocean chapter, leaving her to wonder if *any body* will be left by the time the steamer reaches California: "My little self wholly exhausted by seasickness. Have I to drift to America in skin and bone?" (23). In this passage, seasickness operates as a relentless force that "exhausts" Miss Morning Glory, leading her to question how much of her body will be left once she arrives in America. The line "My little self wholly exhausted by seasickness" lacks a verb, underscoring the narrator's limp, near lifeless state; without a verb, her body cannot *do* anything, after all. Additionally, the possibility of "drift"—which offers a way to survive management's numbing systems, as the next section illuminates—in this instance seems the only way Miss Morning Glory's nauseated, verb-depleted body will reach shore.

While one could easily view Miss Morning Glory's nausea at sea as inconsequential and register it as a big so-what?—after all, even frequent seagoers like Charles Darwin suffered from bouts of seasickness—it is important to place her sickness in the context of turn-of-the-century medical advice for oceangoing tourists. At the time, many viewed seasickness as a failure of the body to defend itself against cruel and contaminating environmental forces. After all, to be "sick" from the sea aligns the ocean's kinetics with potentially harmful material actors like germs, viruses, and other entities that pose threats to human health and well-being. In a 1908 *Literary Digest* article, one doctor notes that "proper food," plenty of rest, and "a careful course of training for a week before sailing" may help prevent sickness on board.[93] A second doctor cautions that individuals should not "weakly succumb" to seasickness, as if one has a choice. Instead, he urges travelers to "fight manfully against it" by lying "well wrapt up on deck" and consuming foods that improve digestion.[94] Indigestion, he believes, is one of the root causes of sickness at sea. According to these medical professionals, seasickness does not occur randomly, as we often think of it today; instead, the doctors cited believe that depleted, feminine, or untrained bodies cannot manage at sea, or at least not *well*. Also, a failure to self-regulate and a lack of physical preparation invites ill health, Progressives believed. Additionally, this logic suggests that since travelers must "fight manfully" to stave off the ocean's bodily assault, women's bodies will inherently suffer the most, particularly Asian women, who were often viewed as more feminine and delicate than "rugged, big boned" American women.[95] Such a view of inherent maladaptability attempts to safeguard oceanic spaces for men, as

it would seem that only a manly man could "fight manfully"
enough against oceanic violence.

It would, at first, appear like Noguchi follows this masculinist
logic of seasickness and unfit bodies, given *Diary*'s focus on Miss
Morning Glory's ill health aboard the *Belgic*. Admitting that she
feels "like a paper bag thrown in a tempest," Miss Morning Glory
acknowledges that her "drifting" body, which the wind "throws"
without direction, is no match for the tempestuous ocean. Her
skin, as thin and porous as a paper bag, can't help but figuratively
drink up the ocean and then, after it is thoroughly waterlogged,
disintegrate in its waves. This unraveling, or loosening up of the
body, takes many forms for Miss Morning Glory, and in contrast
to Van Weyden's hardening and enhanced determination, the
drifting body gives Noguchi's narrator a kind of power. For one,
the humidity and wind begin to undo her hair, once precisely
fashioned in "Japan style" (12). "What a confusion my hair has
suffered! I haven't put it in order since I left the Orient. Such negligence of toilet would be fined by the police in Japan. I was busy
with my hair all the morning" (26–27). While on the steamer, Miss
Morning Glory seems particularly stressed about her inability to
put her hair "in order," since she views it as integral to her cultural
identity as a Nippon woman. "Busy with my hair all morning,"
she struggles to manage it into its former state. Apparently the
sea's "sickness" has made its way into her hair as well, and this elemental interference makes it difficult to remain a Japanese woman
in the legal sense.

Hair remains a concern for Miss Morning Glory long after she
leaves the *Belgic*, as evidenced by the near thirty references to hair
throughout the novel. In one early scene, she laments her failure
to curl her hair with tongs while in California. "Such disobedient
tools! They didn't work at all," she cries before throwing the curler
on the floor in a fit (50). While her untidy locks at first incite frustration in the narrator—enough to make her scream and throw
objects—Miss Morning Glory's hair, loosened by her first trip

across the Pacific and imbued with a kind of life of its own, actually becomes a thing of pleasure for her even though she never regains complete control over it. For example, while reclining on the beach with her friend Ada, who also emerges as a possible love interest for the narrator, Miss Morning Glory says, "[Ada's] head inclined pathetically against my shoulder. My hair, stirred by the sea zephyrs, patted her cheek" (68). In this intimate moment between the two women, the sea wind enlivens Miss Morning Glory's flyaway tendrils, helping to express the desire the narrator feels, but never vocalizes, for Ada. Unlike her experience on the *Belgic*, wherein she seems to mourn the loss of her tidy Japanese hair, she does not try to regulate her wisps after she falls for Ada. Instead, Miss Morning Glory allows her hair to grace Ada's cheek and possibly interlace with Ada's "chestnut" locks, which Miss Morning Glory finds so attractive. In one scene, for example, the narrator "extended my finger-tips behind her, and pulled some wisps of her chestnut hair," aligning loose hair with desirous play. Near the end of the novel, Miss Morning Glory even confesses that her hair, imbued with a (relaxed) life of its own, "lounges down my back" (141). She then arrives at the conclusion that "Disorder is the first step in being a genius" (141). From strict oversight to pleasurable repose, Miss Morning Glory's evolving relationship with her seasick hair represents just one way she comes to let go of management's dizzying procedures.

Several days after she disembarks in San Francisco, Miss Morning Glory continues to feel the ocean's movements in her body, which leaves her in a prolonged state of instability. Still discombobulated after a week, she appears landsick, a form of seasickness that lingers after one has endured a long oceanic voyage, what London refers to in *The Cruise of the Snark* as "the antic behavior of the land" (17). Unable to sleep, she says, "but the same feeling as on the ocean returned. My American bed acted like water, waving at even my slightest motion. . . . Nothing can put me at ease" (40). Here, I read landsickness as the success of Miss Morning Glory's

transformation while at sea, as it leads her to recognize what
Benjamin Bateman calls the "complex other-in-me."[96] The ocean's
movement, a kind of being that extends beyond the ocean itself,
lingers with(in) Miss Morning Glory and refuses to let her body
rest. In Noguchi's memoir, he also says that his soft hotel bed in
San Francisco "imitated" the motion of the sea (29). The ocean
does not abandon Miss Morning Glory or Noguchi, but instead,
its atmosphere continues to permeate their bodies, leaving them
in a state of *dis-ease*. Contemplating her ongoing landsickness,
Miss Morning Glory says, "I was restless all the night long" (41).

Though uncomfortable and terribly exhausted, Noguchi's
narrator, having freshly arrived on the other side of the Pacific,
finds a strange new power in this inability to cope. Unable to
manage in old and familiar ways while in California, she gives
in to freeing unmanageability and drifts to the side of management. Benjamin Bateman refers to this epistemological unbur-
dening as "running out of steam" and argues that more affiliative
relations with the world might be gained by simply giving up,
or of withdrawing from the endless drives to maintain, survive,
and improve: "Running out of steam makes the attenuated self
available for other more sustainable energies."[97] Unable to shake
the water from her body, Miss Morning Glory begins to slide
into moments of play, pleasure, and intense *being-with* that
management cannot articulate, such as when she "rolls" with
Ada on the floor, their poufy dresses rippling in waves (60).
"I don't see how to manage myself sometimes," she confesses
a few pages later when considering how her grandmother,
a traditional Japanese woman, would perceive the diarist
as she "drifts among the ijins [foreigners]" the grandmother
"loathed" (68). Both seasick and landsick—ever changed by the
Pacific's transcorporeal abilities—Miss Morning Glory gradually transmogrifies from hypervigilant self-manager to acqui-
escent drifter, revealing that survival (and even delight) can be
available to those who give up.

These scenes reveal, in other words, that Noguchi's narrator does not have to be doused, sluiced, or nearly drowned to be overcome by the material force of saltwater. Instead, for Miss Morning Glory, who later likens herself to "a cherry blossom smiling softly in the Spring moonlight," the oceanic transformation occurs as a result of her mere approximation to oceanic waters: the steamer, the beach, the California coast, and so on (69). While Miss Morning Glory does not—and, according to London's white masculine logic, *cannot*—undergo the salt cure in the naturalist sense since she is neither a man nor an American, saltwater disorients and changes her body's relation to the world, causing her to move like and with waves wherever she goes. Instead of pursuing vertical improvement and "compulsory productivity," as was the expected Progressive trajectory, Miss Morning Glory floats queerly and almost effortlessly to the side of improvement, which prevents *Diary* from reaching any kind of narrative climax—or resolution.[98] The drift I am describing here resonates with Bateman's configuration of "lateral agency," which signifies a "relaxing or even fading into opportunities for respite or escape."[99] The Pacific offers Miss Morning Glory the material nudge she needs to "fade into" generative presents, and for future-thinking Progressives these indulgent simmerings might not compute.

In addition to these moments in *Diary* when Noguchi interrogates the themes of drift and disorder in Miss Morning Glory's daily life, the novel also reads as seasick at the structural level. Short paragraphs, incomplete sentences, and big gaps in time come together to disorient readers, making them question where Miss Morning Glory's wanderings and observations will take her next. For example, in one entry, Noguchi writes,

> I could not believe that the sparrow of large America could be as small as the Nippon-born.
>
> Horses are large here. Woman's mouth is large, something like that of an alligator. Policeman is too large. (56)

The narrator's surprise that an American and Japanese bird could appear so similar leads her, in the very next paragraph, into a discussion of women's voices and the overwhelming presence of law enforcement in the United States. In these two paragraphs that comprise a mere four sentences, humans, birds, horses, and alligators smear across the same geography, creating the effect of distinct waves cresting above the ocean's surface only to crash into a singular liquid immensity. Despite the startling (and quite pleasurable) leaps in imagery—for example, American women's mouths remind Miss Morning Glory of the open and waiting mouths of hungry reptiles—word repetition ("large") and variations of the infinitive verb "to be" give loose order to these otherwise choppy and discordant sentences. Through a kind of seasick epistemology, Noguchi generates a liquid logic that might throw modern American readers off balance, allowing them to visualize the United States as Miss Morning Glory, the near-immigrant, would perceive it. The choppy structure that leaps between seeming discordant images and ideas reinforces the fact that everything in the new continent is a little *off*, or dizzying, for the narrator; even similarities between Japan and the United States, which should offer comfort in their familiarity, bewilder.

The face of disciplinary management itself—the police—elicits consternation in its overwhelming presence. By letting go and submitting to a watery stream of consciousness, Miss Morning Glory expresses a radical response to management's anxious focus on hard-salted bodies, linear ascension, and steady improvement. The structural drift reflects Probyn's "queasiness in the world," or what I read as a way of knowing the world with a gut feeling— and, in this case, that gut is shaken. Just as Van Weyden creates his own "business-like atmosphere," so, too, does Noguchi's narrator develop a new orientation to and with the world via her seasick writing. In one entry, she speaks of her newfound love of smoking and says, "the smoke seems to be speaking for me" (167). Similarly, her writing—surrounding her, dispersing, and commingling with the atmospheres of others—demonstrates a textural alternative to management's obsession with firm order at all costs.

This oceanic logic of bodily drift, zephyrized hair, and disorder stands in contrast to London's hardy "natural man" philosophy. While both Van Weyden and Miss Morning Glory experience bodily breakdown in the Pacific, London's project requires that men "contain" and then harness the energy of the collapse for useful, manly ends: building boats, navigating difficult waters with surety, and generally subduing erratic human and environmental elements. In other words, Van Weyden pursues what Bateman refers to as the "compulsory productivity of Progressive Era cultural life."[100] Ever focused on productive futures, Van Weyden can't help but compulsively build, improve, and, in general, try to manage with everything he's got. For Miss Morning Glory, on the other hand, being at sea results in ongoing "stirrings," "loungings," and drifts. In the middle of her diary she confesses to feeling "a new stream of blood beginning to swell within my body," a sensation that resonates with the practice of administering hypodermic injections of saltwater to "invigorate" exhausted bodies; she then allows that energy to propel her into open-ended moments of play and discovery:

> I buzzed a silly song.
> I crept into my uncle's room.
> I stole one stalk of his cigars.
> I bit it, aping Mr. Uncle, when my door banged. (73)

As these reflections reveal, the "swelling" in her body, much like the swells of oceanic waves, sends her in curious directions; one moment of play laps into another, and into another, and readers never know where she will end up next. Quite often, those swells peak into play and pleasure, such as when she chews on an unlit cigar while "aping" her uncle. The diarist fails to hesitate—to evaluate former actions and assess the next step—when riding out these swells. Instead, she slides into each activity without much thinking—"I bite," "I crept," "I stole," and "I bit"—and thus manages without quite managing.

However, when considering the narrator's ability to make time for pleasure-drifts, it is important to keep in mind her social and economic standing. As an aristocratic Japanese woman who does not have to work to earn a living, Miss Morning Glory has the luxury of ample leisure time—time in which she can contemplate and then write about the effects of humidity on her hair, among other details of her day-to-day life. Additionally, at the beginning of *Diary*, the narrator comments on her uncle's position as the secretary of the Nippon Mining Company, meaning his presence in the United States—and, subsequently, hers—depends on resource extraction and industrial-scale projects that could potentially result in environmental harm. Her privilege to drift, in other words, results from the wealth her family derives, at least in part, from masculine management. This does not mean we should dismiss the value of Miss Morning Glory's playful embrace of disorder, especially since her narrative reflects Noguchi's more humble experience as a near-immigrant in California who, while there, struggled to make ends meet. Regardless of the narrator's social status, the fact that a seasick "girl"—and an East Asian girl at that—might be capable of managing on American soil at the turn of the twentieth century reveals saltwater's power to confuse, instead of fortify, efforts to regulate and subdue dynamic *human elements* at the turn of the century.

• • •

Even though London, Stephen Crane, and other writers of the naturalist cohort viewed saltwater as a solution capable of transforming American men into imperial men, Miss Morning Glory's brief but charged encounter with the Pacific, though somewhat traumatic at first, directs a queer response to "the natural man," a figure Gail Bederman describes as the entwinement of hard masculinity with whiteness at the turn of the twentieth century.[101] The natural / national man, according to Bederman, was to use his strong, imperial body to lead and manage the country into productive future spaces, like the Pacific. To fail to be a man in this setting is really a failure of embodiment—moreover, a failure to *make* one's body into the "primitive masculine" ideal.[102]

If we consider the word "natural" as a synonym for "belonging," the "natural man" has other implications as well. In essence, a "natural man" in the Progressive sense believes that wherever he is, he belongs, an idea that seems to rationalize conquest by viewing land touched as land already possessed. Neither Noguchi nor Miss Morning Glory become *naturalized* in the United States, and in *Diary* Noguchi seems to experiment with more liquid ways of belonging—or of *becoming natural*—in the new continent. Miss Morning Glory questions her own desires to fit in in the United States when, at the beginning of *Diary*, she asks, "Shall I have to become 'naturalized' in America?" (10). With this question, she demonstrates that naturalization, in both the legal and affiliative senses of the word, is possible for her as an aristocratic Japanese woman. For "primitive men," like London, who wish to guard the country against effeminacy, Miss Morning Glory's question could be read as a threat to notions of American superiority and white male supremacy. After all, by posing the question in a frustrating, hesitative tone ("Shall I *have* to . . ."), Miss Morning Glory dismisses Americanization as a desirous goal, which has the effect of cheapening the exclusionary rhetoric of American citizenship. In other words, she *could* have it, but *does she want it*? Even though her disorienting journey across the Pacific Ocean does not help the narrator answer this question, it does provide her with an unconventional tool for fitting in on the new continent—if she wants to, that is.

In his own autobiography, *The Story of Yone Noguchi*, the author locates affiliative belonging neither in a single nation nor on land, but in the queer, salty waves of the Pacific Ocean. In the Epilogue, Noguchi writes publicly about his love for Charles Warren Stoddard, or "Charley" as he endearingly calls him, who frequently voyaged in the South Seas "to shake off the world's troubles" (253). Choosing to end his memoir with a dedication to the recently deceased Stoddard, with whom Noguchi shared a deep "romantic friendship," Noguchi creates a tonal break in what is otherwise a matter-of-fact memoir.[103] Up to this point, Noguchi's autobiography reads like a chronology of travel observations, friendships, and literary inspirations. Even though he offers surface details of his wife and baby son, these familial summaries carry little emotion and read more like a biographical timeline. In fact, in the paragraphs leading up to his dedication to Stoddard, Noguchi remarks on the near omission of his toddler son, Isamu, and others: "I said nothing about Hifumi, Haruwo, and Masawo, these three children who the present wife of mine, a Japanese, brought to me" (245). Instead, he gives his attention to the man whose memory "I cherish in my inner heart" (245).

What makes the separate section detailing his love for another man so fascinating—and so relevant to this chapter—is not only its vulnerable openness about Noguchi and Stoddard's relationship, but also its reliance on oceanic metaphors to describe that relationship. Just as London's saltwater proves capable of preserving or sustaining the bodies of men like Larsen who raged against Pacific waters before "the frontier [became] conscious of itself," to use Frank Norris's words, it is also capable of nurturing the romantic love that two men had for one another, Noguchi seems to be arguing.[104]

With Noguchi's heartfelt epilogue in mind, I wish to end this project by contemplating the environmental possibilities of loving (another) in the "strange agencies" of the sea—or any perceived *wasteland*, for that matter.[105] In the conclusion, I will briefly contemplate what managing-by-drift might look like while also imagining how situated managements, more broadly, might allow us to survive in (and perhaps even love) warmer, more precarious worlds.

EXILED BIRDS AND ABANDONED BOATS

DRIFTING TOWARD A CONCLUSION ON THE QUEER PACIFIC

Even in these murky waters, we still breathe, turn, float, and feel our bodies into the waves.

—SUSAN PRATT, ET AL., "FATHOM," *ENVIRONMENTAL HUMANITIES* (2020)

n "After Sustainability," Steve Mentz urges ecocritics to "stop dreaming green dreams" in the era of climate change.[1] He instead insists that we should look to the ocean for a new post-sustainability ethics. "As the global climate becomes more unstable," he says, "we have begun to realize that planet-sized ecological questions are really questions about the ocean. Imagining earth as ocean rather than garden enables us to escape pastoral nostalgia."[2] Mentz believes that land-based nostalgic longings, as they have been variously expressed in ecocriticism and nature writing, force us to hold onto a "fantasy about stasis, an imaginary world"; these narrative attempts to restore or recover "lost landscapes" prevent us from conjuring more immersive, open-ended environmental futures.[3] What we need is not sustainability, Mentz concludes, but options, "room to maneuver."[4] In other words, we need to think (and move) like an ocean.

In these final pages of *Sand, Water, Salt*, I maintain that the saltwatery Pacific offers just that: "room to maneuver," or the space to drift into more expansive ecological attunements in the Anthropocene. With its unpredictable currents and fathoms, not to mention its interminglings and fusions of strange agents and agencies, oceans offer liquid visions of non-hierarchical situated managements. Even though managing-by-drift cannot solve every ecological dilemma—after all, complete mastery over the environment is never possible since we are never quite *over* it in a physical or emotional sense—situated managements can at least help us shift our attention from an ethics of fixing to one of *living-with*. Living-with it ("it" being everything—a river, climate change, a grassy road verge, or drought) implies "collaborating in and with the world to point to other possibilities still unknown."[5] In other words, the ocean invites us to manage by listening to, loving, and releasing ourselves gyre-like into (and into, and into, and always-into) the elements.

All of this is not to say we throw up our hands and abandon for good science- and engineering-based methods of managing environments, letting the currents simply pull our dejected and passive bodies out to pelagic depths. Drifting is not an apathetic maneuver, nor does it result in inaction or managerial acquiescence. Instead, let us consider what an ethos of situated managements— one that upwells from the saltwatery Pacific—might look and feel like if we allow it to inform scientific practice. Managing-by-drift implies an openness to "asking a question and engaging with what surfaces" from the fathoms, which runs counter to more methodical, solutions-based forms of land and oceanic management that find their root in the Progressive Era.[6] When managing-by-drift, one is not without care and commitment; instead one drifts-with-awareness, absorbing the sensations and letting those absorptions inspire decision-making. In other words, one can be hard at work and still assume the intellectual and emotional position of the drifter.

The Water Protectors at Standing Rock who actively stood guard over-and-with the elements they held dear are but one example of those who have managed-by-drift. One of those Protectors, Jeanne Dorado, described the Pan-Indigenous movement against the construction of the Dakota Access Pipeline as "a sea change," a description that compares a profound cultural revolution with the transformative power of the ocean. Dorado continues, "The native folks here have never come together like this in agreement over something beautiful, which is love and spirit, and our common future, which is the children."[7] Just being there, standing with others "in agreement over something beautiful," operated as Standing Rock's collective thesis, Dorado maintains. Listening, drifting together around an aqueous commitment: that, too, is a kind of management. New collectives, obligations, and human-nonhuman affiliations develop out of managerial drift, offering those involved the chance to foster intimate, non-national forms of belonging. *Agreeing over something beautiful* builds new relations that exceed the nation, in other words.

We see this in Noguchi's work as well. In the emotional epilogue to *The Story of Yone Noguchi*, Noguchi cites a letter written from Stoddard wherein he compares Noguchi to an exiled seabird, battered by the wind, who lands aboard a ship sailing in the "wave-crested wilderness."[8] The sailors nurse the bird back to health, but it loses its ability to sing. "So thou seemest to me, O Noguchi! . . . They who have found thee, would comfort and caress thee—I most of all—but thy songs are tear-stained, and thou singest only the song of the exile" (249). Creating a kind of conversation with the dead, Noguchi then responds to his friend's letter by comparing Stoddard to "an abandoned boat—perhaps a Hawaiian canoe—terribly tottering on the ocean waves, not knowing whither he was going" (254).

While these references to wind-battered seabirds and directionless canoes might not seem like the stuff of traditional love and romance, I argue that similar to Miss Morning Glory's decision to "drift" in Noguchi's *The American Diary of a Japanese Girl*, they present a challenge to the "natural man's" wholesale possession of the Pacific. Management views loss and listlessness on the ocean as ultimate failures that require remediation—after all, injured bodies and aimless, unmanned canoes will not an empire make. In this tribute to Stoddard, Noguchi envisions the ocean as a space for queer bodies, and those bodies in repose are not guided by imperial aims or productive ends. Their waywardness, when combined with their refusal to articulate clear goals, makes them difficult for Progressive management to index in its rigid lexicon. We may want to track the "tottering" boat and see it to safety, but we can't, and this frustrates us, makes us ever uneasy. In the context of imperialism's patriotic pleas to possess, improve, and master at all costs, the sad and frustrating canoe emerges as a radical concept. It drifts, un-manned, with no one in control. What happens when we turn our eyes away from it, let it go from the line of our sight? And what does this letting go look like in the context of managing the world's oceans, especially since experts frequently remind us that overfishing, species extinction, and plastic pollution—to name only a few environmental issues facing today's marine ecosystems—signal that "the ocean is headed for a collapse"?[9]

When Noguchi recalls a memory of "dozing" with Stoddard in "the deep hollow" of a chair, the arms of the chair "appearing but a pair of oars carrying us into the isle of a dream," he presents today's readers with an opportunity to envision a non-teleological approach to surviving on/with compromised oceanic spaces, one that attempts to collapse the techno-scientific distance between humans and dynamic ecologies in favor of ecological attunement (251). Unlike Wolf Larsen's hierarchical and somewhat predatory relationship with Van Weyden, Noguchi and Stoddard cuddle with one another in the buoyant chair as an "us" in this epilogue, which offers a vision of management rooted in love and care. If we enter that "isle of a dream" and drift into open waters with the two men, unanticipated attachments to humans, animals, and "strange agencies" might occur from which more immersive, justice-oriented environmentalisms can develop. So, let us imagine where that drift-in-the-chair might take the two men—and where it might navigate us in the era of global climate change:

The two restful men exert no energy but exist in a state of being-with one another in the dream-ocean. The chair's "deep hollow," ample enough to accommodate both of their nestling bodies, holds them cozily as they drift without direction. Perhaps the two men, while dozing, float past Larsen's murderous Ghost *ship, an anxious vessel full of rough men always ready to war. Still dozing, eyes parting halfway, maybe Noguchi and Stoddard bob through the wake of Miss Morning Glory's steamer, the* Belgic, *where, below deck, the diarist's uncle excitedly examines blueprints with a fellow mining executive. And still they drift, grazing the bloated belly of a dead fur seal, swimming their way through the fog—or is it gunpowder?—or maybe a baby orca's first breath? If the men's eyes were open, it's possible they could decipher the origin of the haze. But instead they sleep,*

*aware in an unaware sort of way of the liquid ground they are cov-
ering. The chair, the men, swirl around all of this and then some as
they enter the stuff of our current historical moment: nurdles, volca-
nic ash, a lost polar bear, an old flip-flop, holographic smears of crude
oil, king salmon, nuclear fallout, and the sun's intensifying heat. The
chair, now thoroughly saturated and still bearing the weight of two
men in love, angles sideways in this strange new ocean. Their drift
diminishes to drag, and then the chair submerges into the mouth of
the ocean. Their sleep now troubled by a tingly feeling that the world
is off, the men open sponge-like to Pacific depths and drift downward
into the phytoplankton and plastic bits and electric eels, the chair still
crevassing their love. There's no telling how deep they will travel in
the chair's "deep hollow," or whether they will reemerge, reach land.*

Near the end of her own oceanic voyage, Miss Morning Glory
writes, "We have abandoned the land. The ocean has no bottom,"
and this realization frightens her.[10] Thoroughly worn out from
the journey and separated from the firm ground of familiar country, she imagines herself perpetually at sea, and the thought unsettles her. We might recognize Morning Glory's unease in these
Anthropocene times. For us—drifters in the uncertain seas of
climate change—this sense of endless departure upon what seems
a bottomless ocean is very real and no less disquieting, even when
"the disciplines that can fix things" declare that certain doom
can be avoided so long as we take responsibility, adopt a plan,
and act now.[11] While it is difficult to argue with the urgent calls
for developing multiscalar, compassionate, scientific solutions
to the threats climate change poses to humans and nonhumans
alike, there might also be room for alternative epistemologies, or
ways of envisioning (with our scientific eyes closed) other modes
of ecological attunement. Since many of today's environmental
management efforts remain focused on data needs, sustainable
growth, aspirational outcomes, and other values championed by the
Progressive Movement, management philosophy rarely allows itself
to drift into the "deep hollows" to see what else might be possible.

In addition to giving one room to breathe, so to speak, drifting puts one in touch with the world, albeit in a strange way; after all, drifters never know what to expect. In Stoddard's letter to Noguchi, the injured seabird illustrates the usefulness of a drifting ontology for eco-oriented activists and scholars, particularly as we attempt to articulate an ethics rooted in open-ended relations, unexpected encounters, and gentler ways of affiliating with environments deemed compromised. For example, when Stoddard describes Noguchi as a seabird "whirling" through "empty spaces" who, by chance, falls "panting and affrighted upon the ship's reeling deck," he notes that "those who were on board tenderly nursed it, and caressed it, and gave it generous cheer" in hopes that the bird would recover. In the open ocean, the sailors could not have anticipated these "generous" moments of affection they would share with the injured creature. It simply drifted onto their boat, in need of something. Or was it the men who were in need? Either way, the men, the bird, found something to lovingly touch in the middle of the ocean's elemental waste.

ACKNOWLEDGMENTS

Many people helped me write this book, and they deserve an ocean of gratitude. The brilliance and generosity of these individuals motivated me to turn a strange paper about the desert in *McTeague* into a dissertation—and, later, this book.

My fiercely dedicated advisor at the University of South Carolina, Cynthia Davis, believed in *Sand, Water, Salt* well before I did. Cynthia is a model scholar, teacher, and mentor, and I am eternally grateful for her advice and kindness. Catherine Keyser's smart and enthusiastic comments on earlier versions of this project gave me the energy I needed to keep writing when the writing was tough.

Many thanks are due to Brian Glavey, whose wonderful class on American literary modernism inspired the first rusty sentences I wrote for this project. Thomas Lekan and Kevin Trumpeter offered much guidance on the ecocritical stakes of *Sand, Water, Salt*, and I thank them deeply for their sharp insights.

I presented sections of *Sand, Water, Salt* at conferences hosted by the Western Literature Association, the Association for the Study of Literature and the Environment, and the South Atlantic Modern Language Association. I am grateful to those in the audience who asked questions about my work or challenged some of its central claims. This book is more robust because of their feedback.

I am incredibly grateful for the support and kindness of my editors at Texas Tech University Press, Travis Snyder and Joanna Conrad. Many thanks are also due to Christie Perlmutter, Bob Land, and the two anonymous reviewers whose sharp readings and suggestions helped me write a better book.

I also wish to thank Arizona State University's Institute for Humanities Research and Desert Humanities Initiative, especially Celina Osuna and Ron Broglio, who chose to include this book in the Desert Humanities Series.

I owe a debt of gratitude to Gary Reger, my dear friend and fellow desert-lover, who, throughout the writing of this book, cheered me on and offered important critiques of several chapters.

To Kristen, Jennifer, and Jill, for all of the work dates, walks, and cups of coffee. Much of this book was written in your presence, and so many of its pages are infused with our laughter and conversation.

I am endlessly inspired by Jaime and Emily, my dearest friends. You more than anyone get my love of sand, water, and salt.

To my parents for letting me play in the dirt—and for nurturing my love of writing.

To Jeff and Winona, my loves. You are the most important elements.

NOTES

INTRODUCTION

1. Climate fiction, or cli-fi as it is frequently called, is a relatively new genre of environmental literature that focuses on climate change and global warming. Several reviews of *Gold Fame Citrus* categorize it as cli-fi. See Ben Goldfarb, "In *Gold Fame Citrus*, the Nascent Genre Looks to California," *High Country News*, February 2, 2016, and Tim Martin, "*Gold Fame Citrus* Is a Cli-Fi Novel—the Dystopia of Choice in the Era of Climate Change," *NewStatesman*, March 2, 2016.

2. Claire Vaye Watkins, *Gold Fame Citrus* (New York: Riverhead Books, 2015), 20, 11, 14. Hereafter cited in text.

3. Martha Banta, *Taylored Lives: Narrative Productions in the Age of Taylor, Veblen, and Ford* (Chicago: University of Chicago Press, 1993).

4. Donald Worster, *Rivers of Empire: Water, Aridity, and the Growth of the American West* (New York: Oxford University Press, 1992); Marc Reisner, *Cadillac Desert: The American West and Its Disappearing Water* (New York: Viking Press, 1986); Robert H. Wiebe, *The Search for Order, 1877–1920* (New York: Hill and Wang, 1966).

5. Thomas C. Leonard, *Illiberal Reformers: Race, Eugenics, and American Economics in the Progressive Era* (Princeton, NJ: Princeton University Press, 2016), 9.

6. In *The Conquest of Arid America*, William E. Smythe refers to the Western United States as a "clean, blank page" that "awaits" the "goodly heritage of our people" (New York: Harper & Brothers, 1900), xvi.

7. "William Mulholland of Aqueduct Fame Dies," *Los Angeles*

Times, July 23, 1935.

8. Many critics align the Anthropocene with feelings of melancholia. In "Mourning and Melancholia in the Anthropocene," Margaret Ronda writes, "This recursive structure of wish-denial, recognition of guilt, and ceaseless heartache offers a powerful account of how the determined, aggrandized human agency of the Anthropocene might be experienced—the *feeling,* that is, of thinking 'nothing but us.'" *Post45,* June 10, 2013. See also Roy Scranton, "Raising My Daughter in a Doomed World," *New York Times,* July 16, 2018.

9. Donald J. Trump, "Remarks by President Trump after Meeting with Congressional Leadership on Border Security." White House, US Government, January 4, 2019.

10. Jeffrey Jerome Cohen and Lowell Duckert, "Introduction: Eleven Principles of the Elements," *Elemental Ecocriticism: Thinking with Earth, Air, Water, and Fire,* edited by Jeffrey Jerome Cohen and Lowell Duckert (Minneapolis: University of Minnesota Press, 2015), 3.

11. Jane Tomkins, *West of Everything: The Inner Life of Westerns* (New York: Oxford University Press, 1992), 73.

12. Tom Lynch, *Xerophilia: Ecocritical Explorations in Southwestern Literature* (Lubbock: Texas Tech University Press, 2008), 11.

13. Catriona Mortimer-Sandilands, "Unnatural Passions?: Notes toward a Queer Ecology," *Invisible Culture: An Electronic Journal for Visual Culture* 9 (2005), https://www.rochester.edu/in_visible_culture/Issue_9/issue9_sandilands.pdf.

14. The term "situated managements" is influenced by Donna Haraway's groundbreaking concept "situated knowledge." "Situated knowledge," she argues, is a "doctrine of embodied objectivity that accommodates paradoxical and critical feminist science projects: Feminist objectivity means quite

simply situated knowledge" (581). Haraway, "Situated Knowledges: The Science Question in Feminism and the Privilege of Partial Perspective," *Feminist Studies* 14, no. 3 (1988): 575–99.

15. Helen Feder, "Nature and Culture in (and Outside) the Academy," *Western American Literature* 52, no. 3 (2017): xi.

16. Julie Sze, "From Environmental Justice Literature to the Literature of Environmental Justice," in *The Environmental Justice Reader: Politics, Poetics, and Pedagogy*, Joni Adamson, Mei Mei Evans, and Rachel Stein, eds. (Tucson: University of Arizona Press, 2002).

17. Traci Brynne Voyles, *Wastelanding: Legacies of Uranium Mining in Navajo Country* (Minneapolis: University of Minnesota Press, 2015), 7.

18. Nicolas Witschi, *Traces of Gold: California's Natural Resources and the Claim to Realism in Western American Literature* (Tuscaloosa: University of Alabama Press, 2002), 12.

19. Neil Campbell, *The Rhizomatic West: Representing the American West in a Transnational, Global, Media Age* (Lincoln, NE: Bison Books, 2011).

20. Richard Seager et al., "Whither the Hundredth Meridian? The Once and Future Physical and Human Geography of America's Arid-Humid Divide. Part 1: The Story So Far," *Earth Interactions* 22 (2018): 1–24.

21. Powell states, "A broad belt separates the Arid Region of the west from the Humid Region of the east. Extending from the one hundredth meridian eastward to about the isohyetal line of 28 inches, the district of country thus embraced will be subject more or less to disastrous droughts, the frequency of which will diminish from west to east." John Wesley Powell, *Report on the Lands of the Arid Region of the United States* (Washington, DC: Government Printing Office, 1878).

22. Joe Wertz, "The Arid West Moves East, with Big Implications

for Agriculture," National Public Radio Online, August 19, 2018, https://www.npr.org/2018/08/09/637161725/the-arid-west-moves-east-with-big-implications-for-agriculture.

23. Tom Lynch, "Desertification," in *Reading Aridity in Western American Literature*, edited by Jada Ach and Gary Reger (Lanham, MD: Lexington Books, 2020), ix–x.

24. See Stacy Alaimo, "Elemental Love in the Anthropocene," in *Elemental Ecocriticism: Thinking with Earth, Air, Water, And Fire*, Jeffrey Jerome Cohen and Lowell Duckert, eds. (Minneapolis: University of Minnesota Press, 2015), 298–309.

25. Cecilia Tichi defines "machine-age texts" as cultural or literary artifacts that in theme and style reflect Progressive Era gear-and-girder technologies, such as we see in skyscrapers and modern bridges. *Shifting Gears: Technology, Literature, Culture in Modernist America* (Chapel Hill: University of North Carolina Press, 1987).

26. Thomas C. Leonard, *Illiberal Reformers: Race, Eugenics, and American Economics in the Progressive Era* (Princeton, NJ: Princeton University Press, 2016); Linda Nash, *Inescapable Ecologies: A History of Environment, Disease, and Knowledge* (Berkeley: University of California Press, 2006).

27. Linda Nash, *Inescapable Ecologies: A History of Environment, Disease, and Knowledge* (Berkeley: University of California Press, 2006).

28. Bill Brown, *A Sense of Things: The Object Matter of American Literature* (Chicago: University of Chicago Press, 2003); Jane Bennett, *Vibrant Matter: A Political Ecology of Things* (Durham, NC: Duke University Press, 2010); Aaron Jaffe, *The Way Things Go: An Essay on the Matter of Second Modernism* (Minneapolis: University of Minnesota Press, 2014).

29. Cohen and Duckert, "Introduction: Eleven Principles," 13.

30. Bennett, *Vibrant Matter*, ix.

31. Cohen and Duckert, "Introduction: Eleven Principles of

the Elements," 5–6.

32. Ibid., 7.

33. Stacy Alaimo, *Bodily Natures: Science, Environment, and the Material Self* (Bloomington: Indiana University Press, 2010). 2.

34. Ibid., 29.

35. Alaimo, *Bodily Natures,* 29.

36. Alaimo, *Bodily Natures,* 29.

37. Louise Westling, *The Green Breast of the New World: Landscape, Gender, and American Fiction* (Athens: University of Georgia Press, 1996), 167.

38. Ibid., 167–68.

39. C19: Society of Nineteenth-Century Americanists, "Conference," C19 Online, 2017, https://c19conference.wordpress.com/past-conference-programs/.

40. John L. Cowan, "Dry Farming: The Hope of the West," *Century Magazine,* July 1906, 435–46.

41. Jack London, *The Sea-Wolf* (New York: Bantam Dell, 2007 [New York: Macmillan, 1904]).

42. Benjamin Bateman, *The Modernist Art of Queer Survival* (New York: Oxford University Press, 2017).

CHAPTER 1

1. L. Frank Baum, *The Wizard of Oz* (New York: Penguin Books, 1998), 73. Hereafter cited in text.

2. Gale Norton, "Testimony of Secretary of the Interior Gale Norton before the House Committee on Resources on the Arctic Coastal Plain Domestic Energy Security Act of 2003," US Department of the Interior, March 12, 2003.

3. Elena Glasberg, *Antarctica as Cultural Critique: The Gendered Politics of Scientific Exploration and Climate Change* (New York: Palgrave MacMillan, 2012), xxiv.

4. In "Situated Knowledges," Donna Haraway argues that "the world neither speaks itself nor disappears in favor of a

master decoder. . . . [T]he world encountered in knowledge projects is an active entity" (593). "Situated Knowledges: The Science Question in Feminism and the Privilege of Partial Perspectives," *Feminist Studies* 14, no. 3 (1988): 575–99.

5. Mark Dorrian and Frédéric Pousin, "Introduction," in *Seeing from Above: The Aerial View in Visual Culture*, ed. Mark Dorrian and Frédéric Pousin (New York: I. B. Tauris, 2013), 7.

6. Jane Bennett, *Vibrant Matter: A Political Ecology of Things* (Durham, NC: Duke University Press, 2010), ix.

7. James Weems suggests that aerial photography in the 1930s aided the "synoptic gaze" of the Farm Security Administration. "In the repetitive, rectilinear grid work represented in the Illinois photography, [Roy] Stryker discerned a visual tracing of the Jeffersonian land system and the republican agrarian ideals that underlie America's mythic Western expansion. Once they were revealed by the synoptic gaze of the aerial photograph, these cultural patterns could be perceived in other, down-to-earth images of the landscape and its inhabitants" (273). "Aerial Views and Farm Security Administration Photography," *History of Photography* 28, no. 3 (2004): 267–82.

8. Gifford Pinchot, *The Training of a Forester* (Philadelphia: J. B. Lippincott Company, 1914), 66.

9. Ibid., 67.

10. Ibid., 66, 91, 141, 61.

11. Ibid., 42.

12. Ibid., 70.

13. Ibid., 60–61.

14. Ibid., 141.

15. John Burroughs, "The Art of Seeing Things," *American Earth: Environmental Writing since Thoreau* (New York: Library of America, 2008), 146.

16. Ibid., 148.

17. Haraway, "Situated Knowledges," 582.

18. The hovering, all-absorbing eye is reminiscent of Ralph Waldo Emerson's concept of the "transparent eye-ball" in *Nature*: "Standing on the bare ground,—my head bathed by the blithe air, and uplifted into infinite space,—all mean egotism vanishes. I become a transparent eye-ball; I am nothing; I see all; the currents of the Universal Being circulate through me; I am part or particle of God" (8). Emerson, *Nature: Addresses, and Lectures* (Boston: James Munroe Company, 1849).

19. In *Sand, Water, Salt*, "landscape" is largely defined as not only the pictorial representations of rural spaces, as in a landscape painting or photograph, but also as a specific attitude toward place, one that conceives of environments as "inexhaustible storehouses" of artistic inspiration, commodities, natural resources, data, and/or moral guidance. Burroughs, "The Art of Seeing Things," 147.

20. William Eddy, quoted in Earl Mago, "Parade from Mid-Air: Mr. Eddy Details His Plans for Taking Photographs on the 27th," *Anaconda* (MT) *Standard*, April 25, 1897, 14, retrieved from Chronicling America—The Library of Congress, March 22, 2017.

21. Amber Foster, "Nancy Prince's Utopias: Reimagining the African American Utopian Tradition," *Utopian Studies* 24, no. 2 (2013): 332.

22. Data from Foster, "Nancy Prince's Utopias," 332.

23. Writers such as Sutton E. Griggs, who situates his fictional black shadow government in Waco, Texas, for example, appropriates the national mythos of "open spaces" in the West to experiment with black sovereignty and new modes of national belonging. In doing so, Griggs's novel *Imperium in Imperio* disrupts and denaturalizes Anglo-American claims to the West at the turn of the century (Cincinnati: Editor Publishing Company, 1899). For more on

turn-of-the-century utopian fiction, see Foster, "Nancy Prince's Utopias," 329–47; Thomas Galt Peyser, "Reproducing Utopia: Charlotte Perkins Gilman and *Herland*," *Studies in American Fiction* 20, no. 1 (1992): 1–16; Tom Moylan, *Demand the Impossible: Science Fiction and the Utopian Imagination* (New York: Methuen, 1986); Mandy Reid, "Utopia Is in the Blood: The Bodily Utopias of Martin R. Delany and Pauline Hopkins," *Utopian Studies* 22, no. 1 (2011): 91–103; and Pavla Veselá, "Neither Black nor White: The Critical Utopias of Sutton E. Griggs and George S. Schuyler," *Science Fiction Studies* 38, no. 1 (2011): 270–87.

24. Mary Ellen Snodgrass, *The Encyclopedia of Utopian Literature* (Santa Barbara: ABC-CLIO, 1995), xi.

25. Dorrian and Pousin, Introduction, 7.

26. Fox notes, "'Aréalité' is an almost completely obscured French word that curator Thierry Davila . . . brought to my attention when I told him that I was writing about 'the aerial imagination.' He translates it as 'air + reality,' but to my ear it immediately fused 'aerial' and 'reality' in a near palindromic fashion, never mind that I couldn't find it in any number of French dictionaries" (3). *Aereality: Essays on the World from Above* (Berkeley, CA: Counterpoint, 2009). For a local case study of aerial photography's use for land management purposes in the 1930s, see Weems, "Aerial Views."

27. Gilbert Totten Woglom, "Unusual Uses of Photography: I—Aerial Photography," *Scribner's* 22, no. 64 (1897): 617–25.

28. See Woglom, *Parakites: A Treatise on the Making and Flying of Tailless Kites for Scientific Purposes and for Recreation* (New York: G. P. Putnam's Sons, 1896).

29. Woglom, "Unusual Uses of Photography," 619, 621.

30. Several turn-of-the-century American newspaper articles examine the use of aerial photographic devices, often

describing their potential usefulness in the contexts of war and land management. Examples include, but are not limited to, the following: Mago, "Parade from Mid-Air," 14; "Takes Aerial Photographs," *Peninsula* (VA) *Enterprise*, June 4, 1898, 2, retrieved from Chronicling America—The Library of Congress, February 7, 2017; "To Use Kites in Cuba," *Copper Country* (MI) *Evening News*, June 8, 1898, 4, retrieved from Chronicling America—The Library of Congress, February 7, 2017; "Practical Uses for Kite Photographs," *Salt Lake Herald*, November 9, 1897, retrieved from Chronicling America—The Library of Congress, February 2, 2017; "Science in Warfare," *Salt Lake Herald*, March 27, 1898, retrieved from Chronicling America—The Library of Congress, February 7, 2017. Additionally, the Professional Aerial Photographers Association (PAPA) summarizes the evolution of aerial photography in "The History of Aerial Photography," *PAPA International Online*, 2018, https://papainternational. com/history-of-aerial-photos/#:~:text=The%20first%20 known%20aerial%20photograph,%2C%20known%20 as%20%22Nadar%22.&text=(center)%20Nadar's%20earli-est%20surviving%20aerial,1860%2C%20by%20James%20 Wallace%20Black.

31. See Simon Baker's "The Hitherto Impossible in Photography Was Our Specialty," who takes his title from George R. Lawrence's Chicago-based commercial photography business. Among other credits, Lawrence constructed what was, at the turn of the twentieth century, the world's largest camera, weighing in at fourteen hundred pounds. *Air & Space Magazine*, October–November 1988, 64–68.

32. Woglom, "Unusual Uses," 621.

33. Gaston Tissandier, quoted in James Ryan, *Photography and Exploration* (London: Reaktion Books, 2013), 13. For a comprehensive history of nineteenth-century photography

in the United States, see *Photography in Nineteenth-Century America*, ed. Martha A. Sandweiss (Fort Worth, TX: Amon Carter Museum, 1991).

34. James R. Ryan, *Photography and Exploration* (Chicago: University of Chicago Press, 2013), 14.

35. Haraway, "Situated Knowledge," 576.

36. Woglom, "Unusual Uses," 621.

37. Ibid.

38. Erwin Hinckley Barbour, "Laboratory Photography," *Journal of Applied Microscopy* 3 (January 15, 1900): 750.

39. Very little has been written about Lawrence, but scholars will be interested to read Christopher Turner's 2008–2009 article "George R. Lawrence, Aeronaut Photographer," *Cabinet Magazine* 32 (2009), https://www.cabinetmagazine. org/issues/32/turner.php. While Lawrence never published any descriptions of his inventions, two military reports exist that both evaluate and offer diagrams of his "captive airships." See L. H. Chandler, "Report of the Performance of the Photographic Apparatus for Use with Kites," US Navy Department, Bureau of Ordnance, Washington, DC, May 22, 1905; W. H. G. Bullard, A. L. Willard, and J. H. Holden, "Report upon the Kite Photographic Experiments," USS *Maine*, Hampton Roads, Virginia, January 12, 1906. Several of Lawrence's photographs, including *San Francisco in Ruins*, can be found online via the Library of Congress.

40. Simon Baker, "San Francisco in Ruins," *Landscape Magazine* 30, no. 2 (1989), http://robroy.dyndns.info/lawrence/landscape.html.

41. Ibid.

42. Turner, "George R. Lawrence."

43. Marie Thébaud-Sorger, "Thomas Baldwin's *Airopaidia*, or the Aerial View in Color," *Seeing from Above: The Aerial View in Visual Culture*, ed. Mark Dorrian and Frédéric Pousin (New York: I. B. Tauris, 2013), 59.

44. Baker, "San Francisco in Ruins."

45. Marina Warner, "Intimate Communiqués: Melchior Lorck's Flying Tortoise," in *Seeing from Above: The Aerial View in Visual Culture*, ed. Mark Dorrian and Frédéric Pousin (New York: I. B. Tauris, 2013), 13.

46. Sontag, *On Photography* (New York: Picador, 1990), 4.

47. While the majority of the photographs taken of the Animas River contamination are aerial shots, I referenced the following for the purposes of this project. A *CBS News* article included two photographs and two videos, all of which depicted the disaster from above. "EPA Says It Won't Repay Claims for Spill That Caused Yellow Rivers," CBS News, January 13, 2017, https://www.cbsnews.com/news/gold-kin g-mine-spill-colorado-rivers-epa-claims/#:~:text=EPA%20 says%20it%20won't%20repay%20claims,spill%20that%20 caused%20yellow%20rivers&text=DENVER%20 %2D%2D%20The%20Environmental%20Protection,say ing%20the%20law%20prohibits%20it. Sara Jerome's *Water Online* article included an aerial photograph depicting a contaminated Animas River rushing through a canyon: "EPA Wastewater Spill Creates Challenges for Navajo Nation," *Water Online*, August 28, 2015.

48. Timothy Morton, *Hyperobjects: Philosophy and Ecology after the End of the World* (Minneapolis: University of Minnesota Press, 2013).

49. Ibid., 199.

50. Ibid.

51. Bullard, Willard, and Holden, "Report."

52. Chandler, "Report."

53. Morton, *Hyperobjects*, 27.

54. Woglom, "Unusual Uses," 625.

55. Quoted in Richard Holmes, "Gigantic Voyages," *Falling Upwards: How We Took to the Air, an Unconventional History of Ballooning* (New York: Pantheon Books, 2013), 172–73.

56. George R. Lawrence, "Photograph of San Francisco in Ruins from Lawrence Captive Airship, 2,000-Feet above San Francisco Bay overlooking Waterfront," 1906, *The Panoramic Photographs Collection*, Library of Congress, Washington, DC, February 27, 2017; Francis Luis Mora, *Cloud Study from the Connecticut Litchfield Hills*, 1912–1919, Oil on panel, Dallas, Heritage Auctions; Edith Van Dyne, *The Flying Girl* (Chicago: Reilly & Britton Company, 1911).

57. Haraway, "Situated Knowledges," 582.

58. Katharine M. Rogers quotes an 1888 *Aberdeen Daily* article saying that Baum "finds recreation from the cares of an extensive business [*sic*] in the fascinating pursuit, amateur photography. Mr. Baum was proficient in the art and during his stay in the city secured a number of fine negatives of Dakota land and cloud scapes" (20). Rogers then notes that later in his life Baum owned his own darkroom and passed his love of photography along to his children as well (20). Rogers, *L. Frank Baum: Creator of Oz: A Biography* (New York: St. Martin's Press, 2007).

59. Edwin P. Ryland, a close friend of Baum, says that if Baum "had not taken to writing children's books he might have been one of the country's best known technical writers for he had a strong leaning toward technical matters." Quoted in Michael Patrick Hearn, Introduction, *The Annotated Wizard of Oz* (New York: W. W. Norton & Company, 2000), lxxxiv; Charlotte Perkins Gilman, "When We Fly: How the Accomplishment of Aerial Navigation Will Make Necessary a Revision of Human Laws and Customs," *Harper's Weekly*, November 9, 1907, 1650, 1664.

60. Gilman, "When We Fly," 1664.

61. Charlotte Perkins Gilman, *Herland* (Mineola, NY: Dover Publications, 1915), 9.

62. Edith Van Dyne, *The Flying Girl* (Chicago: Reilly and Britton Company, 1911); Edith Van Dyne, *The Flying Girl and*

Her Chum (Chicago: Reilly and Britton Company, 1912).

63. Harry Lincoln Sayler wrote both *The Airship Boys* and *The Aeroplane Boys*, even though the latter was published under the pen name Ashton Lamar. *The Airship Boys* series includes seven books published from 1909 to 1913. Seven books appear in *The Aeroplane Boys* series, published from 1910 to 1913.

64. Van Dyne, *The Flying Girl*, 189.

65. In *Sand, Water, Salt*, I use the term "imperial" and "imperialism" primarily in reference to late nineteenth-century American expansionist policies, wherein territorial appropriation and resource acquisition were but two of its central aims. Scientific expeditions and quest narratives, such as *The Wizard of Oz*, proved fundamental to this larger project. Imperialism, then, as it is used in this project, signals what W. J. T. Mitchell calls the "complicated process of exchange, mutual transformation, and ambivalence" (9) that cohered in turn-of-the-century expansionist practices and enabled the codification of a globalized "empire" in the twentieth century. W. J. T. Mitchell, "Imperial Landscapes," *Landscape and Power* (Chicago: University of Chicago Press, 2002), 1–34. See also Michael Hardt and Antonio Negri, *Empire* (Cambridge, MA: Harvard University Press, 2000).

66. Baum was born and raised in Chittenango, New York, a canal town that connects to the Erie Canal.

67. According to historian Thomas C. Leonard, regardless of Progressives' diverse goals, "all of [them] found a way to make a vocation of reform" (11). *Illiberal Reformers: Race, Eugenics, and American Economics in the Progressive Era* (Princeton, NJ: Princeton University Press, 2016).

68. Fox, *Aereality*, 7.

69. "Plowing the Desert: Salt Lake Road Penetrating a New Waste Region," *Topeka State Journal*, December 26, 1903, 3.

70. William L. Fox, *Terra Antarctica: Looking into the Emptiest*

Continent (Berkeley, CA: Counterpoint, 2007).

71. Ibid., 6.

72. Ibid., 18.

73. Ibid.

74. Nancy Tystad Koupal, "The Wonderful Wizard of the West: L. Frank Baum in South Dakota, 1888–1891," *Great Plains Quarterly* 9 (Fall 1989): 203–15.

75. Ibid., 212.

76. Similar to Martha Banta's "managed life," Leonard in *Illiberal Reformers* refers to the "dismantling" of laissez-faire economics and the subsequent adherence to regulation and reform as "the administrative state" (ix). This description is common among political and economic historians.

77. Thébaud-Sorger, "Thomas Baldwin's *Airopaidia*," 54.

78. See Marie Thébaud-Sorger's reflections on how "air and atmospheric density, the play of wind and fog, all conspire to blur perception and distort attempts at object identification" (56). "Thomas Baldwin's *Airopaidia*."

79. As a branch of the Department of the Interior, the BLM's mission is to "sustain the health, diversity, and productivity of the public lands for human use and enjoyment of present and future generations," which reveals an alignment with such capitalist desires as "productivity," consumption, and conservation (the protection of national resources) over preservation. US Department of the Interior, Bureau of Land Management, "Our Mission," Bureau of Land Management, https://www.blm.gov/about/our-mission, accessed July 17, 2017.

80. Fox, *Terra Antarctica*, xiv.

81. It is also worth noting that in Baum's young adult novel *The Boy Fortune Hunters in China*, written under the pseudonym Floyd Akers, he uses the word "dainty" four times to describe Chinese women. While my own project focuses on the capitalist connotations of fragile china in *The Wizard*

of Oz, scholars might also be interested in exploring Baum's Dainty China Country as it relates to Progressive views on the Chinese and Chinese immigrants. Floyd Akers (L. Frank Baum), *The Boy Fortune Hunters in China* (Chicago: Reilly and Britton Co.), 1909.

82. For a history of the manufacturing and use of porcelain in American building and engineering, see Thomas C. Jester's "Porcelain Enamel," in *Twentieth-Century Building Materials: History and Conservation* (Los Angeles: Getty Publications, 2014), 223–30.

83. In a 1900 article in the *Journal of Applied Microscopy and Laboratory Methods*, the author notes that "dishing" occurred in mid-nineteenth-century microscopes as well: "There were strange iridescent rings around the outside of the field and 'dishing' of the object, which we now condemn as chromatic and spherical aberration" (753). Charles H. Potter, "Laboratory Photography," *Journal of Applied Microscopy and Laboratory Methods* 3 (1900): 748–56.

84. Thébaud-Sorger, "Thomas Baldwin's *Airopaidia*," 93.

85. Cecilia Tichi, *Shifting Gears: Technology, Literature, Culture in Modernist America* (Chapel Hill: University of North Carolina Press, 1987), 45, 54.

86. Daniel Eli Burnstein, *Next to Godliness: Confronting Dirt and Despair in Progressive Era New York City* (Urbana-Champaign: University of Illinois Press, 2006).

87. Tichi, *Shifting Gears*, 16; American Society for Quality, "Continuous Improvement," American Society for Quality, 2017, https://asq.org/quality-resources/continuous-improvement, accessed March 15, 2017.

88. American Society for Quality, "Continuous Improvement."

89. In *Next to Godliness*, Burnstein says, "An individual's level of well-being, comfort, and health reflected both the quality of his or her environment and what we would today term his or her 'lifestyle.' This holistic outlook, which implicitly

recognized a link between impoverished living standards and disease, was an important component of the progressives' semi-utopian vision of the good society, a vision of widespread improvement in individual and community health, well-being, and morality" (141). For more on Progressives' managerial approach to social, environmental, and economic reform, see Leonard, *Illiberal Reformers*; Martha Banta, *Taylored Lives: Narrative Productions in the Age of Taylor, Veblen, and Ford* (Chicago: University of Chicago Press, 1993); Richard Hofstadter, *The Age of Reform: From Bryan to F. D. R.* (New York: Knopf Doubleday, 2011); and Samuel P. Hays, *Conservation and the Gospel of Efficiency: The Progressive Conservation Movement, 1890–1920* (Pittsburgh: University of Pittsburgh Press, 1999).

90. Tichi, *Shifting Gears*, 4.
91. American Society for Quality, "Continuous Improvement."
92. Roger Turner, "Aviation Meteorology: How Flight Safety Depends upon the Repetitious Production of Constantly Expiring Data," paper presented at the Maintainers Conference, Hoboken, NJ, April 2016.
93. Ibid., 2–3.
94. Ibid., 3.
95. For an insightful analysis on the effects of innovation as a "dominant ideology," see Andrew Russell and Lee Vinsel, "Hail the Maintainers," *Aeon*, April 7, 2016.
96. Mitchell, *Landscape and Power*, 16.
97. Bennett, *Vibrant Matter*, xi.
98. Winona LaDuke, "Native American Activist Winona LaDuke at Standing Rock: It's Time to Move on from Fossil Fuels," interviewed by Amy Goodman, *Democracy Now!*, September 12, 2016.
99. Voyles, *Wastelanding: Legacies of Uranium Mining in Navajo Country* (Minneapolis: University of Minnesota Press, 2015).

100. Norton, "Testimony." Following Norton's vision of ANWR as an unwelcoming environment, photographer Subhankar Banerjee notes in the description of his "Arctic Series Photographs" that the television program *60 Minutes* described ANWR as a "hostile wasteland," reinforcing the idea that Arctic spaces are nefarious as well as unproductive. Banerjee, "Arctic Series Photographs," Subhankar Banerjee, http://www.subhankarbanerjee.org/selectphotographs. html, accessed July 1, 2018.

101. Fox, *Aereality*, 3.

102. Norton, "Testimony."

103. Ibid.

104. Ibid.

105. Donald Trump, "Remarks by President Trump at the National Republican Congressional Committee March Dinner," National Building Museum, Washington, DC, March 20, 2018, whitehouse.gov.

106. Ibid.

107. The language quoted in this sentence derives from the 1980 Alaska Lands Act, which consolidated the state's refuge systems, including ANWR. US Congress, Senate, *Alaska National Interest Lands Conservation Act Refuges*, December 2, 1980.

108. Journalist Bill Weir called ANWR the "North American Serengeti" due to its rich biodiversity: "With bears, both brown bears and polar, musk oxen, Arctic foxes and the nests of birds from all 50 states, this place is a North American Serengeti, which is why it was first set aside in 1960 and protected by an act of Congress in 1980." Weir, "Inside Alaska's Battles over Land, Sea, and Life," CNN, July 25, 2018.

109. Fox, *Aereality*, 46.

110. Ibid., 47.

111. Mitchell, *Landscape and Power*, 29–30.

CHAPTER 2

1. Vanessa Agard-Jones, "What the Sands Remember," *GLQ: A Journal of Lesbian and Gay Studies* 18, nos. 2–3 (2012): 325–46, quote at 340. A segment of this chapter was originally published in *Western American Literature*. It has been revised and reprinted here with permission from the publisher. Jada Ach, "'Left All Alone in This World's Wilderness': Queer Ecology, Desert Spaces, and Unmaking the Nation in Frank Norris's *McTeague*," *Western American Literature* 51, no. 2 (Summer 2016): 175–97.

2. Michael Cobb, "Welcome to the Desert of Me," in *Single: Arguments for the Uncoupled* (New York: New York University Press, 2012), 173.

3. Mary Hunter Austin, *The Land of Little Rain* (1903; New York: The Modern Library, 2003), 54.

4. Frank Norris, *McTeague: A Story of San Francisco*, ed. Donald Pizer (1899; New York: Norton, 1997); Mary Hunter Austin, *The Land of Little Rain* (New York: Houghton, Mifflin, & Co., 1903). Hereafter cited in text.

5. In *Politics of Nature*, Bruno Latour describes an "actant" as anything that "modifies other actors through a series of" actions (75). Latour distinguishes "actor," which he deems anthropomorphic, from "actant, which is any "acting agent," be it human or nonhuman (75). Latour, *Politics of Nature: How to Bring the Sciences into Democracy*, translated by Catherine Porter (Cambridge, MA: Harvard University Press, 2004).

6. Heather I. Sullivan, "Dirt Theory and Material Ecocriticism," *Interdisciplinary Studies in Literature and the Environment* 19, no. 3 (2012): 518.

7. Ibid.

8. Ibid., 526.

9. Ednah Aiken, *The River* (Indianapolis: Bobbs-Merrill Company, 1914), 98.

10. Sullivan, "Dirt Theory," 518. See also Stacy Alaimo and Linda Nash for historical overviews of what Alaimo calls "the permeable body" (*Bodily Natures* 89–91) and what Nash refers to as an "inescapable ecology." Alaimo, *Bodily Nature: Science, Environment, and the Material Self* (Bloomington: Indiana University Press, 2010); Nash, *Inescapable Ecologies: A History of Environment, Disease, and Knowledge* (Berkeley: University of California Press, 2007).

11. "Spotless Town Campaign On," *Arizona Republican*, April 4, 1914, retrieved from Chronicling America—The Library of Congress, November 20, 2019.

12. Nicolas Witschi, *Traces of Gold: California's Natural Resources and the Claim to Realism in Western American Literature* (Tuscaloosa: University of Alabama Press, 2002), 12.

13. Lauren Berlant and Lee Edelman, *Sex, or the Unbearable* (Durham, NC: Duke University Press, 2013), xi.

14. Grosz, *Chaos, Territory, Art: Deleuze and the Framing of the Earth* (New York: Columbia University Press, 2008).

15. Many ecocritics and historians have shaped my new materialist reading in this chapter. In many ways, my project, which focuses on queer human-sand relationships in the context of Progressive Era land management, picks up where these scholars have left off. Annette Kolodny's groundbreaking *The Lay of the Land: Metaphor as Experience and History in American Life and Letters* (1984) examines how the use of feminine and maternal metaphors to describe the New World represents a "uniquely American 'pastoral impulse,'" one that fosters an exploitive human-environmental relationship that has persisted since the arrival of white settlers. In Martha Banta's *Taylored Lives: Narrative Productions in the Age of Taylor, Veblen, and Ford* (1993), she extrapolates what she terms the Progressive Era's "managed life," offering a top-down vision of scientific management and literary

manifestations thereof. James C. Scott's wide-ranging global historical analysis, *Seeing Like a State: How Certain Schemes to Improve the Human Condition Have Failed* (1998), interrogates the relationship between managerial legibility and state power in the twentieth century. Of particular interest to my project is Scott's focus on the inception of scientific forestry and land management in Europe, especially his suggestion that local practices do not always align with state agendas. "There will always be a shadow land-tenure system lurking beside and beneath the official account in the land-records office. We must never assume that local practice conforms with state theory" (49). Similar to Scott, Julia E. Daniel's ecocritical literary analysis, *Building Natures: Modern American Poetry, Landscape Architecture, and City Planning,* explores park management in the early twentieth century. In her chapter titled "Marianne Moore and the National Park Service," she explores Moore's "park poem" "An Octopus" and argues that the poet "recognizes, rather than ignores, the human presence that both crafts and moves through the crafted landscape" of Mount Rainier National Park (153). All four of these authors examine land and landscape management through the lens of gender, cultural studies, global and European history, poetics, and modernist studies, paving the way for my queer Progressive Era approach to environmental management in American fiction. Kolodny, *The Lay of the Land: Metaphor as Experience and History in American Life and Letters* (Chapel Hill: University of North Carolina Press, 1984); Banta, *Taylored Lives: Narrative Productions in the Age of Taylor, Veblen, and Ford* (Chicago: University of Chicago Press, 1993); Scott, *Seeing Like a State: How Certain Schemes to Improve the Human Condition Have Failed* (New Haven, CT: Yale University Press, 1998); Daniel, *Building Natures: Modern American Poetry, Landscape Architecture, and City Planning*

(Charlottesville: University of Virginia Press, 2017).

16. Here, the word "vibrant" alludes to Jane Bennett's *Vibrant Matter: A Political Ecology of Things*. In this work, Bennett argues for the "vitality of matter and the lively powers of material formations" (vii) (Durham, NC: Duke University Press, 2010).

17. Among many other sources that refer to the southwestern US desert as an "empire," see "Desert Empire Is Discovered by Explorers from the North," *Imperial Valley Press* (El Centro, CA), December 19, 1908, retrieved from Chronicling America—The Library of Congress; "Plans to Water Vast Dry Area," *Fair Play* (Ste. Genevieve, MO), September 25, 1920, retrieved from Chronicling America—The Library of Congress; "Means Reclamation of Desert Empire," *Salt Lake Tribune*, March 12, 1910, retrieved from Chronicling America—The Library of Congress. (All sources retrieved November 20, 2019.)

18. "Savage People on Good Roads Move," *Arizona Republican*, September 8, 1916, retrieved from Chronicling America—The Library of Congress, November 20, 2019.

19. Ibid.

20. United States Department of Transportation, Federal Highway Administration, "Zero Milestone—Washington, DC," *Highway History*, fhwa.dot.gov, accessed November 15, 2017.

21. Ibid.

22. Mel Y. Chen, *Animacies: Biopolitics, Racial Mattering, and Queer Affect* (Durham, NC: Duke University Press, 2012).

23. "Car Performs Thrilling Feats," *Evening Capital News* (Boise, ID), September 24, 1916, retrieved from Chronicling America—The Library of Congress, November 20, 2019.

24. Ibid.

25. Scott Harrison, "Where Is Death Valley Dodge?," *Los*

Angeles Times, September 25, 2013.

26. Austin, *Earth Horizon* (Santa Fe: Sunstone Press, 1932). See also J. Smeaton Chase, *California Desert Trails* (Boston: Houghton, Mifflin & Co., 1919), 263. In *Earth Horizon*, Austin refers to automobile culture in the desert two other times, and she seems saddened by the encroachment of cars in areas once considered remote. In one passage, she says, "you can reach the land itself by motor bus from Los Angeles in a few hours. But on the life there, the unforgettable life, modern America has laid a greedy, vulgarizing hand" (234). In yet another passage, she mentions that "long stretches of the road" between points of interest used to "ramble along the shallow dry beds of seasonal streams." Such winding roads have "long since straightened for automobiles" (187). Similarly, travel writer J. Smeaton Chase comments on the problems sand poses for locomotion in his 1919 work *California Desert Trails*: "The sand probably overlies a rocky abutment of the adjacent foothills, and has been heaped there by that scarifying wind, the terror of railway employees whose lines are cast in the division which includes the San Gorgonio Pass" (5).

27. J. M. Murdoch, "The Lure of Death Valley," *Goodwin's Weekly: A Thinking Paper for Thinking People* (Salt Lake City, UT), February 25, 1911, retrieved from Chronicling America—The Library of Congress, November 19, 2019.

28. See Kevin Starr, *Material Dreams: Southern California through the 1920s* (New York: Oxford University Press, 1991).

29. See Mark Seltzer's alignment of the male body with the "procreative force of the machine" in *Bodies and Machines* (New York: Routledge, 1992), 27.

30. In *Land*, Austin refers to the essence of the desert as "desertness." Here is one example in the introductory chapter: "And yet—and yet—is it not perhaps to satisfy expectation

that one falls into the tragic key in writing of desertness? The more you wish of it the more you get, and in the mean time lose much of pleasantness" (9–10).

31. In a January 13, 2018, *New York Times* article by Hiroko Tabuchi, "Uranium Miners Pushed Hard for a Comeback. They Got Their Wish," Tabuchi says, "[E]mboldened by the Trump Administration's embrace of corporate interests, the uranium mining industry is renewing a push into the areas adjacent to Mr. Holiday's Navajo Nation home: the Grand Canyon watershed to the west, where a new uranium mine is preparing to open, and the Bears Ears National Monument to the north."

32. Chris Packard, *Queer Cowboys and Other Erotic Male Friendships in Nineteenth-Century American Literature* (New York: Palgrave Macmillan, 2005), 1.

33. John P. O'Grady, *Pilgrims to the Wild: Everett Ruess, Henry David Thoreau, John Muir, Clarence King, and Mary Austin* (Salt Lake City: University of Utah Press, 1993).

34. Ibid., 125.

35. Ibid.

36. Catriona Mortimer-Sandilands and Bruce Erickson, "Introduction: A Genealogy of Queer Ecologies," *Queer Ecologies: Sex, Nature, Politics, Desire* (Bloomington: Indiana University Press, 2010), 13, 14. See also Mortimer-Sandilands, "Unnatural Passions? Notes toward a Queer Ecology," *Invisible Culture: An Electronic Journal for Visual Culture* 9 (2005), https://www.rochester.edu/in_visible_culture/Issue_9/issue9_sandilands.pdf.

37. Denise Cruz, "Reconsidering *McTeague*'s 'Mark' and 'Mac': Intersections of U.S. Naturalism, Imperial Masculinities, and Desire between Men," *American Literature* 78, no. 3 (2006): 488.

38. Mortimer-Sandilands and Erickson, "Introduction," 13.

39. Ibid.

40. United States Congress, Senate, S. 32, Yellowstone Act of 1872, 42nd Congress, 2nd Session (Washington, DC: Government Printing Office, 1872). *America's National Park System: The Critical Documents*, https://www.nps.gov/parkhistory/online_books/anps/anps_1c.htm.

41. Jennifer Fleissner, "The Great Indoors: Regionalism, Feminism, and Obsessional Domesticity," in *Women, Compulsion, Modernity: The Moment of American Naturalism* (Chicago: University of Chicago Press, 2004), 85.

42. Tom Lynch, *Xerophilia: Ecocritical Explorations in Southwestern Literature* (Lubbock: Texas Tech University Press, 2008), 22, 33.

43. David McGlynn, "*McTeague*'s Gilded Prison," *Rocky Mountain Review* 62, no. 1 (2008): 39.

44. Ibid., 38.

45. Norris writes, "What strange sixth sense stirred in McTeague at this time? What animal cunning, what brute instinct clamored for recognition and obedience? What lower faculty was it that roused his suspicion, that drove him out into the night a score of times between dark and dawn, his head in the air, his eyes and ears keenly alert?" (215). And again on page 226, he braids McTeague's "strange sixth sense" with his "brute instinct": "What! It was warning him again, that strange sixth sense, that obscure brute instinct. It was aroused again and clamoring to be obeyed. Here, in these desolate barren hills, twenty miles from the nearest human being, it stirred and woke and rowelled him to be moving on."

46. McGlynn, "*McTeague*'s Gilded Prison," 38.

47. Cruz, "Reconsidering," 507.

48. Noreen Giffney and Myra J. Hird, "Introduction: Queering the Non/Human," in *Unnatural Predators: Queer Theory Meets Environmental Studies in Bram Stoker's* Dracula, ed. Noreen Giffney and Myra J. Hird (Burlington, VT:

Ashgate, 2008), 4.

49. Robert Azzarello, *Queer Environmentality: Ecology, Evolution, and Sexuality in American Literature* (Burlington, VT: Ashgate, 2012).

50. Ibid., 28.

51. Mortimer-Sandilands and Erickson, "Introduction," 14, 20.

52. Ibid., 20.

53. Mortimer-Sandilands and Erickson, "Introduction," 39.

54. United States Congress, The Yellowstone Act of 1872.

55. In "Queer Ecology," Morton explains that "ecological phenomena display . . . infinite strangeness. By contrast, Masculine Nature is 'unperversion.' Organicism articulates desire as erasure, erasure-desire. Organicism wants nature 'untouched,' subject to no desire." He goes on to say that "[Masculine Nature's] desire for 'virginity' is in fact a desire." The ethos of "Masculine Nature," according to Morton, elides the landscape of agency or desire by characterizing it as an already-mapped space that requires human care in the form of regulation, management, and enforcement. Desire's only purpose within this schema is to keep the environment *intact* ("virginal") and under careful surveillance. Morton, "Guest Column: Queer Ecology," *Publications of the Modern Language Association of America* 125, no. 2 (2010): 279.

56. Agard-Jones, "What the Sands Remember," 325–26.

57. United States Congress, Yellowstone Act of 1872.

58. Ibid.

59. Ibid.

60. O'Grady, *Pilgrims to the Wild*, xi.

61. Agard-Jones, "What the Sands Remember," 340.

62. Giffney and Hird, "Introduction," xvii.

63. Michael O'Rourke, "Series Editor's Preface: The Open," in *Queering the Non/Human*, ed. Noreen Giffney and Myra J. Hird (Burlington, VT: Ashgate, 2008), xvii.

64. Sullivan, "Dirt Theory," 515.

65. Cruz, "Reconsidering," 507.

66. Ibid.

67. Ibid.

68. Bruce Erickson, "'fucking close to water': Queering the Production of the Nation," in *Queer Ecologies: Sex, Nature, Politics, Desire*, ed. Catriona Mortimer-Sandilands and Bruce Erickson (Bloomington: Indiana University Press, 2010), 323.

69. Ibid., 327.

70. Rebecca Nisetich, "The Nature of the Beast: Scientific Theories of Race and Sexuality in *McTeague*," *Studies in American Naturalism* 4, no. 1 (2009): 18.

71. Cobb, *Welcome to the Desert*, 173.

72. Ibid., 170–71.

73. Lee Clark Mitchell, *Determined Fictions: American Literary Naturalism* (New York: Columbia University Press, 1989), 3.

74. Ibid., 78.

75. National Park Service, "Death Valley National Park," US Department of the Interior, NPS.gov, November 27, 2013.

76. United States Congress, Senate, S. 21, California Desert Protection Act of 1994, 103rd Congress, 43rd Session (Washington, DC: Government Printing Office, 1994).

77. William Cronon, *Changes in the Land: Indians, Colonists, and the Ecology of New England* (New York: Hill and Wang, 2003), 58.

78. Latour, *Politics of Nature*, 81.

79. In *Wastelanding*, an environmental history of uranium mining in the Southwest, Traci Brynne Voyles writes, "Long before uranium was commonly known for its associations with both nuclear power and nuclear bombs, and long before atomic power took hold of the American public imagination as a fearsome signifier of new human relationships to technology, to the environment, and to each other,

uranium was mostly considered waste. Miners came across it when they blasted apart carnotite, a composite rock that can often be recognized by characteristic streaks of red, black, and bright yellow, to get at the real prize: vanadium, which was used to strengthen steel alloys in a range of products, from automobile parts to gun barrels" (2). *Wastelanding: Legacies of Uranium Mining in Navajo Country* (Minneapolis: University of Minnesota Press, 2015).

80. Sarah Jaquette Ray argues that Austin and other nature writers often engage in primitivism by depicting Indigenous relations with the environment in strictly harmonious and romantic terms. "The genre of nature writing," Ray says, "for the most part has been a genre invested in whiteness and American empire. The nature essay extends natural history and travel writing, forms that have their own roots in imperial expansion, erasure of native populations, and appropriation of natural resources. Even Mary Austin's modernist appreciation for Native American ways of being in the land has been resoundingly critiqued as primitivist—projecting onto Native peoples the ecological vision of harmony that she valorizes, at the cost of recognizing the trauma of dispossession and how that attenuated Native relations." Ray, "Nature Writing and the American West," in *A History of Western American Literature*, ed. Susan Kollin (New York: Cambridge University Press, 2015), 83. In *The Environmental Imagination*, Lawrence Buell comments on Austin's "essentializing" tendencies when it comes to writing about indigeneity (79). "Austin was only too ready to represent herself as the authoritative voice of the West and of Native American culture," he says (79). Buell, *The Environmental Imagination: Thoreau, Nature Writing, and the Formation of American Culture* (Cambridge, MA: The Belknap Press of Harvard University Press, 1995).

81. O'Grady, *Pilgrims to the Wild*, 125.

82. Buell, *Environmental Imagination*, 177.
83. Gary Reger, "The Deserts of Los Angeles: Two Topographies," *Boom California*, May 24, 2017.
84. Charles Nordhoff, *California: For Health, Pleasure, and Residence, A Book for Travellers and Settlers* (New York: Harper & Brothers, 1873), 32.
85. Buell argues that Austin also engages in "self-projection" in *Land* when she attempts to describe the people who make their home in the desert, such as a Paiute artist and medicine man. In other words, she sees herself everywhere in the desert. *Environmental Imagination*, 80.
86. Austin, *Earth Horizon*, 182.
87. In *The Future of Environmental Criticism: Environmental Crisis and the Literary Imagination*, Lawrence Buell notes that despite the fact that "place" is an "indispensable concept" in ecocriticism, "one cannot theorize scrupulously about place without confronting its fragility, including the question of whether 'place' as traditionally understood means anything anymore at a time when fewer and fewer of the world's population live out their lives in locations that are not shaped to a great extent by translocal—ultimately global—forces" (62–63). What's more, he argues that "place can become regressive and repressive when it is thought of in essentialized terms as an unchanging unitary entity, as in ethnocentric appeals to *Heimat* or local patriotism" (145–46). Timothy Morton also theorizes on the shortcomings of "place" in the age of global capitalism, remarking that blind attachment to "the local" over the global or hyperobjective cannot lead to political action. In *Ecology without Nature: Rethinking Environmental Aesthetics*, he says, "In social structure and in thought, goes the argument, place has been ruthlessly corroded by space: all that is solid melts into air. But unless we think about it some more, the cry of 'place!' will resound in empty space, to no effect. It is a question of

whether you think that the 're-enchantment of the world' will make nice pictures, or whether it is a political practice" (10–11). Buell, *The Future of Environmental Criticism* (Malden, MA: Blackwell, 2005); Timothy Morton, *Ecology without Nature: Rethinking Environmental Aesthetics* (Cambridge, MA: Harvard University Press, 2007).

88. In "Nature Writing and the American West," Ray compares Austin to both Henry David Thoreau and John Muir in her portrayal of "an emptied landscape . . . so favored by the romantic nature writers" (90).

89. David N. Cassuto, *Dripping Dry: Literature, Politics, and Water in the Desert Southwest* (Ann Arbor: University of Michigan Press, 2001), 41–42.

90. Cecilia Tichi, *Shifting Gears: Technology, Literature, Culture in Modernist America* (Chapel Hill: University of North Carolina Press, 1987).

91. Austin, *Earth Horizon,* 234.

92. Stacy Alaimo, "The Undomesticated Nature of Feminism: Mary Austin and the Progressive Women Conservationists," *Studies in American Fiction* 26, no. 1 (1998): 73.

93. Buell, *The Environmental Imagination,* 49.

94. Smythe, *The Conquest of Arid America* (New York: Harper & Brothers, 1900), ix.

95. In *Dripping Dry,* Cassuto writes, "Linking women with the land and classifying both as reproductive agents and tools of the patriarchy allowed their use and abuse in the name of the common good. They become resources, and natural resources are, by definition, national assets" (40). The use of the word "virginal," then, to describe natural spaces rich in resources furthers patriarchal notions of sexuality that align "virgin" with "good" and "pure."

96. John Muir, *Our National Parks* (Boston: Houghton, Mifflin and Co., 1900), 2, 3.

97. Samuel W. Ball, "The Conservation of Social Energy," *The*

Progressive Woman 6, no. 75 (n.d.): 4.

98. Ibid.

99. Nordhoff, *California*, 63.

100. Rebecca McWilliams Evans, "Unnatural History: Ecological Temporality in Post–1945 American Literature" (PhD diss., Duke University, 2016), 28.

101. National Park Service, "Joshua Tree: Foundation Document," National Park Service, nps.gov, accessed December 20, 2017.

102. Timothy Morton, *Dark Ecology: For a Logic of Future Coexistence* (New York: Columbia University Press, 2016), 29.

103. Bennett, *Vibrant Matter*, xiv.

104. See Bennett, *Vibrant Matter*.

105. Chase, *California Desert Trails*.

106. Ibid., 5.

107. The National Museum of the United States Army, "The Weather Bureau," nmusa.org, 2018, accessed January 17, 2018.

108. Bennett, *Vibrant Matter*, 16.

109. According to clean energy policy analyst Joel Stronberg, industrial sand entangles with many of our contemporary material desires, including roadway systems (cement), building materials (concrete and mortar), glass, and even electronics (silica). "Frac sand" is also used in the natural gas fracking process. "Sand Milling in America: It's Not Just about the Sand," *Civil Notion*, April 12, 2017. See also Vince Beiser, *The World in a Grain: The Story of Sand and How It Transformed Civilization* (New York: Penguin Random House, 2018).

110. Brian Thill, *Waste*, Object Lessons Series (New York: Bloomsbury, 2015), 53.

111. In "Nuclear Ontologies," Gabrielle Hecht describes the challenges of defining a *thing* as nuclear: "Such questions are problems of ontology, not merely of rhetoric. The nuclearity

of a nation, a program, a technology, or a material—that is, the degree to which any of these things count as 'nuclear'— can never be defined in simple, clear-cut, scientific terms. Rather, nuclearity is a technopolitical spectrum that shifts in time and space. It is a historical and geographical condition, as well as a scientific and technological one. And nuclearity, in turn, has significant consequences for politics, culture, and health. Degrees of nuclearity structure global control over the flow of radioactive materials; they constitute the conceptual bedrock of anti-nuclear movements; they affect regulatory frameworks for occupational health and compensation for work-related illnesses. This matter of degree is crucial; nuclearity is not an on-off condition. Nuclear ontologies have a history, and a geography" (251). Hecht, "Nuclear Ontologies," in *Energy Humanities: An Anthology*, ed. Imre Szeman and Dominic Boyer (Baltimore: Johns Hopkins University Press, 2017).

112. Claire Vaye Watkins, *Gold Fame Citrus* (New York: Riverhead Books, 2015), 85.

113. In *The Tainted Desert: Environmental Ruin in the American West*, Valerie L. Kuletz argues that "the ironic and continuing designation of this resource-rich terrain as wasteland in fact represents a very important means of justifying the relentless plunder of the region through highly environmentally destructive extractive technologies" (New York: Routledge, 1998), 13.

114. Evans, "Unnatural History," 50.

115. Hannes Bergthaller, Rob Emmet, Adeline Johns-Putra, et al., "Mapping Common Ground: Ecocriticism, Environmental History, and the Environmental Humanities," *Environmental Humanities* 5, no. 1 (2014): 261–76, quote at 265.

CHAPTER 3

1. Richard White, *The Organic Machine: The Remaking of the*

Columbia River (New York: Hill and Wang, 1996), 79. A segment of this chapter was originally published in *Ecozon@: European Journal of Literature, Culture and Environment*. It has been revised and reprinted here with permission from the publisher. Jada Ach, "Land 'under the Ditch': Channeling Water through Owen Wister's *The Virginian*," *Ecozon@: European Journal of Literature, Culture and Environment* 9, no. 1 (2018): 111–28.

2. William Phipps Blake, *The Imperial Valley and the Salton Sink* (San Francisco: John J. Newbegin, 1915), 18.

3. Sarah Winnemucca, *Life among the Piutes: Their Wrongs and Claims* (Reno: University of Nevada Press, 1994), 156.

4. Examples of water-related environmental disasters impacting the West in recent years include the failed emergency spillways in Oroville, California (2017), leaked crude oil from the newly finished Dakota Access Pipeline in South Dakota (2017), and the toxic wastewater spill at Gold King Mine (2015), to name just a few.

5. LeMenager, *Living Oil: Petroleum Culture in the American Century* (New York: Oxford University Press, 2014), 185.

6. This physical hardening resonates with Stacy Alaimo's transcorporeal theory, wherein bodies and natures flow into and through one another, materially altering both. In this sense, the men's dry, thirsty bodies physically *become* men via their intimate interactions with Wyoming's semiarid ecology. *Bodily Natures: Science, Environment, and the Material Self* (Bloomington: Indiana University Press, 2010).

7. Historian Kevin Starr developed the term "irrigation novel" to refer to fictional works that take water development as a central element of the plot. Examples might include Frank Norris's *The Octopus: A Story of California* (1901), Harold Bell Wright's *The Winning of Barbara Worth* (1911), Jack London's *The Valley of the Moon* (1913), Aiken's *The River* (1916), and Mary Hunter Austin's *The Ford* (1917). Kevin

Starr, *Material Dreams: Southern California through the 1920s* (New York: Oxford University Press, 1990).

8. In his envirotech history titled "Generating Infrastructural Invisibility: Insulation, Interconnection, and Avian Excrement in the Southern California Power Grid" (2015), Benson states, "Infrastructural inversion—the analytic practice of bringing the background into the foreground—requires a kind of focus that often escapes me" (121). *Environmental Humanities* 6 (2015): 103–30.

9. In this chapter, the term "animated" is used to describe the lively quality, or what Jane Bennett might refer to as "vibrancy," of both living and nonliving things. I do not always equate animacy with agency, as the latter presumes a willfulness or intent that need not exist for a thing to *matter*. In *Animacies*, critic Mel Y. Chen says that in the realm of critical theory, "animacy . . . has been described variously as a quality of agency, awareness, mobility, and liveness" (2). Jane Bennett, *Vibrant Matter: A Political Ecology of Things* (Durham, NC: Duke University Press, 2010); Mel Y. Chen, *Animacies: Biopolitics, Racial Mattering, and Queer Affect* (Durham, NC: Duke University Press, 2012).

10. "Ednah Aiken and 'The River,'" *Book News Monthly* 33, no. 6 (February 1916): 281–82.

11. Robert H. Wiebe, *The Search for Order, 1877–1920* (New York: Hill and Wang, 1967), 166.

12. Ednah Robinson Aiken, *The River* (Indianapolis: Bobbs-Merrill, 1914), 2–3. Hereafter cited in text.

13. Bennett, *Vibrant Matter*, ix.

14. White, *The Organic Machine*, xi.

15. Gifford Pinchot, *The Fight for Conservation* (New York: Doubleday, Page & Co., 1910), 5.

16. Samuel P. Hays, *Conservation and the Gospel of Efficiency* (Pittsburgh: University of Pittsburgh Press, 1999), 30.

17. The various approaches to Western water history noted in

this passage can be attributed to environmental historians Samuel P. Hays, Philip Fradkin, Donald Worster, Marc Reisner, Richard White, Donald J. Pisani, Daniel C. McCool, and Patricia Nelson Limerick. Spanning sixty years of water history, works by these historians demonstrate that as water flows through American history, its meaning and value continue to change. See Hays, *Conservation and the Gospel of Efficiency*; Fradkin, *A River No More: The Colorado River and the West* (Oakland: University of California Press, 1981); Worster, *Rivers of Empire: Water, Aridity, and the Growth of the American West* (New York: Oxford University Press, 1985); Reisner, *Cadillac Desert: The American West and Its Disappearing Water* (New York: Penguin, 1993); White, *The Organic Machine*; Pisani, "Beyond the Hundredth Meridian: Nationalizing the History of Water in the United States," *Environmental History* 5, no. 4 (2000): 466–82; McCool, *Native Waters: Contemporary Indian Water Settlements and the Second Treaty Era* (Tucson: University of Arizona Press, 2006); and Limerick, *A Ditch in Time: The City, the West, and Water* (Golden, CO: Fulcrum Publishing, 2012).

18. See Mark Seltzer, *Bodies and Machines* (New York: Routledge, 1992); David N. Cassuto, *Dripping Dry: Literature, Politics, and Water in the Desert Southwest* (Ann Arbor: University of Michigan Press, 1993); and Paul Formisano, "Presley's Pauses: Unearthing Force in California's Land and Water Regimes and Frank Norris's *The Octopus*," *Journal of Ecocriticism* 7, no. 1 (2015): 1–18. See also *Words on Water: Literary and Cultural Representations*, which looks at the symbolic and material significance of water from a global perspective. Edited by Maureen Devine and Christa Grewe-Volpp (Trier, Germany: WVT Wissenschaftlicher Verlag Trier, 2008), the collection of critical essays "entail[s] looking at water in its various forms as a part of our cultural

identity and heritage, understanding historical perceptions of water including political and economic aspects, as well as religious and spiritual perceptions of water past and present" (3). For a study on representations of water in Western films, see Mary Pinard, "Haunted by Waters: The River in American Films of the West," in *The Landscape of Hollywood Westerns: Ecocriticism in an American Film Genre*, ed. Deborah A. Carmichael (Salt Lake City: University of Utah Press, 2006).

19. Pinchot, *The Fight for Conservation*, 72.

20. Winnemucca, *Life among the Piutes*; Scott Lankford, "Sarah Winnemucca," in *Tahoe beneath the Surface: The Hidden Stories of America's Largest Mountain Lake* (Rockland, CA: Sierra College Press, 2016), 49–73.

21. Reisner, *Cadillac Desert*, 111.

22. Limerick, *A Ditch*, 264.

23. Ibid.

24. Cassuto, *Dripping Dry*, 37. Cassuto's compelling work, which combines environmental history with literary criticism, focuses on water's power to shape culture in Southern California. This chapter picks up where Cassuto left off by animating water's material power to enter bodies and elicit human desire.

25. White, *The Organic Machine*, 79.

26. Timothy Morton, *Dark Ecology: For a Logic of Future Coexistence* (New York: Columbia University Press, 2016).

27. Owen Wister, *The Virginian: A Horseman of the Plains* (1902; New York: Penguin Books, 1988), 62. Hereafter cited in text.

28. As a popular land management and conservation practice, "rewilding" is "the scientific argument for restoring big wilderness based on the regulatory roles of large predators" (Soulé and Noss). In this chapter, the term represents Wister's narrative strategy of naturalizing mechanical and

manmade systems. See Michael Soulé and Reed Noss, "Rewilding and Biodiversity as Complementary Goals for Continental Conservation," *Wild Earth* 22 (Fall 1998): 1–11.

29. According to Ashley Carse, "Infrastructure implies artifice; nature traditionally signifies its absence" (540). "Nature as Infrastructure: Making and Managing the Panama Canal Watershed," *Social Studies of Science* 42, no. 4 (2012): 539–63.

30. Here I'm gesturing toward the recent emergence of a materially oriented ecocriticism described by Jeffrey Jerome Cohen and Lowell Duckert as "elemental ecocriticism." In their collection of essays, *Elemental Ecocriticism: Thinking with Earth, Air, Water, and Fire*, Cohen and Duckert suggest that elements emerge as vibrant cultural actants in their own right (Minneapolis: University of Minnesota Press, 2015).

31. In addition to documenting Paiute relations with water that existed before "the best land [was] taken from them," Winnemucca's *Life among the Piutes* shines a light on Indigenous laborers who engaged in ditch and dam work for various water projects in the West, both on and off reservation land (122).

32. Edward Powers, *War and the Weather* (Chicago: Knight & Leonard, 1890), 6.

33. Ibid.

34. Ibid., 5.

35. Powers, *War and the Weather*, 11; John L. Cowan, "Dry Farming—The Hope of the West: A Method of Producing Bountiful Crops without Irrigation in Semi-Arid Regions," *Century Magazine*, July 1906, 435.

36. In Cowan's "Dry Farming," published in 1906, he states that "Nearly one third of the entire area of the United States, exclusive of Alaska and our insular possessions, consists of

vacant public lands regarded as naturally unsuited to cultivation on account of insufficient rainfall" (435).

37. Powers, *War and the Weather*, 5.

38. Ibid., 145.

39. Chapter 11 of the *California Water Plan*, most recently
updated in 2013, is titled "Precipitation Enhancement."
The chapter outlines California's current cloud seeding program, whereby silver iodide and other "seeding agents" are
injected into clouds "to produce more rainfall or snowfall
than they would produce naturally" (5). Wyoming's own
Weather Modification Project holds a similar goal of aug-
menting snowfall via cloud seeding. Cloud seeding has been
a common practice in Western states since at least the 1950s.
California Department of Water Resources, "Precipitation
Enhancement," *California Water Plan* 3 (2013): 5–15; Wyoming Water Development Commission, "Background," in
Wyoming Weather Modification Pilot Project, Wyoming
Water Development Commission Online, April 20, 2016,
https://wwdc.state.wy.us/weathermod/background.html.

40. Nebraska State Historical Society, "Melbourne, the
Rainmaker," Nebraska State Historical Society Online,
April 2010, https://history.nebraska.gov/publications/
melbourne-rainmaker.

41. Seltzer, *Bodies and Machines*, 164. It should be noted that
engineers, land managers, and administrators of various
types figure prominently in turn-of-the-century American
literature, including in Edith Wharton's *Ethan Frome* (1911)
and Edward Mandell House's *Philip Dru: Administrator: A
Story of Tomorrow, 1920–1935* (1912).

42. Daniel Belgrad, "'Power's Larger Meaning': The Johnson
County War as Political Violence in an Environmental Context," *Western Historical Quarterly* 33 (Summer 2002): 168.

43. Cowan, "Dry Farming," 436–37.

44. Ibid., 445.

45. Karen Bakker, "Water: Political, Biopolitical, Material," in *Water Worlds*, special issue of *Social Studies of Science* 42, no. 2 (2012): 617.

46. Cowan, "Dry Farming," 440.

47. Ibid., 442.

48. Ibid., 441.

49. Cowan notes that due to its "hardness," durum wheat prospered in the arid West (441). "It will not thrive in humid environments, requiring for its most perfect development a dry climate and a semiarid land" (441). In Latin, *durum* means "hard."

50. In landscape management, "softscapes" are the organic materials (plants, soils, flowers, pools, etc.) used to create landscapes. "Hardscapes," on the other hand, exist as the foundational materials (rock, metal, wood) that structure landscape design. At the 2016 C19 Conference, David Phillips and Judith Madera used the term "softscape" to denote watery ecotones such as swamps and marshes, a fitting contrast to the hard bodies and environments that populate *The Virginian*. Madera and Phillips, "On Edge Effects," C19: The Society of Nineteenth-Century Americanists Conference, State College, PA, March 19, 2016.

51. Seltzer, *Bodies and Machines*, 164.

52. Cowan, "Dry Farming," 436.

53. Seltzer, *Bodies and Machines*, 164.

54. Ibid. See also Pisani, "Beyond the Hundredth Meridian."

55. In the Yellowstone Act of 1872, which designated Yellowstone National Park as the first national park in the United States, Congress explains that these lands should be "reserved and withdrawn from settlement, occupancy, or sale under the laws of the United States." United States, S 32, Yellowstone Act of 1872, 42nd Congress, 2nd Session, Washington, DC: Government Printing Office, 1872.

56. John Muir, *Our National Parks* (Boston: Houghton, Mifflin

and Company, 1901), 1.

57. Carolyn Finney, *Black Spaces, White Faces: Reimagining the Relationship of African Americans to the Great Outdoors* (Chapel Hill: University of North Carolina Press, 2014), 28.

58. "Map of Wyoming with Special Reference to Shoshone Irrigation Company's Lands" (ca. 1900), *CB&Q: Building an Empire*, Chicago: Newberry Library, http://publications. newberry.org/cbqempire/items/show/153, accessed August 20, 2016.

59. "Cancer-Riddled Wind River Reservation Fights EPA over Uranium Contamination," *Indian Country Today*, January 19, 2012.

60. See Jennifer Tuttle, "Indigenous Whiteness and Wister's Invisible Indians," in *Reading* The Virginian *in the New West*, ed. Melody Graulich and Stephen Tatum (Lincoln: University of Nebraska Press, 2003), 89–112; and Louis Owens, "White for a Hundred Years," in *Reading* The Virginian *in the New West*, ed. Melody Graulich and Stephen Tatum (Lincoln: University of Nebraska Press, 2003), 72–88.

61. On the first page of *Life among the Piutes*, Winnemucca notes, "I was a very small child when the first white people came into our country. They came like a lion, yes, like a roaring lion, and have continued so ever since, and I have never forgotten their first coming" (5).

62. Peña, "Endangered Landscapes and Disappearing Peoples? Identity, Place, and Community in Ecological Politics," in *Environmental Justice Reader: Politics, Poetics, and Pedagogy*, ed. Joni Adamson (St. Louis: Turtleback Books, 2002), 70.

63. In *Vibrant Matter*, Bennett uses the term "assemblage" to describe an agentive, interactive conception of ecologies. "Actor-members" compose an assemblage, and "over time . . . the members themselves undergo internal alteration" (35). Unlike Timothy Morton's meshy "hyperobject,"

wherein individual members are rarely distinct, Bennett's "actor-members" retain their distinctness and "never melt into a collective body" (35). Morton, *Hyperobjects: Philosophy and Ecology after the End of the World* (Minneapolis: University of Minnesota Press, 2012).

64. McCool, *Native Waters*, 19.

65. Marta Banta, *Taylored Lives: Narrative Productions in the Age of Taylor, Veblen, and Ford* (Chicago: University of Chicago Press, 1993), 27.

66. Ibid., 28.

67. William E. Smythe, *The Conquest of Arid America* (New York: Harper & Brothers, 1900), 162.

68. Ibid., emphasis added.

69. Stacy Alaimo, *Bodily Natures: Science, Environment, and the Material Self* (Bloomington: Indiana University Press, 2010), 29.

70. According to Adamson, Evans, and Stein, environmental justice movements stand at the intersection of "ecological and social justice concerns." They continue, "We define environmental justice as the right of all people to share equally in the benefits bestowed by a healthy environment. We define the environment, in turn, as the places in which we live, work, play, and worship. Environmental justice initiatives specifically attempt to redress the disproportionate incidence of environmental contamination in communities of the poor and/or communities of color, to secure for those affected the right to live unthreatened by the risks posed by environmental degradation and contamination, and to afford equal access to natural resources that sustain life and culture." Joni Adamson, Mei Mei Evans, and Rachel Stein, "Introduction," in *The Environmental Justice Reader: Politics, Poetics, and Pedagogy*, ed. Joni Adamson, Mei Mei Evans, and Rachel Stein (Tucson: University of Arizona Press, 2002), 4.

71. The Office of Indian Affairs is today the Bureau of Indian Affairs and is managed by the Department of the Interior.

72. Smythe, *The Conquest of Arid America*, xvii.

73. McClure, "[Post]Indian Princess and Voice of the Paiutes," *MELUS* 24, no. 2 (Summer 2002): 29.

74. Ibid., 31.

75. Peña, "Endangered Landscapes," 22–23.

76. Alaimo, *Bodily Natures*, 29.

77. Ibid.

78. Ibid., 15.

79. Ibid., 63.

80. Ibid. Also, Lankford suggests in "Sarah Winnemucca" that cholera was most likely the "major epidemic" that had killed the Paiutes who had remained at Pyramid Lake. "Even the sacred waters of Lake Tahoe, the Paiutes told themselves, had been poisoned. Famine soon followed this new plague" (66–67).

81. Abigail Millings, et al., "Holding Back the Tears: Individual Differences in Adult Crying Proneness Reflect Attachment Orientation and Attitudes to Crying." *Frontiers in Psychology* 7, no. 1003 (July 2016).

82. Shani Gelstein, et al., "Human Tears Contain a Chemosignal," *Science* 331, no. 6014 (January 2011), 226–30.

83. Susan Bernardin, "The Lessons of a Sentimental Education: Zitkála-Šá's Autobiographical Narratives, *Western American Literature* 32, no. 3 (1997): 212–38. For more on Zitkála-Šá's use of sentimental modes in her autobiographical writing, see Penelope Myrtle Kelsey, "Zitkála-Šá, Sentiment, and Tiospaye: Reading Dakota Rhetorics of Nation and Gender," in *Tribal Theory in Native American Literature: Dakota and Haudenosaunee Writing and Indigenous Worldviews* (Lincoln: University of Nebraska Press, 2008), 62–75; and Cari Carpenter, *Seeing Red: Anger, Sentimentality, and American Indians* (Columbus: Ohio State

University Press, 2008).

84.   In *Tribal Theory*, Kelsey refers to Bernardin's work on sen-
      timentality in Zitkála-Šá's fiction, adding that her melding
      of sentimentalism with self-narration reflects both gendered
      and Dakota modes of self-expression (66). Rob Nixon's
      "slow violence" refers to "violence that is neither spectacular
      nor instantaneous but instead incremental, whose calami-
      tous repercussions are postponed for years or decades or
      centuries." Nixon, "Slow Violence," *The Chronicle of Higher
      Education*, June 26, 2011.

85.   Abby Goodnough and Scott Atkinson, "A Potent Side
      Effect to the Flint Water Crisis: Mental Health Problems,"
      New York Times, April 30, 2016.

86.   H. T. Cory, *The Imperial Valley and the Salton Sink* (San
      Francisco: J. J. Newbegin, 1915), 1513.

87.   Andrew Russell and Lee Vinsel, "Hail the Maintainers,"
      Aeon Magazine, April 7, 2015, https://aeon.co/essays/
      innovation-is-overvalued-maintenance-often-matters-more.

88.   Cory, *The Imperial Valley*, 1516.

89.   In *Native Waters*, Daniel McCool defines the first treaty era
      as occurring between 1850 and 1871. The first treaty era, he
      notes, concerned the appropriation of Native lands, whereas
      the second treaty era, beginning in the late 1970s and con-
      tinuing to today, concerns water (8). In *Fluid Arguments:
      Five Centuries of Western Water Conflict* (2001), Char Miller
      says that in both treaty eras, "the written agreements result-
      ing from the negotiations were intended to be permanent
      settlements to long-standing conflicts. . . . In the first treaty
      era the commitments made were seldom honored; although
      it is too early to make conclusive generalizations, the second
      treaty era has initially met with mixed success in meeting
      agreed-upon commitments" (125). Miller, *Fluid Arguments*
      (Tucson: University of Arizona Press, 2001).

90.   Smythe, *The Conquest of Arid America*, 285.

91. Cecilia Tichi, *Shifting Gears: Technology, Literature, Culture in Modernist America* (Chapel Hill: University of North Carolina Press, 1987).

92. In *The River*, Aiken states, "[Innes] found the open space of the trapezium swarming with strange dark faces. So silent their coming, she had not heard the arrival of the tribes. . . . She isolated the Cocopahs, stately as bronze statues, their long hair streaming, or wound, mud-caked under brilliant head-cloths. Forgathering with them were men of other tribes; these must be the Yumans and Deguinos, the men needed on the river. Tom had told her that the long-haired tribes were famous for their water-craft. These were the men who were to work on the rafts, weave the great mattresses. A squad of short-haired Pimas with their squaws and babies and their gaudy bundles, gaped at the fair-haired woman as she passed. . . . These were the brush-cutters to replace the stampeding peons. This, then, meant the beginning of real activity" (266–67). See 74, 250–52, and 278.

93. "There is a second element of security not inferior to the land itself. It is the element of human labor. This is the soul of the security, as land and water are its physical body" (Smythe, *The Conquest of Arid America*, 263–64).

94. Cory, *The Imperial Valley*, 1513, 1397.

95. Helen Hunt Jackson, *Ramona* (New York: Grosset & Dunlap, 1884).

96. Smythe, *The Conquest of Arid America*, 285, 264.

97. Ibid., 243.

98. Robert Crifasi, *A Land Made from Water: Appropriation and the Evolution of Colorado's Landscape, Ditches, and Water Institutions* (Boulder: University of Colorado Press, 2015), 57.

99. White defines "the organic machine" as "an energy system which, although modified by human interventions, maintains its natural, its 'unmade' qualities" (*The Organic*

Machine, ix).

100. Crifasi, *A Land Made from Water,* 56.

101. Zitkála-Šá, *American Indian Stories* (Washington, DC: Hayworth Publishing House, 1921), 9. See also Charles Eastman's *Indian Boyhood,* wherein the Santee Dakota author reflects on the drastic decrease in waterfowl along the Assiniboine River that results from white hunting practices, or what he terms the "wholesale methods of destruction" (253). Eastman's observations offer chilling details on how the expansionist ethos impacted river ecologies in South Dakota (New York: Doubleday, Page & Company, 1911).

102. See, for example, "My Time at Standing Rock," *Stand. Earth,* December 20, 2016, https://www.stand.earth/latest/my-time-standing-rock; and Isiah Holmes, "Dakota Access Contractor with Blackwater Ties Heads Protester Surveillance, Violence Escalates," *The Fifth Column,* November 26, 2016, https://thefifthcolumnnews.com/2016/11/dakota-access-contractor-with-blackwater-ties-heads-protester-surveillance-violence-escalates/.

103. Chief Arvol Looking Horse, "Standing Rock Is Everywhere: One Year Later," *The Guardian,* February 22, 2018.

CHAPTER 4

1. Claire de Pratz, "The Salt Cure," *Contemporary Review* 79, no. 3 (1901): 401.

2. Jack London, *The Sea-Wolf* (New York: Bantam Dell, 2007), 124. Hereafter cited in text.

3. Hester Blum, "The Prospect of Oceanic Studies," *PMLA* 125, no. 3 (May 2010): 670–77, quote at 670.

4. In London's *The Sea-Wolf,* the narrator frequently describes the immensity of the Pacific Ocean using words like "vast," "expansive," and "illimitable." For example: "Coming from no man knew where in the illimitable Pacific, it was

travelling north on its annual migration" (120).

5. "On the Broad Pacific," *National Tribune*, February 27, 1908, retrieved from Chronicling America—The Library of Congress, March 14, 2018.

6. Ibid.

7. Steve Mentz and Martha Elena Rojas, "Introduction: 'The Hungry Ocean,'" in *The Sea and Nineteenth-Century Anglophone Literary Culture*, ed. Steve Mentz and Martha Elena Rojas, (Routledge: New York, 2017), 1–14. Additionally, in his book *Shipwreck Modernity: Ecologies of Globalization, 1550–1719* (Minneapolis: University of Minnesota Press, 2015), Mentz coins the term "blue humanities," which refers to film, literature, and art focused on oceanic spaces.

8. In *Facing Facts*, David Shi uses the term "savage realist" to describe naturalist writers such as London, Stephen Crane, and Theodore Dreiser whose writing exposes "sordid facts and primitive passions" (212). David Shi, *Facing Facts: Realism in American Thought and Culture, 1850–1920* (New York: Oxford University Press, 1995).

9. Lee Clark Mitchell, "'And Rescue Us from Ourselves': Becoming Someone in Jack London's *The Sea-Wolf*," *American Literature* 70, no. 2 (1998): 317–35.

10. Edwin Emerson Jr. states in a 1905 *Sunset Magazine* article that London "loathed and abominated the Japanese. More than these he did not hesitate to show his feelings. Any one [*sic*] who has ever lived among the Japanese, and who has learned to appreciate their dominant trait of hiding their own feelings, cannot but realize that a man coming among them with such a disposition need never hope to get any thing [*sic*] out of them. Not even true impressions." Emerson, "When East Meets West," *Sunset Magazine*, October 1905, 515–30.

11. London, "If Japan Awakens China," *Sunset Magazine*, December 1909, 597–601.

12. Yonejirō Noguchi, "No Yellow Peril in China," *Sunset Magazine*, July 1910, 14–16.

13. Helen M. Rozwadowski, "Scientists Writing and Knowing the Ocean," in *The Sea and Nineteenth-Century Anglophone Literary Culture*, ed. Steve Mentz and Martha Elena Rojas (New York: Routledge, 2017), 29.

14. Ibid.

15. "Stone Giants of the South Seas," *San Francisco Call*, February 19, 1899, retrieved from Chronicling America—The Library of Congress, March 18, 2018.

16. Margherita Arlina Hamm, "Hail! The Conquering Hero Comes!" *The Anaconda Standard*, September 19, 1899, 14, retrieved from Chronicling America—The Library of Congress.

17. Basil Hall Chamberlain and W. B. Mason, *A Handbook for Travellers in Japan* (London: Albermarle Street, 1894), 2.

18. Thomas J. Osborne, "Pacific Eldorado: Rethinking Greater California's Past," *California History* 87, no. 1 (2009): 33.

19. Hamm, "Hail!"

20. Ibid.

21. "On the Broad Pacific."

22. "Self-contained bodies" is a reference to Linda Nash's research on conceptions of health and embodiment during the Progressive Era. The "self-contained body," which is opposed to rather than in harmony with the environment, is discussed later in this chapter. Linda Nash, *Inescapable Ecologies: A History of Environment, Disease, and Knowledge* (Berkeley: University of California Press, 2006), 12, 13. In *Diary*, Miss Morning Glory observes that "everything reveals a huge scale of measurement" in the United States. "The continental spectacle is different from that of our islands" (37).

23. In Frederick Jackson Turner's well-known historical work *The Significance of the Frontier in American History* (1893),

he argues that the movement westward shaped American identity. Relying on oceanic metaphors, such as "waves," to describe American migrations into the West, Turner believed that the frontier was largely closed in the 1890s, and he worried about what this might mean for American character. Turner, *The Significance of the Frontier in American History* (1893; New York: Henry Holt and Company, 1920).

24. Mark Kurlansky, *Salt: A World History* (New York: Penguin Books, 2003), 257.

25. In an 1896 article titled "Lake of Salt," the Salt Mining Company of San Francisco describes a saline deposit in Needles, California, as having a "gem-like radiance" covering "the ground like an immense incrustation of diamonds" (*Record-Union* [Sacramento, CA], January 24, 1896). Kurlansky notes in *Salt* that "As Americans moved west, they shipped salt from the East, just as the settlers in the East had shipped it from England" (252). He also says that salt mined in California was "of low quality, and it did not compete with Liverpool salt, which came as ballast on the British ships that bought California wheat" (283).

26. Salt extraction and salt production are two different processes. Extraction involves the mining of salt and usually occurs in inland regions. Salt production, however, refers to the evaporation of saltwater to "produce" sea salt, and usually occurs in coastal and marshland ecologies. Salt is both extracted and produced in the United States.

27. Gregory Rosenthal, *Beyond Hawai'i: Native Labor in the Pacific World* (Berkeley: University of California Press, 2018), 20.

28. Timothy LeCain, *The Matter of History: How Things Create the Past* (New York: Cambridge University Press, 2017), 130.

29. Jane Bennett, *Vibrant Matter: A Political Ecology of Things*

(Durham, NC: Duke University Press, 2009).

30. In *Politics of Nature*, Bruno Latour describes an "actant" as anything that "modifies other actors through a series of" actions (75). Latour distinguishes "actor," which he deems anthropomorphic, from "actant," which is any "acting agent," be it human or nonhuman (75). Latour, *Politics of Nature: How to Bring the Sciences into Democracy*, translated by Catherine Porter (Cambridge, MA: Harvard University Press, 2004).

31. Kurlansky, *Salt*, 283. See also Rosenthal, who describes the extent of Indigenous labor involved in Hawaiian salt production. "To make so much salt required massive amounts of human labor. Stewart did not report on how many workers produced salt at Āliapa'akai, but later sources from the 1830s through the mid-nineteenth century describe maka'āinana labor in the thousands (as many as two thousand workers in one instance) working in and around the [salt] lake making crystals for exports to passing ships" (*Beyond Hawai'i*, 21).

32. See Kripa Ram Haldiya, Murli Lal Mathur, Raman Sachdev, and Habibulla N. Saiyed, "Risk of High Blood Pressure in Salt Workers Working near Salt Milling Plants: A Cross-Sectional and Interventional Study," *Environmental Health* 4 (2005): 13; Kripa Ram Haldiya, Murli Lal Mathur, Raman Sachdev, and Habibulla N. Saiyed, "Knowledge, Attitude, and Practices Related to Occupational Health Problems among Salt Workers Working in the Desert of Rajasthan, India," *Journal of Occupational Health* 47, no. 1 (2005): 85–88.

33. Jack London, *The Cruise of the Snark* (New York: Macmillan, 1911), 6.

34. London highlights Wolf Larsen's Scandinavian roots in several passages and thus aligns Larsen's oceanic endurance with a kind of idealized "white-skinned" lineage. Additionally, Van Weyden often admires Larsen's hyperwhite body,

noting that his biceps moved "like a living thing under its white sheath" (143).

35. "The Salt Water Cure," *Hopkinsville Kentuckian*, June 16, 1908, 3, retrieved from Chronicling America—The Library of Congress, March 20, 2018.

36. de Pratz, "The Salt Cure," 401–5.

37. Ibid., 408.

38. Ibid.

39. *Santa Fe New Mexican*, January 18, 1901, 2, retrieved from Chronicling America—The Library of Congress, March 18, 2018.

40. William Dean Howells, *Criticism and Fiction* (New York: Harper & Brothers, 1891), 126, quoted in Shi, *Facing Facts*, 117.

41. Fleissner, *Women, Compulsion, Modernity: The Moment of American Naturalism* (Chicago: University of Chicago Press, 2004), 98.

42. See Cecilia Tichi, "House of Progress, House of Shame," in *Jack London: A Writer's Fight for a Better America* (Chapel Hill: University of North Carolina Press, 2015), 125–56; Mitchell, "'And Rescue Us from Ourselves'"; and Jonathan Auerbach, "Between Men of Letters: Homoerotic Agon in *The Sea-Wolf*," in *Male Call: Becoming Jack London* (Durham, NC: Duke University Press, 1996), 178–226.

43. According to critic Regina Schober, "The ocean, in its incalculable temperament, speaks to the epistemological crisis reflected in naturalist fiction. . . . Water imagery in literary naturalism draws on but also transforms the rhetoric of scientific sea exploration of its time." Schober, "'A Problem in Small Boat Navigation': Ocean Metaphors and Emerging Data Epistemology in Stephen Crane's 'The Open Boat' and Jack London's 'The Heathen,'" *Studies in American Naturalism*, no. 1 (2017): 71.

44. Ibid.

45. Mark Seltzer, *Bodies and Machines* (New York: Routledge, 1992), 150.

46. In "Things Alive," London says that college men "live largely in an atmosphere of book-congealed minds" (*Yale Monthly Magazine* 1, no. 1 (1906): 76–79, quote on 76). London describes San Francisco as a city with a "dusty existence," highlighting the lack of saltwater—and, hence, hardness—in metropolitan spaces (*The Sea-Wolf,* 1).

47. Wolf's eyes are described in oceanic terms several times throughout the novel, such as when Van Weyden says that "his eyes, clear blue this morning as the sea, were sparkling with light" (73). Also, see Hester Blum's description of "the sea eye" in *The View from the Masthead: Maritime Imagination and Antebellum American Sea Narratives* (Chapel Hill: University of North Carolina Press, 2008).

48. Mitchell, "'And Rescue Us from Ourselves,'" 324.

49. Auerbach, "Between Men of Letters," 193.

50. Jay Williams describes London's employment at a pickle factory: "In the cannery he stuffed pickles into jars for ten cents per hour in shifts that stretched from twelve to eighteen hours daily. . . . Though escaping injury at the cannery, he saw coworkers disfigured by machinery that lacked safety equipment" (31). Jay Williams, *Oxford Handbook of Jack London* (New York: Oxford University Press, 2017).

51. London, "The Yellow Peril," in *Revolution and Other Essays* (New York: Macmillan, 1909).

52. In several naturalist works, authors describe women's skin as softer and more permeable than men's bodies, which puts women's bodies at risk. Chapter 3 of this book explored how feminine bodies in Wister's *The Virginian* become heavy and sluggish when they take on water. In *McTeague,* Trina becomes poisoned (or "stained") when her fingers absorb turpentine paint. Additionally, London's Mercedes, who weighs down the sled with her belongings in *The Call of*

the Wild, leads her team to a watery death. These and other examples align women's bodies with the perils of porousness.

53. London, *The Cruise of the Snark*, 339. See also Jennifer C. Aronica and Scott A. Norton, "The Snark and the Skin: Jack London's Pacific Voyage," *Journal of the American Medical Association: Dermatology* 151, no. 9 (2015): 1016.

54. Stacy Alaimo, *Bodily Natures: Science, Environment, and the Material Self* (Bloomington: Indiana University Press, 2010), 15.

55. Wayne Rozen, "Great White Hope: Not Great, No Hope," *New York Times*, July 4, 2010.

56. Nash, *Inescapable Ecologies*, 12, 13.

57. Ibid., 12.

58. In "The Yellow Peril," London states, "The menace to the Western world lies, not in the little brown man, but in the four hundred millions of yellow men should the little brown man undertake their management" (597).

59. London, *The Cruise of the Snark*, 170.

60. Gail Bederman, *Manliness and Civilization: A Cultural History of Gender and Race in the United States* (Chicago: University of Chicago Press, 1995), 71.

61. It is worth noting that, as a child, Theodore Roosevelt's first taxidermy project was a seal head he purchased on Broadway. Later, as governor of New York, Roosevelt promoted "the strenuous life," and the preservation of dead animal bodies—particularly those deemed rare or hard to get, like seals—allowed men the opportunity to *manage* the wild, so to speak. When Pacific fur seal numbers began to decline as a result of pelagic sealing, Roosevelt actually advocated for "exterminating the herd ourselves in the most humane way possible." Theodore Roosevelt, "Sixth State of the Union Address," December 3, 1906.

62. See Briton Cooper Busch, *The War against the Seals: A*

History of the North American Seal Fishery (Montreal: McGill–Queen's University Press, 1985).

63. London, *The Cruise of the Snark*.

64. Ibid., 329.

65. In *Hyperobjects: Philosophy and Ecology at the End of the World* (Minneapolis: University of Minnesota Press, 2013), Timothy Morton suggests that viscosity is one of the key qualities of "hyperobjects": "They are *viscous*, which means that they 'stick' to beings that are involved with them" (1).

66. Yone Noguchi, *The Story of Yone Noguchi* (Philadelphia: George W. Jacobs and Company, 1914), 88. Hereafter cited in text.

67. Mark Fisher, *Capitalist Realism: Is There No Alternative?* (Seattle: Zero Books, 2009), 45.

68. W. Heinemann, "All at Sea," *The Guardian*, November 30, 1904.

69. Mitchell, "'And Rescue Us from Ourselves,'" 327.

70. Donna Campbell, *Resisting Regionalism: Gender and Naturalism in American Fiction, 1885–1915* (Athens: Ohio University Press, 1997).

71. Noguchi, *The Story of Yone Noguchi*, 26.

72. Tichi, *Jack London*, 178.

73. Charles Warren Stoddard, *The Island of Tranquil Delights: A South Sea Idyl, and Others* (Boston: H. B. Turner, 1904), 14. London in *The Cruise of the Snark* echoes this idea that the Pacific exists as a playground of sorts for men: "And the picture of that coloured sea and that flying sea-god Kanaka becomes another reason for the young man to go west, and farther west, beyond the Baths of Sunset, and still west till he arrives home again" (59).

74. In *America's Asia: Racial Form and American Literature, 1893–1945*, Colleen Lye says that in London's early stories set in the Pacific, "'Japan' simply designates the outer horizon of an expansive oceanic world, which is London's

stage for adventure" (12). By refusing to land in Japan, or to acknowledge Japanese claim over certain Pacific islands, London extends an American colonialist mentality into Pacific spaces, Lye continues. Lye, "A Genealogy of the 'Yellow Peril': Jack London, George Kennan, and the Russo-Japanese War," *America's Asia* (Princeton, NJ: Princeton University Press, 2004).

75. London, *The Cruise of the Snark*, 10.

76. Amy Sueyoshi, "Miss Morning Glory: Orientalism and Misogyny in the Queer Writings of Yone Noguchi," *Amerasia Journal* 37, no. 2 (2011): 2–27, quote at 4.

77. Ibid.

78. Ibid.

79. In *Eating the Ocean*, theorist Elspeth Probyn describes seasickness as a "queasiness in the world" (Durham, NC: Duke University Press, 2016).

80. See Edward Marx, "Afterword," in *The American Diary of a Japanese Girl: An Annotated Edition*, ed. Edward Marx and Laura E. Franey (Philadelphia: Temple University Press, 2007), 144, 140–142. Amy Sueyoshi has written extensively about Noguchi's queer sexuality. In "Miss Morning Glory," she describes *Diary* as both a "secretly gay text" and "one of Asian America's earliest queer texts" (14). She continues, "Morning Glory's affair with her love interest Oscar took on distinct parallels with Noguchi's own exchanges with Stoddard" (14). See also Amy Sueyoshi, "Finding Fellatio," in *Embodying Asian American Sexualities*, ed. Gina Masequesmay and Sean Metzger (Lanham, MD: Lexington Books, 2009), 157–72.

81. John Hicks argues that Noguchi "prefigured Beat Generation writers such as Jack Kerouac." Hicks, *The Literature of California: Native American Beginnings to 1945* (Berkeley: University of California Press, 2001), 198.

82. See Yone Noguchi, *The Voice of the Valley* (San Francisco: W.

Doxey, 1897).

83. Bederman, *Manliness and Civilization*, 279.

84. Critics have called London an American (Tichi, *Jack London*), Californian (Osborne, "Pacific Eldorado"), and Pacific Rim writer (Williams, *Oxford Handbook*), among other labels. Edward Marx tells us that Noguchi was inspired by the New Woman novel as it emerged in Japan, Europe, and the United States (143). See also Marx, "Afterword," 137.

85. Sueyoshi, "Miss Morning Glory," 4.

86. Marx, "Afterword," 144.

87. Ibid.

88. Noguchi, *The Story of Yone Noguchi*, 26.

89. "Today," Williams says, "globalization—the formation of capital and culture and the migration and transplantation of peoples regardless of national boundaries—and imperialism are necessary parts of our understanding of what it means to use the label Pacific Rim or Pacific writer" (*Oxford Handbook of Jack London*, 2). The phrase "American literature as world literature" is taken from the book title *Shades of the Planet: American Literature as World Literature*, ed. Wai Chi Dimock and Lawrence Buell (Princeton, NJ: Princeton University Press, 2007).

90. Dimock and Buell, "Introduction," *Shades of the Planet*.

91. William Boelhower, "The Rise of the Atlantic Studies Matrix," *American Literary History* 20, nos. 1–2 (March 2008): 83–101.

92. Probyn, *Eating the Ocean*, 19.

93. "Vacation Trips to Europe," *Literary Digest*, April 18, 1908, 569.

94. Ibid.

95. Miss Morning Glory notes that Ada is not a typical American woman. In particular, her nose—"an inspiration, like the snow-capped peak of O Fuji San"—contrasts with the "rugged, big bone" noses of other women (52).

96. Bateman, *The Modernist Art of Queer Survival* (New York: Oxford University Press, 2017), 11.

97. Ibid., 7.

98. Ibid., 5.

99. Ibid., 11–12.

100. Ibid., 5.

101. See Crane's "The Open Boat," in *The Open Boat and Other Stories* (New York: Scholarly Press, 1898). For a discussion of "the natural man," see Bederman's *Manliness and Civilization*.

102. Bederman, *Manliness and Civilization*, 71.

103. In "Finding Fellatio," Amy Sueyoshi calls Noguchi's relationship with Stoddard a "romantic friendship": "Yone's unique relationship with Charles has largely gone unnoticed, perhaps because of the lack of evidence detailing explicit genital contact or maybe even due to the influence of presentist notions of Asian/American male asexuality that make it nearly impossible to imagine immigrants as love machines." She continues, "the best conclusion for these affairs might very well be romantic friendship" (165).

104. Frank Norris, "The Frontier Gone at Last," in *The Responsibilities of the Novelist and Other Essays* (New York: Doubleday Page and Company, 1903), 73.

105. Stacy Alaimo says that "embedded onto-epistemologies, provisional knowledge practices, performances of exposure, and imaginative dissolves diverge from the predominant paradigm of sustainability by staying low, remaining open to the world, and becoming attuned to strange agencies." Alaimo, *Exposed: Environmental Politics and Pleasures in Posthuman Times* (Minneapolis: University of Minnesota Press, 2016), 174.

CODA

1. Steve Mentz, "After Sustainability," *PMLA* 127, no. 3 (2012): 591.
2. Ibid., 587.
3. Ibid.
4. Ibid.
5. Susan Pratt, Camila Marambio, et al., "Fathom," *Environmental Humanities* 12, no. 1 (May 2020): 176.
6. Ibid., 176.
7. Jeanne Dorado, quoted in Ariel Zambelich and Cassi Alexandra, "In Their Own Words: The 'Water Protectors' of Standing Rock," National Public Radio, December 11, 2016. Accessed April 11, 2020, NPR.org.
8. Yone Noguchi, *The Story of Yone Noguchi* (Philadelphia: George W. Jacobs and Company, 1914), 248. Hereafter cited in text.
9. The World Wildlife Foundation argues that "In many parts of the world, the ocean is headed for a collapse" due to the human-caused degradation of coral reefs, as well as the decrease in marine animals, among other issues. WWF, "Why Is Our Ocean at Risk?" *World Wildlife Foundation Global*, 2017, accessed 30 July 2018.
10. Yone Noguchi, *The American Diary of a Japanese Girl* (New York: F. A. Stokes, 1902), 27.
11. In *Exposed*, Stacy Alaimo describes "engineering, the sciences, and maybe architecture and urban planning" as "the disciplines that can fix things" (171). These managerial disciplines, she notes, promote a "new gospel of efficiency" similar to that extolled by turn-of-the-century Progressives (171).

BIBLIOGRAPHY

Ach, Jada. "Land 'Under the Ditch': Channeling Water through Owen Wister's *The Virginian*." *Ecozon@: European Journal of Literature, Culture and Environment* 9, no. 1 (2018): 111–28.

———. "'Left All Alone in This World's Wilderness': Queer Ecology, Desert Spaces, and Unmaking the Nation in Frank Norris's *McTeague*." *Western American Literature* 51, no. 2 (Summer 2016): 175–97.

Ach, Jada, and Gary Reger, eds. *Reading Aridity in Western American Literature*. Lanham, MD: Lexington Press, 2020.

Adamson, Joni, Mei Mei Evans, and Rachel Stein. Introduction to *The Environmental Justice Reader: Politics, Poetics, and Pedagogy*. Edited by Joni Adamson, Mei Mei Evans, and Rachel Stein. Tucson: University of Arizona Press, 2002.

Agard-Jones, Vanessa. "What the Sands Remember." *GLQ: A Journal of Lesbian and Gay Studies* 18, nos. 2–3 (2012): 325–46.

Ahtone, Tristan. "Cancer-Riddled Wind River Reservation Fights EPA over Uranium Contamination." *Indian Country Today*, January 19, 2012. Accessed August 19, 2018. https://indiancountrytoday.com/archive/cancer-riddled-wind-rive r-reservation-fights-epa-over-uranium-contamination.

Aiken, Ednah Robinson. *The River*. Indianapolis: Bobbs-Merrill Company, 1914.

Akers, Floyd [pseud.]. *The Boy Fortune Hunters in China*. Chicago: Reilly and Britton Co., 1909.

Alaimo, Stacy. *Bodily Nature: Science, Environment, and the Material Self*. Bloomington: Indiana University Press, 2010.

———. "Elemental Love in the Anthropocene." In *Elemental Ecocriticism: Thinking with Earth, Air, Water, and Fire*. Edited by Jeffrey Jerome Cohen and Lowell Duckert, 298–309.

Minneapolis: University of Minnesota Press, 2015.

———. *Exposed: Environmental Politics and Pleasures in Post-human Times*. Minneapolis: University of Minnesota Press, 2016.

———. "The Undomesticated Nature of Feminism: Mary Austin and the Progressive Women Conservationists." *Studies in American Fiction* 26, no. 1 (1998).

American Society for Quality. "Continuous Improvement." American Society for Quality, 2017. Accessed March 15, 2017. https://asq.org/quality-resources/continuous-improvement.

Aronica, Jennifer C., and Scott A. Norton. "The Snark and the Skin: Jack London's Pacific Voyage." *Journal of the American Medical Association: Dermatology* 151, no. 9 (2015).

Arvol Looking Horse, Chief. "Standing Rock Is Everywhere: One Year Later." *The Guardian*, February 22, 2018.

Auerbach, Jonathan. "Between Men of Letters: Homoerotic Agon in *The Sea-Wolf*." In *Male Call: Becoming Jack London*, 178–226. Durham, NC: Duke University Press, 1996.

Austin, Mary Hunter. *The Land of Little Rain*. New York: The Modern Library, 2003 [1903].

———. *Earth Horizon*. Santa Fe, NM: Sunstone Press, 1932.

Azzarello, Robert. *Queer Environmentality: Ecology, Evolution, and Sexuality in American Literature*. Burlington, VT: Ashgate, 2012.

Baker, Simon. "The Hitherto Impossible in Photography Was Our Specialty." *Air & Space Magazine*, October–November 1988, 64–68.

———. "San Francisco in Ruins." *Landscape Magazine* 30, no. 2 (1989). http://robroy.dyndns.info/lawrence/landscape.html.

Bakker, Karen. "Water: Political, Biopolitical, Material." In *Water Worlds*. Edited by Jessica Barnes and Samer Alatout. Special issue, *Social Studies of Science* 42, no. 2 (2012).

Ball, Samuel W. "The Conservation of Social Energy." *The Progressive Woman* 6, no. 75 (n.d.): 4.

Banerjee, Subhankar. "Arctic Series Photographs." Subhankar

Banerjee, 2018. Accessed July 1, 2018. http://www.subhankar-banerjee.org/selectphotographs.html.

Banta, Martha. *Taylored Lives: Narrative Productions in the Age of Taylor, Veblen, and Ford*. Chicago: University of Chicago Press, 1993.

Barbour, Erwin Hinckley. "Laboratory Photography." *Journal of Applied Microscopy* 3 (January 15, 1900).

Bateman, Benjamin. *The Modernist Art of Queer Survival*. New York: Oxford University Press, 2017.

Baum, L. Frank. *The Wonderful Wizard of Oz*. New York: Penguin Books, 1998 [1900].

Bederman, Gail. *Manliness and Civilization: A Cultural History of Gender and Race in the United States*. Chicago: University of Chicago Press, 1995.

Beiser, Vince. *The World in a Grain: The Story of Sand and How It Transformed Civilization*. New York: Penguin Random House, 2018.

Belgrad, Daniel. "'Power's Larger Meaning': The Johnson County War as Political Violence in an Environmental Context." *Western Historical Quarterly* 33 (Summer 2002).

Bennett, Jane. *Vibrant Matter: A Political Ecology of Things*. Durham, NC: Duke University Press, 2010.

Benson, Etienne. "Generating Infrastructural Invisibility: Insulation, Interconnection, and Avian Excrement in the Southern California Power Grid." *Environmental Humanities* 6 (2015): 103–30.

Bergthaller, Hannes, Rob Emmet, Adeline Johns-Putra, et al. "Mapping Common Ground: Ecocriticism, Environmental History, and the Environmental Humanities." *Environmental Humanities* 5, no. 1 (2014): 261–76.

Berlant, Lauren, and Lee Edelman. *Sex, or the Unbearable*. Durham, NC: Duke University Press, 2013.

Bernardin, Susan. "The Lessons of a Sentimental Education: Zitkála-Šá's Autobiographical Narratives." *Western American*

Literature 32, no. 3 (1997): 212–38.

Blake, William Phipps. *The Imperial Valley and the Salton Sink.* San Francisco: John J. Newbegin, 1915.

Blum, Hester. "The Prospect of Oceanic Studies." *PMLA* 125, no. 3 (May 2010): 670–77.

———. *The View from the Masthead: Maritime Imagination and Antebellum American Sea Narratives.* Chapel Hill: University of North Carolina Press, 2008.

Boelhower, William. "The Rise of the Atlantic Studies Matrix." *American Literary History* 20, nos. 1–2 (March 2008): 83–101.

Brown, Bill. *A Sense of Things: The Object Matter of American Literature.* Chicago: University of Chicago Press, 2003.

Buell, Lawrence. *The Environmental Imagination: Thoreau, Nature Writing, and the Formation of American Culture.* Cambridge, MA: The Belknap Press of Harvard University Press, 1995.

———. *The Future of Environmental Criticism.* Malden, MA: Blackwell, 2005.

Bullard, W. H. G., A. L. Willard, and J. H. Holden. "Report upon the Kite Photographic Experiments." USS *Maine*, Hampton Roads, Virginia, January 12, 1906.

Burnstein, Daniel Eli. *Next to Godliness: Confronting Dirt and Despair in Progressive Era New York City.* Urbana-Champaign: University of Illinois Press, 2006.

Burroughs, John. "The Art of Seeing Things." *American Earth: Environmental Writing since Thoreau.* New York: Library of America, 2008.

Busch, Briton Cooper. *The War against the Seals: A History of the North American Seal Fishery.* Montreal: McGill–Queen's University Press, 1985.

C19: Society of Nineteenth-Century Americanists. "Conference." C19 Online, 2017. Accessed August 20, 2018. https://c19conference.wordpress.com/past-conference-programs/.

California Department of Water Resources. "Precipitation

Enhancement." *California Water Plan* 3 (2013): 5–15.

Campbell, Donna. *Resisting Regionalism: Gender and Naturalism in American Fiction, 1885–1915.* Athens: Ohio University Press, 1997.

Campbell, Neil. *The Rhizomatic West: Representing the American West in a Transnational, Global, Media Age.* Lincoln, NE: Bison Books, 2011.

"Car Performs Thrilling Feats." *Evening Capital News* (Boise, ID). September 24, 1916. Retrieved from Chronicling America— The Library of Congress.

Carpenter, Cari. *Seeing Red: Anger, Sentimentality, and American Indians.* Columbus: Ohio State University Press, 2008.

Carse, Ashley. "Nature as Infrastructure: Making and Managing the Panama Canal Watershed." *Social Studies of Science* 42, no. 4 (2012): 539–63.

Cassuto, David N. *Dripping Dry: Literature, Politics, and Water in the Desert Southwest.* Ann Arbor: University of Michigan Press, 2001.

Chamberlain, Basil Hall, and W. B. Mason. *A Handbook for Travellers in Japan.* London: Albermarle Street, 1894.

Chandler, L. H. "Report of the Performance of the Photographic Apparatus for Use with Kites." US Navy Department, Bureau of Ordnance. Washington, DC, May 22, 1905.

Chase, J. Smeaton. *California Desert Trails.* Boston: Houghton, Mifflin & Co., 1919.

Chen, Mel Y. *Animacies: Biopolitics, Racial Mattering, and Queer Affect.* Durham, NC: Duke University Press, 2012.

Cobb, Michael. "Welcome to the Desert of Me." In *Single: Arguments for the Uncoupled.* New York: New York University Press, 2012.

Cohen, Jeffrey Jerome, and Lowell Duckert. "Introduction: Eleven Principles of the Elements." *Elemental Ecocriticism: Thinking with Earth, Air, Water, and Fire.* Edited by Jeffrey Jerome Cohen and Lowell Duckert. Minneapolis: University of Minnesota Press, 2015.

Cory, H. T. *The Imperial Valley and the Salton Sink*. San Francisco: J. J. Newbegin, 1915.

Cowan, John L. "Dry Farming: The Hope of the West." *Century Magazine* (July 1906): 435–46.

Crane, Stephen. "The Open Boat." In *The Open Boat and Other Stories*. New York: Scholarly Press, 1898.

Crifasi, Robert. *A Land Made from Water: Appropriation and the Evolution of Colorado's Landscape, Ditches, and Water Institutions*. Boulder: University of Colorado Press, 2015.

Cronon, William. *Changes in the Land: Indians, Colonists, and the Ecology of New England*. New York: Hill and Wang, 2003.

Cruz, Denise. "Reconsidering *McTeague*'s 'Mark' and 'Mac': Intersections of U.S. Naturalism, Imperial Masculinities, and Desire between Men." *American Literature* 78, no. 3 (2006).

Daniel, Julia E. *Building Natures: Modern American Poetry, Landscape Architecture, and City Planning*. Charlottesville: University of Virginia Press, 2017.

de Pratz, Claire. "The Salt Cure." *Contemporary Review* 79, no. 3 (1901): 401.

"Desert Empire Is Discovered by Explorers from the North." *Imperial Valley Press* (El Centro, CA), December 19, 1908. Retrieved from Chronicling America—The Library of Congress.

Devine, Maureen, and Christa Grewe-Volpp, eds. *Words on Water: Literary and Cultural Representations*. Trier, Germany: WVT Wissenschaftlicher Verlag Trier, 2008.

Dimock, Wai Chi, and Lawrence Buell. "Introduction." In *Shades of the Planet: American Literature as World Literature*. Edited by Wai Chi Dimock and Lawrence Buell. Princeton, NJ: Princeton University Press, 2007.

Dorado, Jeanne. Quoted in Ariel Zambelich and Cassi Alexandra, "In Their Own Words: The 'Water Protectors' of Standing Rock." National Public Radio, December 11, 2016. Accessed

April 11, 2020. NPR.org.

Dorrian, Mark, and Frédéric Pousin. "Introduction." In *Seeing from Above: The Aerial View in Visual Culture*. Edited by Mark Dorrian and Frédéric Pousin. New York: I. B. Tauris, 2013.

Eastman, Charles. *Indian Boyhood*. New York: Doubleday, Page & Company, 1911.

Eddy, William. Quoted in Earl Mago, "Parade from Mid-Air: Mr. Eddy Details His Plans for Taking Photographs on the 27th." *Anaconda* (MT) *Standard*, April 25, 1897, 14. Retrieved from Chronicling America—The Library of Congress.

"Ednah Aiken and 'The River.'" *Book News Monthly* 33, no. 6 (February 1916): 281–82.

Emerson, Edwin, Jr. "When East Meets West." *Sunset Magazine* (October 1905): 515–30.

Emerson, Ralph Waldo. *Nature: Addresses, and Lectures*. Boston: James Munroe Company, 1849.

Erickson, Bruce. "'fucking close to water': Queering the Production of the Nation." In *Queer Ecologies: Sex, Nature, Politics, Desire*. Edited by Catriona Mortimer-Sandilands and Bruce Erickson. Bloomington: Indiana University Press, 2010.

Evans, Rebecca McWilliams. "Unnatural History: Ecological Temporality in Post–1945 American Literature." PhD diss., Duke University, 2016.

Feder, Helen. "Nature and Culture in (and Outside) the Academy." Western American Literature 52, no. 3 (2017).

Finney, Carolyn. *Black Spaces, White Faces: Reimagining the Relationship of African Americans to the Great Outdoors*. Chapel Hill: University of North Carolina Press, 2014.

Fisher, Mark. *Capitalist Realism: Is There No Alternative?* Seattle: Zero Books, 2009.

Fleissner, Jennifer. "The Great Indoors: Regionalism, Feminism, and Obsessional Domesticity." In *Women, Compulsion, Modernity: The Moment of American Naturalism*. Chicago: University of Chicago Press, 2004.

Formisano, Paul. "Presley's Pauses: Unearthing Force in California's Land and Water Regimes and Frank Norris's *The Octopus*." *Journal of Ecocriticism* 7, no. 1 (2015): 1–18.

Foster, Amber. "Nancy Prince's Utopias: Reimagining the African American Utopian Tradition." *Utopian Studies* 24, no. 2 (2013).

Fox, William L. *Aereality: Essays on the World from Above*. Berkeley, CA: Counterpoint, 2009.

———. *Terra Antarctica: Looking into the Emptiest Continent*. Berkeley, CA: Counterpoint, 2007.

Fradkin, Philip. *A River No More: The Colorado River and the West*. Oakland: University of California Press, 1981.

Gelstein, Shani, et al. "Human Tears Contain a Chemosignal." *Science* 331, no. 6014 (January 2011): 226–30.

Giffney, Noreen, and Myra J. Hird. "Introduction: Queering the Non/Human." In *Unnatural Predators: Queer Theory Meets Environmental Studies in Bram Stoker's* Dracula. Edited by Noreen Giffney and Myra J. Hird. Burlington, VT: Ashgate, 2008.

Gilman, Charlotte Perkins. *Herland*. Mineola, NY: Dover Publications, 1915.

———. "When We Fly: How the Accomplishment of Aerial Navigation Will Make Necessary a Revision of Human Laws and Customs." *Harper's Weekly*, November 9, 1907, 1650, 1664.

Glasberg, Elena. *Antarctica as Cultural Critique: The Gendered Politics of Scientific Exploration and Climate Change*. New York: Palgrave MacMillan, 2012.

Goldfarb, Ben. "In *Gold Fame Citrus*, the Nascent Genre Looks to California." *High Country News*, February 2, 2016.

Goodnough, Abby, and Scott Atkinson. "A Potent Side Effect to the Flint Water Crisis: Mental Health Problems." *New York Times*, April 30, 2016.

Griggs, Sutton E. *Imperium in Imperio*. Cincinnati: Editor

Publishing Company, 1899.

Grosz, Elizabeth. *Chaos, Territory, Art: Deleuze and the Framing of the Earth*. New York: Columbia University Press, 2008.

Haldiya, Kripa Ram, Murli Lal Mathur, Raman Sachdev, and Habibulla N. Saiyed. "Knowledge, Attitude, and Practices Related to Occupational Health Problems among Salt Workers Working in the Desert of Rajasthan, India." *Journal of Occupational Health* 47, no. 1 (2005): 85–88.

———. "Risk of High Blood Pressure in Salt Workers Working near Salt Milling Plants: A Cross-Sectional and Interventional Study." *Environmental Health* 4 (2005): 4–13.

Hamm, Margherita Arlina. "Hail! The Conquering Hero Comes!" *The Anaconda Standard*, September 19, 1899. 14. Retrieved from Chronicling America—The Library of Congress.

Haraway, Donna. "Situated Knowledges: The Science Question in Feminism and the Privilege of Partial Perspective." *Feminist Studies* 14, no. 3 (1988): 575–99.

Hardt, Michael, and Antonio Negri. *Empire*. Cambridge, MA: Harvard University Press, 2000.

Harrison, Scott. "Where Is Death Valley Dodge?" *Los Angeles Times*, September 25, 2013.

Hays, Samuel P. *Conservation and the Gospel of Efficiency: The Progressive Conservation Movement, 1890–1920*. Pittsburgh: University of Pittsburgh Press, 1999.

Hearn, Michael Patrick. *The Annotated Wizard of Oz*. New York: W. W. Norton & Company, 2000.

Hecht, Gabrielle. "Nuclear Ontologies." In *Energy Humanities: An Anthology*. Edited by Imre Szeman and Dominic Boyer. Baltimore: Johns Hopkins University Press, 2017.

Heinemann, W. "All at Sea." *The Guardian*. November 30, 1904.

Hicks, John. *The Literature of California: Native American Beginnings to 1945*. Berkeley: University of California Press, 2001.

Hofstadter, Richard. *The Age of Reform: From Bryan to F. D. R.*

New York: Knopf Doubleday, 2011.

Holmes, Isiah. "Dakota Access Contractor with Blackwater Ties Heads Protester Surveillance, Violence Escalates." The Fifth Column, November 26, 2016. Accessed December 16, 2018. https://thefifthcolumnnews.com/2016/11/dakota-access-contractor-with-blackwater-ties-heads-protester-surveillance-violence-escalates/.

Holmes, Richard. "Gigantic Voyages." In *Falling Upwards: How We Took to the Air, an Unconventional History of Ballooning*, 172–73. New York: Pantheon Books, 2013.

Howells, William Dean. *Criticism and Fiction*. New York: Harper & Brothers, 1891.

Jackson, Helen Hunt. *Ramona*. New York: Grosset & Dunlap, 1884.

Jaffe, Aaron. *The Way Things Go: An Essay on the Matter of Second Modernism*. Minneapolis: University of Minnesota Press, 2014.

Jester, Thomas C. "Porcelain Enamel." In *Twentieth-Century Building Materials: History and Conservation*, 223–30. Los Angeles: Getty Publications, 2014.

Kelsey, Penelope Myrtle. "Zitkála-Šá, Sentiment, and Tiospaye: Reading Dakota Rhetorics of Nation and Gender." In *Tribal Theory in Native American Literature: Dakota and Haudenosaunee Writing and Indigenous Worldviews*, 62–75. Lincoln: University of Nebraska Press, 2008.

Kolodny, Annette. *The Lay of the Land: Metaphor as Experience and History in American Life and Letters*. Chapel Hill: University of North Carolina Press, 1984.

Koupal, Nancy Tystad. "The Wonderful Wizard of the West: L. Frank Baum in South Dakota, 1888–1891." *Great Plains Quarterly* 9 (Fall 1989): 203–15.

Kuletz, Valerie L. *The Tainted Desert: Environmental Ruin in the American West*. New York: Routledge, 1998.

Kurlansky, Mark. *Salt: A World History*. New York: Penguin

Books, 2003.

LaDuke, Winona. "Native American Activist Winona LaDuke at Standing Rock: It's Time to Move on from Fossil Fuels." Interviewed by Amy Goodman, *Democracy Now!* September 12, 2016.

"Lake of Salt." *Record-Union* (Sacramento, CA), January 24, 1896.

Lankford, Scott. "Sarah Winnemucca." In *Tahoe beneath the Surface: The Hidden Stories of America's Largest Mountain Lake*, 49–73. Rockland, CA: Sierra College Press, 2016.

Latour, Bruno. *Politics of Nature: How to Bring the Sciences into Democracy.* Translated by Catherine Porter. Cambridge, MA: Harvard University Press, 2004.

Lawrence, George R. "Photograph of San Francisco in Ruins from Lawrence Captive Airship, 2,000-Feet above San Francisco Bay overlooking Waterfront." *The Panoramic Photographs Collection.* Library of Congress. Washington, DC, 1906.

LeCain, Timothy. *The Matter of History: How Things Create the Past.* New York: Cambridge University Press, 2017.

LeMenager, Stephanie. *Living Oil: Petroleum Culture in the American Century.* New York: Oxford University Press, 2014.

Leonard, Thomas C. *Illiberal Reformers: Race, Eugenics, and American Economics in the Progressive Era.* Princeton, NJ: Princeton University Press, 2016.

Limerick, Patricia Nelson. *A Ditch in Time: The City, the West, and Water.* Golden, CO: Fulcrum Publishing, 2012.

London, Jack. *The Cruise of the Snark.* New York: Macmillan, 1911.

———. "If Japan Awakens China," *Sunset Magazine*, December 1909, 597–601.

———. *The Sea-Wolf.* New York: Bantam Dell, 2007 [Macmillan, 1904].

———. "Things Alive." *Yale Monthly Magazine* 1, no. 1 (1906): 76–79.

———. "The Yellow Peril." In *Revolution and Other Essays.* New

York: Macmillan, 1909.

Lye, Colleen. "A Genealogy of the 'Yellow Peril': Jack London, George Kennan, and the Russo-Japanese War." In *America's Asia: Racial Form and American Literature, 1893–1945.* Princeton, NJ: Princeton University Press, 2004.

Lynch, Tom. "Desertification." In *Reading Aridity in Western American Literature.* Edited by Jada Ach and Gary Reger, ix–x. Lanham, MD: Lexington Books, 2020.

———.*Xerophilia: Ecocritical Explorations in Southwestern Literature.* Lubbock: Texas Tech University Press, 2008.

Madera, Judith, and David Phillips. "On Edge Effects." C19: The Society of Nineteenth-Century Americanists Conference. State College, PA, March 19, 2016.

"Map of Wyoming with Special Reference to Shoshone Irrigation Company's Lands" (ca. 1900). *CB&Q: Building an Empire.* Chicago: Newberry Library. Accessed August 20, 2016. http://publications.newberry.org/cbqempire/items/show/153.

Martin, Tim. "*Gold Fame Citrus* Is a Cli-Fi Novel—the Dystopia of Choice in the Era of Climate Change." *NewStatesman,* March 2, 2016.

Marx, Edward. "Afterword." In *The American Diary of a Japanese Girl: An Annotated Edition.* Edited by Edward Marx and Laura E. Franey. Philadelphia: Temple University Press, 2007.

McClure, Andrew S. "[Post]Indian Princess and Voice of the Paiutes." *MELUS* 24, no. 2 (Summer 2002).

McCool, Daniel C. *Native Waters: Contemporary Indian Water Settlements and the Second Treaty Era.* Tucson: University of Arizona Press, 2006.

McGlynn, David. "*McTeague's* Gilded Prison." *Rocky Mountain Review* 62, no. 1 (2008).

"Means Reclamation of Desert Empire." *Salt Lake Tribune,* March 12, 1910. Retrieved from Chronicling America—The Library of Congress.

Mentz, Steve. "After Sustainability." *PMLA* 127, no. 3 (2012).

———. *Shipwreck Modernity: Ecologies of Globalization, 1550–1719.* Minneapolis: University of Minnesota Press, 2015.

Mentz, Steve, and Martha Elena Rojas. "Introduction: 'The Hungry Ocean.'" In *The Sea and Nineteenth-Century Anglophone Literary Culture.* Edited by Steve Mentz and Martha Elena Rojas, 1–14. Routledge: New York, 2017.

Miller, Char. *Fluid Arguments: Five Centuries of Western Water Conflict.* Tucson: University of Arizona Press, 2001.

Millings, Abigail, et al. "Holding Back the Tears: Individual Differences in Adult Crying Proneness Reflect Attachment Orientation and Attitudes to Crying." *Frontiers in Psychology* 7, no. 1003 (July 2016).

Mitchell, Lee Clark. "'And Rescue Us from Ourselves': Becoming Someone in Jack London's *The Sea-Wolf.*" *American Literature* 70, no. 2 (1998): 317–35.

———. *Determined Fictions: American Literary Naturalism.* New York: Columbia University Press, 1989.

Mitchell, W. J. T. "Imperial Landscapes." In *Landscape and Power,* 1–34. Chicago: University of Chicago Press, 2002.

Mora, Francis Luis. *Cloud Study from the Connecticut Litchfield Hills,* 1912–1919. Oil on panel. Dallas, Heritage Auctions.

Morton, Timothy. *Dark Ecology: For a Logic of Future Coexistence.* New York: Columbia University Press, 2016.

———. *Ecology without Nature: Rethinking Environmental Aesthetics.* Cambridge, MA: Harvard University Press, 2007.

———. "Guest Column: Queer Ecology." *Publications of the Modern Language Association of America* 125, no. 2 (2010).

———. *Hyperobjects: Philosophy and Ecology after the End of the World.* Minneapolis: University of Minnesota Press, 2013.

Moylan, Tom. *Demand the Impossible: Science Fiction and the Utopian Imagination.* New York: Methuen, 1986.

Muir, John. *Our National Parks.* Boston: Houghton, Mifflin and Co., 1900.

Murdoch, J. M. "The Lure of Death Valley." *Goodwin's Weekly:*

A Thinking Paper for Thinking People (Salt Lake City, UT). February 25, 1911. Retrieved from Chronicling America—The Library of Congress.

Nash, Linda. *Inescapable Ecologies: A History of Environment, Disease, and Knowledge*. Berkeley: University of California Press, 2006.

National Museum of the United States Army. "The Weather Bureau," 2018. nmusa.org.

National Park Service. "Death Valley National Park." US Department of the Interior. NPS.gov.

———. "Joshua Tree: Foundation Document." US Department of the Interior. NPS.gov.

Nebraska State Historical Society. "Melbourne, the Rainmaker." Nebraska State Historical Society Online. April 2010. https://history.nebraska.gov/publications/melbourne-rainmaker.

Nisetich, Rebecca. "The Nature of the Beast: Scientific Theories of Race and Sexuality in *McTeague*." *Studies in American Naturalism* 4, no. 1 (2009).

Nixon, Rob. "Slow Violence." *The Chronicle of Higher Education*, June 26, 2011.

Noguchi, Yonejirō. *The American Diary of a Japanese Girl*. New York: F. A. Stokes, 1902.

———. "No Yellow Peril in China." *Sunset Magazine*. July 1910, 14–16.

———. *The Story of Yone Noguchi*. Philadelphia: George W. Jacobs and Company, 1914.

———. *The Voice of the Valley*. San Francisco: W. Doxey, 1897.

Nordhoff, Charles. *California: For Health, Pleasure, and Residence, A Book for Travellers and Settlers*. New York: Harper & Brothers, 1873.

Norris, Frank. "The Frontier Gone at Last." In *The Responsibilities of the Novelist and Other Essays*. New York: Doubleday Page and Company, 1903.

———. *McTeague: A Story of San Francisco*. Edited by Donald

Pizer. New York: Norton, 1997 [1899].

Norton, Gale. "Testimony of Secretary of the Interior Gale Norton before the House Committee on Resources on the Arctic Coastal Plain Domestic Energy Security Act of 2003." US Department of the Interior, March 12, 2003.

O'Grady, John P. *Pilgrims to the Wild: Everett Ruess, Henry David Thoreau, John Muir, Clarence King, and Mary Austin.* Salt Lake City: University of Utah Press, 1993.

"On the Broad Pacific." *National Tribune,* February 27, 1908. Retrieved from Chronicling America—The Library of Congress.

O'Rourke, Michael. "Series Editor's Preface: The Open." In *Queering the Non/Human.* Edited by Noreen Giffney and Myra J. Hird. Burlington, VT: Ashgate, 2008.

Osborne, Thomas J. "Pacific Eldorado: Rethinking Greater California's Past." *California History* 87, no. 1 (2009).

Owens, Louis. "White for a Hundred Years." In *Reading* The Virginian *in the New West.* Edited by Melody Graulich and Stephen Tatum, 72-88. Lincoln: University of Nebraska Press, 2003.

Packard, Chris. *Queer Cowboys and Other Erotic Male Friendships in Nineteenth-Century American Literature.* New York: Palgrave Macmillan, 2005.

Peña, Devon G. "Endangered Landscapes and Disappearing Peoples? Identity, Place, and Community in Ecological Politics." In *Environmental Justice Reader: Politics, Poetics, and Pedagogy.* Edited by Joni Adamson, Mei Mei Evans, and Rachel Stein. St. Louis: Turtleback Books, 2002.

Peyser, Thomas Galt. "Reproducing Utopia: Charlotte Perkins Gilman and *Herland.*" *Studies in American Fiction* 20, no. 1 (1992): 1–16.

Pinard, Mary. "Haunted by Waters: The River in American Films of the West." In *The Landscape of Hollywood Westerns: Ecocriticism in an American Film Genre.* Edited by Deborah A. Carmichael. Salt Lake City: University of Utah Press, 2006.

Pinchot, Gifford. *The Fight for Conservation*. New York: Doubleday, Page & Co., 1910.

———. *The Training of a Forester*. Philadelphia: J. B. Lippincott Company, 1914.

Pisani, Donald J. "Beyond the Hundredth Meridian: Nationalizing the History of Water in the United States." *Environmental History* 5, no. 4 (2000): 466–82.

"Plans to Water Vast Dry Area." *Fair Play* (Ste. Genevieve, MO), September 25, 1920. Retrieved from Chronicling America—The Library of Congress.

"Plowing the Desert: Salt Lake Road Penetrating a New Waste Region." *Topeka State Journal*, December 26, 1903, 3.

Potter, Charles H. "Laboratory Photography." *Journal of Applied Microscopy and Laboratory Methods* 3 (1900).

Powell, John Wesley. *Report on the Lands of the Arid Region of the United States*. Washington, DC: Government Printing Office, 1878.

Powers, Edward. *War and the Weather*. Chicago: Knight & Leonard, 1890.

"Practical Uses for Kite Photographs." *Salt Lake Herald*, November 9, 1897. Retrieved from Chronicling America—The Library of Congress.

Pratt, Susan, Camila Marambio, et al. "Fathom." *Environmental Humanities* 12, no. 1 (May 2020).

Probyn, Elspeth. *Eating the Ocean*. Durham, NC: Duke University Press, 2016.

Professional Aerial Photographers Association. "The History of Aerial Photography." *PAPA International Online*, 2018. https://papainternational.com/history-of-aerial-photos/#:~:text=The%20first%20known%20aerial%20photograph,%2C%20known%20as%20%22Nadar%22.&text=(center)%20Nadar's%20earliest%20surviving%20aerial,1860%2C%20by%20James%20Wallace%20Black.

Ray, Sarah Jaquette. "Nature Writing and the American West."

In *A History of Western American Literature*. Edited by Susan Kollin. New York: Cambridge University Press, 2015.

Reger, Gary. "The Deserts of Los Angeles: Two Topographies." *Boom California*, May 24, 2017.

Reid, Mandy. "Utopia Is in the Blood: The Bodily Utopias of Martin R. Delany and Pauline Hopkins." *Utopian Studies* 22, no. 1 (2011): 91–103.

Reisner, Marc. *Cadillac Desert: The American West and Its Disappearing Water*. New York: Viking Press, 1986.

Rogers, Katharine M. *L. Frank Baum: Creator of Oz: A Biography*. New York: St. Martin's Press, 2007.

Ronda, Margaret. "Mourning and Melancholia in the Anthropocene." *Post45*, June 10, 2013.

Roosevelt, Theodore. "Sixth State of the Union Address." December 3, 1906.

Rosenthal, Gregory. *Beyond Hawai'i: Native Labor in the Pacific World*. Berkeley: University of California Press, 2018.

Rozen, Wayne. "Great White Hope: Not Great, No Hope." *New York Times*, July 4, 2010.

Rozwadowski, Helen M. "Scientists Writing and Knowing the Ocean." In *The Sea and Nineteenth-Century Anglophone Literary Culture*. Edited by Steve Mentz and Martha Elena Rojas. New York: Routledge, 2017.

Russell, Andrew, and Lee Vinsel. "Hail the Maintainers." *Aeon*, April 7, 2016.

Ryan, James R. *Photography and Exploration*. Chicago: University of Chicago Press, 2013.

"The Salt Water Cure." *Hopkinsville Kentuckian*, June 16, 1908, 3. Retrieved from Chronicling America—The Library of Congress.

Sandilands, Catriona Mortimer. "Unnatural Passions?: Notes toward a Queer Ecology." *Invisible Culture: An Electronic Journal for Visual Culture* 9 (2005), https://www.rochester.edu/in_visible_culture/Issue_9/issue9_sandilands.pdf.

Sandilands, Catriona Mortimer, and Bruce Erickson. "Introduction: A Genealogy of Queer Ecologies." In *Queer Ecologies: Sex, Nature, Politics, Desire*. Bloomington: Indiana University Press, 2010.

Sandweiss, Martha A., ed. *Photography in Nineteenth-Century America*. Fort Worth, TX: Amon Carter Museum, 1991.

"Savage People on Good Roads Move." *Arizona Republican*, September 8, 1916. Retrieved from Chronicling America— The Library of Congress.

Schober, Regina. "'A Problem in Small Boat Navigation': Ocean Metaphors and Emerging Data Epistemology in Stephen Crane's 'The Open Boat' and Jack London's 'The Heathen.'" *Studies in American Naturalism*, no. 1 (2017).

"Science in Warfare." *Salt Lake Herald*, March 27, 1898. Retrieved from Chronicling America—The Library of Congress.

Scott, James C. *Seeing Like a State: How Certain Schemes to Improve the Human Condition Have Failed*. New Haven, CT: Yale University Press, 1998.

Scranton, Roy. "Raising My Daughter in a Doomed World." *New York Times*, July 16, 2018.

Seager, Richard, et al. "Whither the Hundredth Meridian? The Once and Future Physical and Human Geography of America's Arid-Humid Divide. Part 1: The Story So Far." *Earth Interactions* 22 (2018): 1–24.

Seltzer, Mark. *Bodies and Machines*. New York: Routledge, 1992.

Shi, David. *Facing Facts: Realism in American Thought and Culture, 1850–1920*. New York: Oxford University Press, 1995.

Smythe, William E. *The Conquest of Arid America*. New York: Harper & Brothers, 1900.

Snodgrass, Mary Ellen. *The Encyclopedia of Utopian Literature*. Santa Barbara: ABC-CLIO, 1995.

Sontag, Susan. *On Photography*. New York: Picador, 1990.

Soulé, Michael, and Reed Noss. "Rewilding and Biodiversity as Complementary Goals for Continental Conservation." *Wild*

Earth 22 (Fall 1998): 1–11.

"Spotless Town Campaign On." *Arizona Republican*, April 4, 1914. Retrieved from Chronicling America—The Library of Congress.

Starr, Kevin. *Material Dreams: Southern California through the 1920s*. New York: Oxford University Press, 1991.

Stoddard, Charles Warren. *The Island of Tranquil Delights: A South Sea Idyl, and Others*. Boston: H. B. Turner, 1904.

"Stone Giants of the South Seas." *San Francisco Call*, February 19, 1899. Retrieved from Chronicling America—The Library of Congress.

Stronberg, Joel. "Sand Milling in America: It's Not Just about the Sand." *Civil Notion*, April 12, 2017.

Sueyoshi, Amy. "Finding Fellatio." In *Embodying Asian American Sexualities*. Edited by Gina Masequesmay and Sean Metzger, 157–72. Lanham, MD: Lexington Books, 2009.

———. "Miss Morning Glory: Orientalism and Misogyny in the Queer Writings of Yone Noguchi." *Amerasia Journal* 37, no. 2 (2011): 2–27.

Sullivan, Heather I. "Dirt Theory and Material Ecocriticism." *Interdisciplinary Studies in Literature and the Environment* 19, no. 3 (2012).

Sze, Julie. "From Environmental Justice Literature to the Literature of Environmental Justice." In *The Environmental Justice Reader: Politics, Poetics, and Pedagogy*. Edited by Joni Adamson, Mei Mei Evans, and Rachel Stein. Tucson: University of Arizona Press, 2002.

"Takes Aerial Photographs." *Peninsula* (VA) *Enterprise*, June 4, 1898, 2. Retrieved from Chronicling America—The Library of Congress.

Thébaud-Sorger, Marie. "Thomas Baldwin's *Airopaidia*, or the Aerial View in Color." *Seeing from Above: The Aerial View in Visual Culture*. Edited by Mark Dorrian and Frédéric Pousin. New York: I. B. Tauris, 2013.

Thill, Brian. *Waste.* Object Lessons Series. New York: Bloomsbury, 2015.

Tichi, Cecilia. "House of Progress, House of Shame." In *Jack London: A Writer's Fight for a Better America*, 125–56. Chapel Hill: University of North Carolina Press, 2015.

———. *Shifting Gears: Technology, Literature, Culture in Modernist America*. Chapel Hill: University of North Carolina Press, 1987.

Tissandier, Gaston. Quoted in James Ryan, *Photography and Exploration*. London: Reaktion Books, 2013.

"To Use Kites in Cuba." *Copper Country* (MI) *Evening News*, June 8, 1898, 4. Retrieved from Chronicling America—The Library of Congress.

Tomkins, Jane. *West of Everything: The Inner Life of Westerns*. New York: Oxford University Press, 1992.

Trump, Donald J. "Remarks by President Trump after Meeting with Congressional Leadership on Border Security." White House, US Government, January 4, 2019.

Turner, Christopher. "George R. Lawrence, Aeronaut Photographer." *Cabinet Magazine* 32 (2009). https://www.cabinetmagazine.org/issues/32/turner.php.

Turner, Frederick Jackson. *The Significance of the Frontier in American History*. New York: Henry Holt and Company, 1920 [1893].

Turner, Roger. "Aviation Meteorology: How Flight Safety Depends upon the Repetitious Production of Constantly Expiring Data." Paper presented at the Maintainers Conference. Hoboken, NJ, April 2016.

Tuttle, Jennifer. "Indigenous Whiteness and Wister's Invisible Indians." In *Reading* The Virginian *in the New West*. Edited by Melody Graulich and Stephen Tatum, 89–112. Lincoln: University of Nebraska Press, 2003.

United States Congress. Senate. S. 21. California Desert Protection Act of 1994, 103rd Congress, 43rd Session. Washington, DC:

Government Printing Office, 1994.

United States Congress. Senate. S. 32. Yellowstone Act of 1872. 42nd Congress, 2nd Session. Washington, DC: Government Printing Office, 1872. *America's National Park System: The Critical Documents*, https://www.nps.gov/parkhistory/online_books/anps/anps_1c.htm.

United States Department of Transportation. Federal Highway Administration. "Zero Milestone—Washington, DC." *Highway History*. fhwa.dot.gov.

"Vacation Trips to Europe." *Literary Digest*, April 18, 1908, 569.

Van Dyne, Edith [pseud.]. *The Flying Girl*. Chicago: Reilly & Britton Company, 1911.

———. *The Flying Girl and Her Chum*. Chicago: Reilly and Britton Company, 1912.

Veselá, Pavla. "Neither Black nor White: The Critical Utopias of Sutton E. Griggs and George S. Schuyler." *Science Fiction Studies* 38, no. 1 (2011): 270–87.

Voyles, Traci Brynne. *Wastelanding: Legacies of Uranium Mining in Navajo Country*. Minneapolis: University of Minnesota Press, 2015.

Warner, Marina. "Intimate Communiqués: Melchior Lorck's Flying Tortoise." In *Seeing from Above: The Aerial View in Visual Culture*. Edited by Mark Dorrian and Frédéric Pousin. New York: I. B. Tauris, 2013.

Watkins, Claire Vaye. *Gold Fame Citrus*. New York: Riverhead Books, 2015.

Weems, James. "Aerial Views and Farm Security Administration Photography." *History of Photography* 28, no. 3 (2004): 267–82.

Weir, Bill. "Inside Alaska's Battles over Land, Sea, and Life." CNN, July 25, 2018.

Wertz, Joe. "The Arid West Moves East, with Big Implications for Agriculture." NPR.org. https://www.npr.org/2018/08/09/637161725/the-arid-west-moves-east-with-big-implications-for-agriculture.

Westling, Louise. *The Green Breast of the New World: Landscape, Gender, and American Fiction*. Athens: University of Georgia Press, 1996.

White, Richard. *The Organic Machine: The Remaking of the Columbia River*. New York: Hill and Wang, 1996.

Wiebe, Robert H. *The Search for Order, 1877–1920*. New York: Hill and Wang, 1966.

"William Mulholland of Aqueduct Fame Dies." *Los Angeles Times*, July 23, 1935.

Williams, Jay. *Oxford Handbook of Jack London*. New York: Oxford University Press, 2017.

Winnemucca, Sarah. *Life among the Piutes: Their Wrongs and Claims*. Reno: University of Nevada Press, 1994.

Wister, Owen. *The Virginian: A Horseman of the Plains*. New York: Penguin Books, 1988 [1902].

Witschi, Nicolas. *Traces of Gold: California's Natural Resources and the Claim to Realism in Western American Literature*. Tuscaloosa: University of Alabama Press, 2002.

Woglom, Gilbert Totten. *Parakites: A Treatise on the Making and Flying of Tailless Kites for Scientific Purposes and for Recreation*. New York: G. P. Putnam's Sons, 1896.

———. "Unusual Uses of Photography: I—Aerial Photography." *Scribner's* 22, no. 64 (1897): 617–25.

World Wildlife Foundation. "Why Is Our Ocean at Risk?" World Wildlife Foundation Global, 2017.

Worster, Donald. *Rivers of Empire: Water, Aridity, and the Growth of the American West*. New York: Oxford University Press, 1992.

Wyoming Water Development Commission. "Background." In Wyoming Weather Modification Pilot Project, Wyoming Water Development Commission Online. Accessed April 20, 2016. https://wwdc.state.wy.us/weathermod/background.html.

Zitkála-Šá. *American Indian Stories*. Washington, DC: Hayworth Publishing House, 1921.

INDEX

administrative power, 4, 26
administrative state, 17, 53–54, 254n76
aereality, 38, 45, 70, 248n26
Agard-Jones, Vanessa, 89, 90
agriculture, 2, 4, 14, 15, 67, 77, 108, 111, 131, 138, 140, 144, 158, 172. *See also* dry farming; farming techniques
Aiken, Ednah, 75, 128, 130, 131–32, 151, 168, 170, 283n92
Alaimo, Stacy, 15, 19, 110, 295n105, 296n11; social justice and physical environments, 20, 160, 163; transcorporeal materialism, 20, 163, 164, 272n6
Alaska Lands Act (1980), 69, 257n107
Alaska National Wildlife Refuge, 103
alkali dust, 79, 82, 89, 92–93, 102, 105
American expansionism, 129, 135, 155, 157, 159–60, 162, 165, 166, 174, 176, 184, 205, 212, 253n65
American identity-making, 75
Anglo-American settlement, 6, 10, 80, 159, 176, 207, 247–48n23
apocalypse/apocalyptic fiction, 1, 5, 176
applied microscopy, 33, 255n83
aqueducts, 5
Arapaho tribe, 156
Arctic National Wildlife Refuge (ANWR), 67, 68, 69, 257n100, 107, 108

Arvol Looking Horse (Chief), 177
Atkinson, Scott, 167
Auerbach, Jonathan, 13, 197
Austin, Mary Hunter, 5, 8, 11, 82, 103, 108, 267n80, 269n88; and the desert, 26, 27, 80, 94, 98, 106–7, 110–15, 118–19, 121; *Earth Horizon*, 79–80, 109, 116, 261–62n26; environmentalism, 107, 108, 109, 114; *The Land of Little Rain*, 26, 27, 75, 81, 105, 106–7, 110, 112, 120–24, 262–63n30, 268n85; land-oriented management, 107, 108, 118–20; Progressivism, 109; and sand, 76, 94, 105–6, 114, 116–17, 121
Austin, Stafford Wallace, 108
Azzarello, Robert, 87–88

Badlands National Park, 40
Baker, Simon, 41–42
Bakker, Karen, 146
Ball, Samuel, 113–14
ballooning, 39, 40, 46, 47, 51, 53, 57
Bankhead Highway, 77–78
Bankhead, John H., 77
Banta, Martha, 4, 16, 158, 259–60n15
Barbour, Erwin Hinckley, 40
Bateman, Benjamin, 22, 29, 223, 224, 226
Baum, L. Frank, 49, 57, 60, 252n58, 253n66; and aereality, 25, 38–39, 45, 46, 47, 54, 65; and continuous

319

ABOUT THE AUTHOR

Jada Ach is a lecturer for the Leadership and Integrative Studies Program at Arizona State University. Her research has appeared in *Western American Literature, Ecozon@: European Journal of Literature, Culture and Environment,* and *Studies in the Novel.* Along with Gary Reger, Ach coedited the essay collection *Reading Aridity in Western American Literature.*